ARATOR

Would the Founding Fathers
recognize today's bloated government and elastic Constitution as the
same system they established?
Probably not, suggests M. E.
Bradford in his introduction to this new edition of *Arator*, for "we live
now in almost total contradiction of the political precedent of our
Revolution." He adds that "one justification for reconsidering the career
of John Taylor of Caroline, Virginia's strictest republican, is that he
foresaw most of the changes that have come to pass, understood their
causes, and fought them with all the energy and intellect at his command."
John Taylor rose to the rank of
lieutenant colonel in the Revolutionary army, then served in the Virginia
House of Delegates and the U.S. Senate. But it was as a thinker and
author, rather than active statesman, that Taylor's career was most
significant. He was perhaps the foremost philosopher of the conservative
Jeffersonians, and James A. Beard wrote of Taylor's work that "it
deserves to rank among the two or three really historic contributions to
political science which have been produced in the United States."
Arator was Taylor's most popular
and influential work. Bradford places it in the tradition of the *De Agri
Cultura* of Cato the Censor, the special hero of the old Whigs. Its author
was the president of the Virginia Agricultural Society, a planter's planter,
treating advice on farming as a species of moral instruction. But
"because *Arator* is about the social order of an agricultural republic, and
not just about farming," Bradford explains, "Taylor includes in it
materials on the relation of agriculture to the American economy, on
agriculture and politics, and on the enemies of the agrarian republic—
the freeloaders who would batten upon the farmer, mechanic,
and small tradesman."
Neglected in recent years, Taylor's
Arator deserves our renewed attention.

M. E. Bradford is Professor of
English at the University of Dallas. In 1977 he was a Senior Research
Fellow of the National Endowment for the Humanities.

John Taylor of Caroline

ARATOR

Being a Series of
Agricultural Essays, Practical and Political:
In Sixty-Four Numbers

by John Taylor

Edited and with an
Introduction by M. E. Bradford

INDIANAPOLIS

Liberty*Classics* is a publishing imprint of Liberty Fund, Inc., a foundation established to encourage study of the ideal of a society of free and responsible individuals.

The cuneiform inscription that serves as the design motif for our endpapers is the earliest known written appearance of the word "freedom" (*ama-gi*), or liberty. It is taken from a clay document written about 2300 B.C. in the Sumerian city-state of Lagash.

This edition of *Arator* follows the text of the edition published in Petersburg, Virginia, in 1818 by Whitworth & Yancey for John M. Carter. For further information, see "A Note on the Text," pp. 47-48.

Library of Congress Catalog Card No.: 76-58030
ISBN 0–913966–26–6
58

CONTENTS

NOTES

A VIRGINIA CATO:
JOHN TAYLOR OF CAROLINE
AND THE AGRARIAN REPUBLIC
By M. E. Bradford

Though the people of these United States have lived under the same Constitution and with the same basic organs of government for almost two centuries, it is unlikely that many of the contemporary inheritors of that continuous experience would recognize the original form and function of their country as the federal union which their fathers made. The means by which the model has been altered are, of course, quite clear: circumstantial adaptation, statutory and constitutional amendment or accretion, and (worst of all) ingenious legal "construction." This much is understood by the ordinary citizen every time his life is disrupted by some egregious court decision or bureaucratic directive. During the two hundred years something foreign has been injected into the American political bloodstream: something private, ideological, and abstract, deriving its power from authorities outside the historic American context. But how this corruption occurred, and by what particular stages, he cannot say: how it came to be so complete that we live now in almost total contradiction of the political precedent of our Revolution. One justification for reconsidering the career of John Taylor of Caroline, Virginia's strictest republican, is that he foresaw most of the changes that have come to pass, understood their causes, and fought them with all the energy and intellect at his command.

John Taylor was born into a distinguished Virginia family, the son of James and Anne (Pollard) Taylor of Caroline County, and great-grandson of the first of his line to settle in the colony.[1] Three years after his birth (December 1753), Taylor's father died. The responsibility for his upbringing devolved upon his uncle, Edmund Pendleton, who himself played a large role in our nation's history. Taylor was educated in Donald Robertson's academy (where James Madison was at the same time enrolled), at the College of William and Mary, and in Pendleton's law offices. He had inherited a small property, and in 1774 he received a license to practice his uncle's profession. But before he could begin to become well established as a lawyer, events in the larger world drew him away from Virginia's familiar scene and into the Continental Army, in which he served in several states, rising to the rank of major before, in a period of false economy, he resigned in disgust with the inefficiency of the national government and returned home for service in the Virginia House of Delegates. Later, in 1781, he was

---

[1] The only biography is Henry H. Simms' *Life of John Taylor: The Story of a Brilliant Leader in the Early Virginia State Rights School* (Richmond: William Byrd Press, 1932).

appointed lieutenant-colonel of the state militia and saw his last fighting under the command of Lafayette against Hessian mercenaries who were a part of that fateful invasion which had its quietus at Yorktown.

In the years following the Revolution, Taylor emerged rapidly as one of the principal citizens of the Old Dominion. Though he had sold his patrimony in 1776 and had suffered from the depreciation of state and continental paper currency, he received an ample grant of Western lands for his service under arms. He made a fortune at law and became, in his courtroom oratory and pleadings before the bench, the peer of any Virginia attorney—all of this during the "golden age" of the Virginia bar. His fees ran sometimes to $10,000 a year; and almost all of this income he invested in the land of his native county. Furthermore, in 1783 he made a fine marriage to his cousin Lucy Penn, the daughter of the wealthy attorney and planter, John Penn of North Carolina, a signer of the Declaration of Independence. With his own substance and what this union brought, during the following year he became an active planter himself. And until the day of his death (August 21, 1824) he continued one of the most successful farmers in the upper South— achieving his fame as a cultivator in an era of agricultural depression, often upon depleted soils.

Taylor came finally to own several plantations, thousands of undeveloped acres in western Kentucky, and over one hundred fifty slaves. But his showplace and home was at Hazlewood on the Rappahannock, where he greeted visitors with simplicity and taste, generous hospitality, and serious conversation—particularly on the subjects of political philosophy and agricultural reform. A guest thus described him and his estate as they appeared in 1814: "I found an old grey-headed gentleman in an old-fashioned dress, plain in his manners, full of politics and conversational debate. He lives about three miles from . . . Port Royal, Virginia, on the finest farm I have ever seen."[2] A rich man, Taylor the planter soon retired almost completely from his legal practice. Furthermore, even before he had achieved such independence, he was (as early as 1793) the acknowledged spokesman for his county and much of the surrounding territory.[3] And so well was he regarded by other Virginians who had observed him in the courts, in the development of the agricultural societies (in which he played a major role), in the councils of the Episcopal church (of which he was a faithful communicant), or in the legislature (where he served from 1779 to 1781, 1783 to 1785, and 1796 to 1800), that his neighbors sent him three times (1793–94, 1803, and 1822–24) to complete unexpired terms in the United States Senate. They would have sent him for longer stays had he been willing.

Yet though a man of mark, especially as a political philosopher—a man whose "disinterested principles" were, according to John Randolph of Roanoke, "the only bond of union among Republicans"[4]—Taylor preferred

---

[2] A letter from John to David Campbell, quoted in Manning Dauer and Hans Hammond, "John Taylor: Democrat or Aristocrat?" *Journal of Politics* 6 (November 1944): 386; see also 381–403.

[3] Simms, *op. cit.,* p. 58.

[4] Quoted in Benjamin F. Wright, "The Philosopher of Jeffersonian Democracy," *American Political Science Review* 22 (November 1928): 870.

on principle to tend his own cultivated garden and leave the rewards of office and the national arena to men driven by grander ambitions and larger images of themselves.[5] Only when his duty required was he drawn away from his primary vocation as agriculturalist. But on that role, and the politics which made possible the patriarchal planter, his pen was never still, never cut off from the larger world. Indeed, writing from this positive privacy, from the platform and persona which establishment at Hazlewood afforded him, he could speak with more authority than it was possible for a professional politician to achieve. For John Taylor of Caroline, during his maturity, became the classic figure of "old republican" theory: the exemplar of an almost Roman *virtus*, the Virginia Cato, who soldiers, enforces the law, writes in its defense and of the life it secures, and serves the state well when called to office because he has something better to do—because there are lands and people of whose good he is a faithful steward. Like his ancient prototype, he shaped the pattern of his life into an illustration of what he taught. Even in his writing and in the occasional public service.

On the national stage Taylor was remarkably consistent with the posture he assumed within Virginia. And he identified with that point of view throughout his career. All that he attempted follows from what he perceived the Revolution to have been about: from his view of mercantilism and of earlier English history; and from

---

[5] See Loren Baritz, *City on a Hill: A History of Ideas and Myths in America* (New York: Wiley & Sons, 1964), pp. 201–2. The book contains a full chapter on Taylor's pastoral vision.

his understanding of republican political theory, in both its modern and its ancient varieties.[6] We had cast off oppressive, centralized control of the colonies by an exploitative British authority. To put in its place a new authority with the power to threaten either our station or our liberties, an "energetic" government bound to be controlled by faction, seemed to him ridiculous in the extreme. Hence his horror at the official subdivision of American society into classes or interests, his lifetime devotion to the sovereignty of the states (guaranteed, in his view, by the language of the Declaration), and his uneasiness about the new Constitution of 1787–88.[7]

Taylor approved of the Union—a union facing outward, toward the "candid world." It was necessary to preserve the liberties of the people in their natural communities by making possible the coexistence of the thirteen separate commonwealths which had, in concert, won freedom from the hegemony of King George and his feckless Parliament. But his career in national politics began with opposition to ratification of the Philadelphia instrument—effective opposition. His objections in this case foreshadow his subsequent role in the conversation of American politics. The Constitution lacked a bill of rights, particularly a specific statement on the body of powers not surrendered by the states. The preamble contained language contradicting the procedures of adoption, amendment, and national elections. The states act in these

---

[6] Simms, *op. cit.*, p. 211. He stresses the impact of the Revolution on Taylor's politics.

[7] See Taylor's *Tyranny Unmasked* (Washington City, D.C.: Davis and Force, 1822), p. 8, for remarks on the Declaration as creating states.

matters, the people through them. The power of direct taxation granted the federal government also gave Taylor pause. Yet, with the Bill of Rights, Virginia's instrument of ratification (which interpreted what precisely they had agreed upon), and Mr. Jefferson's politically successful insistence upon an "inactive," unconsolidated, nonenergetic reading of the original text, Taylor put his trust in the written national bond, strictly construed. And gave to it his continuing, vocal devotion.

The federal Constitution, in Taylor's conception, was political law—as opposed to local, civil, and other law, which is designed to restrain the citizen in his own community.[8] For the Constitution was basically a law to restrict the conduct of legislators and other public servants —*a law to limit law*—and therefore a means of preventing, within the new nation, a recurrence of those abuses that had brought Americans to revolution in the first place. This emphasis on what the branches and subdivisions of government *could not do* was what Taylor spoke of as "principle" in American politics. It looks to what he perceived as the weakness of the eighteenth-century British system, and of relatively free societies, ancient and modern. In these cultures the liberty of elected or legitimate representatives to reflect the national will to a sovereign had converted into a susceptibility to factious combination, resentment, and schism; into an instrument for the transfer of power and wealth, with some theoret-

---

[8] See Eugene Ten Broeck Mudge, *The Social Philosophy of John Taylor of Caroline* (New York: Columbia University Press, 1939), pp. 111–16, for the distinction between civil and political law.

ical and extrinsic imperative definitive of the common
good brought in as an excuse for innovation. Artificial
aristocracy is the inevitable consequence—consolidation,
monopoly, special privilege, jobbery, patronage, and theft
by taxation. In its hands government becomes a "canni-
bal." Federalism was the American name for politics
according to this model. For Taylor, it was a negation of
all that he had fought for, from the Revolution on.[9]

There were, of course, many kinds of Federalists: some
out of trust for the leaders of the Revolution, some out
of fear of anarchy, some from dreams of national glory,
and some in hopes of wealth. These plus the occasional
Federalists who were simply determined to have a national government capable of defending itself against
attack were all (except for perhaps this last group) expressions of one side of the deep division always present
in republican political theory. Taylor bespeaks the opposing tradition. In simple terms, the former doctrine
associates with city-state republics—cosmopolitan, commercial, secular, and atomistic. Venice is such a republic,
and Carthage; also most of the Greek cities of antiquity,
at some stage in their development. Early Switzerland and
Rome before the *Principate* belong to the opposing stream
of influence. They are closed, rural, religious, and corporate societies: places where the achievement of honor by
one citizen is, through the social identity, a gift to all.

Though familiar to the generation that won our independence, "small" and "extended" were only counters,

---

[9] See Taylor's *New Views of the Constitution of the United States*
(Washington City, D.C.: Way and Gideon, 1823) on the lesson of 1776.

convenient terms for the conversion of this dispute into a simple modern idiom. *Convenient but misleading counters.* Yet, by 1787, they were conventional and have since confused our relation to republican theory. A large republic, Publius forgets, may be homogenous, agrarian, unimperial, defended by a citizen army, and xenophobic. A small "free society" may, on the other hand, be polyglot, externally aggressive, impious, served by mercenaries, and united only by a common mendacity: a nest of asocial individualism. But in the corporate society of the agrarian republic, liberty and unity consort well enough.[10] The envious hatreds of party and class can be held to a minimum. And a considerable inequality of status and function can be justified to all because of the anterior identity dependent on these natural roles, binding levels and orders into a tribal whole: a voluntary bond which is supportive of their respective private selves, within which their personal dignity must be achieved, if it is to be achieved at all.

Thus the thought of John Taylor comes of honorable and ancient origins. He speaks for what Michael Oakeshott calls the "civil-association"—as opposed to the "enterprise-association"—theory of the state: the "mode of association . . . in terms of non-instrumental rules of conduct, called the law.' "[11] Unlike the Federalists, he

---

[10] On Taylor's full political theory, and on the special qualities of his republicanism, I am much indebted to Andrew Nelson Lytle's "John Taylor and the Political Economy of Agriculture," *American Review* 3 (September 1934): 432–47, 3 (October 1934): 630–43, 4 (November 1934): 94–99.

[11] Michael Oakeshott, "Talking Politics," *National Review*, December 5, 1975, p. 1426.

understands law and government as protecting what is, not as creating what is yet to be—as "nomocratic," not "teleocratic."[12] Failure to offer such protection was the fatal error of Bute and Townshend, Lords North and (George) Germaine. America, after the Revolution, had achieved a government which corrected central failings of the British system: had protected an already *known* security of property and personal liberty in already self-governing communities. By achieving, through a political law to limit government and a strictly federal separation of powers, a stability never experienced in Britain or in the Rome of Cato the Censor (the closest approximation in human history to Taylor's ideal republic), the United States had become something original in the "science of politics."[13] Our "new secular order" (as opposed to new theology) forestalled the instability inherent in the "balance-of-power" regimes praised in commercial republican theory: in regimes where the guarantees of order are converted by natural declension into the engines of ex-

---

[12] Oakeshott develops this distinction between the *societas* and *universitas* in his *On Human Conduct* (Oxford: Clarendon Press, 1975), pp. 199–206. The character of the latter type of society is that it holds together only because of a common project affirmed by its members, not because of some sanction attached to its simple existence.

[13] References to Roman history are everywhere in Taylor's works. See, for instance, p. 3 of *Tyranny Unmasked* (Augustus as a vile consolidator) and p. 28 of *Construction Construed, and Constitutions Vindicated* (Richmond: Shepherd and Pollard, 1820), an allusion to Sallust on Jugurtha. But the best illustration of Taylor's use of Roman history is his *An Inquiry into the Principles and Policy of the Government of the United States* (1814). I cite the edition of Loren Baritz (Indianapolis: Bobbs-Merrill Co., 1969), pp. 17, 25, 31, 61, 66, 122, 137, 140, 152, 158, 169, 171, 200, 208, 234, 247–48, 251, 287, 343, 355, 361, 364, 444, 472, 478, 503, 526, 531.

ploitation. But its newness rested finally on an argument from history, on crystallized depositions from what Patrick Henry called "the lamp of experience," and not on private speculation.[14] Even though Taylor criticized John Adams for ignoring what was innovative and an improvement upon European precedent in American politics, no political thinker of importance in the first two generations of our national existence was less *a priori*, less concerned with being abstractly inventive. Taylor had no doubt of what a republic should be. He had seen the answer—in Virginia.

Taylor's struggles in the arena of national politics with the friends of concentrated power, the aristocracy of "paper and patronage," seem on the surface to be extremely various. But the issues dividing him from the champions of unlimited federal sovereignty are always the same. As he writes in *Construction Construed, and Constitutions Vindicated*, "To define the nature of government truly, I would say that a power of distributing property, able to gratify avarice and monopoly, designated a bad one; and that the absence of every such power designated a good one."[15] Alexander Hamilton's financial plan for supporting the new government was the original of all such Federalist mischief. From the moment

---

[14] On this species of political reasoning, see H. Trevor Colbourn, *The Lamp of Experience: Whig History and the Intellectual Origins of the American Revolution* (Chapel Hill: University of North Carolina Press, 1965); see also my essay, "A Teaching for Republicans: Roman History and the Nation's First Identity," *Intercollegiate Review* 11 (Winter–Spring 1976): 67–81.

[15] *Construction Construed*, p. 15.

of their proposal (and especially as senator, in 1793 and '94), Taylor fought the idea of a national bank and the assumption of state debts by the central government. He found no constitutional sanction for federal charters for private businesses or sponsorship of schemes for internal improvement. For one thing, all such proposals seemed to operate at the expense of the South. Land and labor would have to pay the debts the government made by borrowing from this federally protected enterprise. Taxes would pay for credit—but not taxes on banks. Furthermore, a few eminent Federalists seemed to own most of the banknotes or stock and to enjoy most of the benefits of credit. The entire plan smacked of mercantilist protectionism. Like the "country" or "old Whigs" in England, Taylor saw it a "conspiracy" against the landed interest. And that interest was basic to his version of a healthy American republic.

Taylor also deplored the Federalist attempt to raise a "new model" army. Militia should be the shield of a free society. A large standing army was a threat to self-government, a patronage system, the basis for an artificial aristocracy (i.e., without roots), and contrary to the best republican precedent.[16] Especially after the friends of President Adams passed, early in 1798, their great "gag rule," the Alien and Sedition Acts. In December of that year, Taylor carried his fight against such usurpations

---

[16] On the Federalists' "army plot," see Richard Kohn, *Eagle and Sword: The Beginnings of the Military Establishment in America* (New York: Free Press, 1975).

into the Virginia Assembly, where he had secured a seat
in order to bring forward and ensure the passage of the
Virginia version of what we now know as the Virginia
and Kentucky Resolutions. Jefferson was probably the
source of this remonstrance, and a great many of his sup-
porters had a part in the official assertion of the states'
reserved powers to restrict infringements upon the national compact by the national government. Similarly
they (Madison included) had had a part in planning violent resistance, if violence proved their only answer. But
Taylor had been in the field, in his section of Virginia,
before Jefferson had formulated either his plans of battle
or his language of protest. Taylor won victory for the
Jeffersonians in debate. And, upon recognition that disunion and civil war were the only alternative courses
open to his friends if the political process collapsed any
further, he had, after carrying the Resolution of '98,
taken a major role in completing the "interposition of
1800," the election of Thomas Jefferson as President. In
Taylor's view, all of this labor was loyalty to the bond
of national identity, an attempt to preserve the always
fragile balance between the contradictory impulses
toward concentration and fragmentation which went into
the making of our peculiar system of "one and many."[17]
Yet, as he had preferred conflict to subservience in 1776,
and rebellion to usurpation in 1798, so he persisted when
dark days came again: persisted in warning that the

---

[17] See Thomas Ritchie, "To the Reader," in *Construction Construed,*
p. ii.

Union, though preferable, could be preserved only on the
terms of its original negotiation;[18] and was liable to corruption so long as the spokesmen for its members or
components continued to imagine that they might find, in
a fusion of the commerce, general welfare, and "necessary and proper" clauses of the Philadelphia instrument,
seeds of a "sovereign power," in the Old World sense of
those words.[19] The honorable blood spilled in the Revolution required nothing less of its heirs.

But after 1800 there were respite and an interlude of
hope. Jefferson's victory had been peacefully accepted by
those who, two years before, had seemed to threaten military subversion of the electoral process. Furthermore, the
new chief magistrate had sounded precisely the proper
note in his inaugural address: the minimum of government, the minimum of expense, peace—and thus an administration made strong by its devotion to the law. How
well Taylor thought of Jefferson's first-time performance
he specified in his pamphlet *A Defence of the Measures of
the Administration of Thomas Jefferson* (1804).[20] Bad
Federalist laws were repealed. Retrenchment was in
process. There remained only one major problem when
this retrospect was done: the Louisiana Purchase (1803).
Taylor was able to defend the prudence of this acquisi-

---

[18] See Thomas Gordon Lloyd, "The Danger Not Yet Over: The Political Thought and Practice of John Taylor of Caroline" (Ph.D. diss.,
Claremont, 1973), pp. 95–127, for a summary of the evidence that Taylor
considered secession a serious possibility.

[19] See *Construction Construed*, p. 333. The entire book deals with the
myth of sovereignty. For Taylor, only God can be called sovereign.

[20] *A Defence of the Measures of the Administration of Thomas Jefferson* (Washington, D.C.: Samuel H. Smith, 1804).

tion, and (in the last three chapters of his pamphlet) to detail its positive republican effects. But not its constitutionality under the treaty-making powers. Furthermore, the treaty with France contained irregular and unconstitutional stipulations about what was to be done with Louisiana after the purchase was complete. Friendship moved Taylor to attempt a legal apology. But only his argument from consequences stands the test. Jefferson knew all of this as well as Taylor, which is why he sought after-the-fact authority, in both laws and amendments to the Constitution, for what he had done.

In most respects the Jefferson years were the quietest times in Taylor's adult life. And the season of his closest work on agriculture. True, he did not care for the embargo against trade with offending European powers. Nor for other measures taken by his friend from Albemarle to avoid our entanglement with the side effects of the Napoleonic Wars. But he accepted their necessity. While serving briefly in the United States Senate, he argued through to adoption the Twelfth Amendment—on procedures for electing the President and Vice President. He put his mind to other needed changes in the body of political law, especially in regard to the judicial power. Thus he continued to distrust governmental power even though (in questions of extending the franchise and reapportioning the legislature) he exhibited confidence in his Virginia neighbors—except for a few Federalists and certain Democratic-Republicans who had elements in their thought which linked them to the opposing camp. One of these was James Madison. Taylor and the other "old Republicans" did not forget the business he had done, with John Jay and Hamilton, under the mask of Publius, or his direct role in the drafting and ratification of the Constitution. Yet, rather than split his party, Taylor offered no active opposition to Madison's election in 1808. And once the transition was accomplished, he encouraged better-trusted friends, such as James Monroe, to accept places in the new administration. But on the question of foreign war, though the danger of Federalist recovery made him moderate about his opposition once the conflict had begun, he broke officially with the national leadership.[21] He became a member of the Republican minority, the Tertium Quids.

Taylor's reservations about the effect of war on republican institutions are well supported in history and are a basic component of old-Whig doctrine. War would profit contractors, certain "kept" industries and business firms, those desiring federal or military appointments, and the friends of arbitrary "emergency" power. Government would, once "under the gun," be free to plead "reasons of state." Liberty would become exceptional. Social, economic, and political life would be disrupted: the cities filled, families broken, and inflation promoted. And "real property" (i.e., the landed interest) would be called upon to pay the bill.[22] That the necessities of war could be used to effect an internal transformation of the republic made Taylor happy to learn of the Treaty of Ghent.[23] Indeed,

---

[21] On this period, see Russell Kirk, *John Randolph of Roanoke: A Study in American Politics* (Chicago: Henry Regnery Co., 1964), pp. 111–18.

[22] A commonplace of old-Whig theory since the early seventeenth century. Walpole's power rested on his ability to avoid expensive wars.

[23] Simms, *op. cit.*, pp. 131–32.

it seemed to him that commercial and territorial wars were inimical to the basic nature and best interests of organic, agrarian republics: counterproductive even though the other sort of republic, commercial and "progressive," appeared to thrive on such conflicts. Civil war waged on principle and wars of self-defense might have a healthy effect on a nomocratic, basically rural republic, but not dreams of Manifest Destiny or designs for the forcible annexation of Canada—real factors in the thinking of the War Hawks of 1812. Empire had been the "big idea," the telos, that undid the Romans. And in the American context its representatives were clearly responding to Federalist ideology.[24]

In Taylor's remaining years there were even greater national questions to arrest his attention and stimulate his pen. The old heresies of excessive patronage and the Bank (reestablished in 1816) continued to draw his fire. The analogy between the protective tariff and the English corn laws was too obvious for him to overlook.[25] Proposals for federally sponsored improvements—canals, roads, and port facilities—were also clearly special-interest legislation. But the major threats to the Constitution came from other quarters: from the claims of inclusive review powers by the Supreme Court and from the debate surrounding the Missouri Compromise. Than Taylor's, there is no other more rigorous critique of the process by which John Marshall led the other justices to reach for the authority to interpret their own functions.

---

[24] See the analysis of Daniel Webster's reply to Hayne in Richard Weaver, "Two Orators," *Modern Age* 14 (Summer–Fall 1970): 226–42.
[25] *Construction Construed*, p. 323.

And no other sharper warning of what must follow from allowing Congress to predetermine the internal policies to be adopted by soon-to-be sovereign states.

In the matter of the Supreme Court's appellate jurisdiction, Taylor goes back to Philadelphia and the ratification debates. His point is that the powers seized by Marshall are conventional, and (in most cases) subject to reduction by the Congress at any time. The great cases come under his rigorous scrutiny: *Marbury* v. *Madison*, *Martin* v. *Hunter's Lessee*, *Cohens* v. *Virginia*, *McCulloch* v. *Maryland*. In his opinion on the last of these questions, Chief Justice Marshall makes broad use of the aforementioned "necessary and proper" clause of the Constitution; and, by what Taylor calls "the golden rule of construction," he forces a branch of the National Bank on a state reluctant to allow for its presence. Taylor foresees where that argument must tend—to a government (or a court) which will undertake whatever measures that answer to the ideological compulsions of its members: its "uncivil," or "purpose-association" theory of law. And all in the name of interpretation. How potent the magic of that word may be we have learned to our everlasting regret.

Taylor saw most of it coming—the moralistic tyranny of an activist judiciary—and he drew a scathing analogy between the "broad constructionists" and the three faithless sons in the central fable of Swift's *Tale of a Tub*.[26] In Swift each son inherits a coat made of a portion of his father's mantle. In Taylor the three garments are the

---

[26] *New Views of the Constitution*, pp. 298–316.

federal, the state, and the shared powers granted under the Constitution. In both narratives each heir has, in violation of the provisions of the will, by addition or subtraction, altered the original. And particularly Swift's Lord Peter, who is the counterpart of the Virginian's "Judge Construction" (Marshall). These rascals, says Taylor, are the authorities the Federalists should have cited in their violations of the patrimony: Peter, Martin, and Jack—all tempted astray, all ruined in the end, near mad, and unable to live together under the ancestral roof. Yet Taylor knew that this trend would be hard to check —even his fellow southerners, with New England in near rebellion during the War of 1812, had looked to the courts to check such recalcitrance. Furthermore, efforts to impeach arbitrary judges (like Justice Chase) had not gone well. The Sage of Hazlewood took a long view, however. Eventually his countrymen would heed his alarm. And some of them have. He is nowhere more instructive to our times than in his warnings that the judicial power must be restrained and that proper knowledge of the nation's early history will provide most of the needed chains.

On the Missouri Compromise and its dreadful augury Taylor is equally persuasive. The planter of Caroline heard the fire bell in the night as clearly as his friend at Monticello. And, like Jefferson, he knew better than to take the sudden discovery of the "moral question" of slavery by certain Yankee politicians as anything more than a political maneuver, an attempt to collapse the Virginia Dynasty by recruiting new Federalists in the West. We should remember that many on the frontier feared

the extension of slavery because it brought Negroes with
it, and also because it expanded the network of talent
and deference later called "the Slave Power." Northern
commercial and political leaders chafed at the three-fifths
ratio. They chafed at the limits placed on the ambitious
of their region by the hegemony of the South. Sectional
division was their only hope—a politics of suspicion and
fear.[27] And with it a precedent for disrupting or inter-
fering with the internal affairs of a state: for redefining
the compact (and "republican government" with it) without the assent of those with whom it had been drawn.
Southerners must be made to feel that their stake in the
Union would be, from 1820 on, a diminished one: that
the federal territories did not belong to them as to other
full citizens of the Republic. Submission or disunion must
be their only alternatives. For Taylor, the pattern he had
recognized since the drafting of the Constitution was
finally complete: "The great pecuniary favor granted by
congress to certificate-holders, begat banking; banking
begat bounties to manufacturing capitalists; bounties to
manufacturing capitalists begat an oppressive pension
list; these partialities united to beget the Missouri project;
that project begat the idea of using slavery as an instrument for effecting a balance of power; when it is put in
operation, it will beget new usurpations of internal power

---

[27] See Lytle, *op. cit.*, on this portion of Taylor's thought. See also
Robert E. Shalhope, "Thomas Jefferson's Republicanism and Antebellum
Southern Thought," *Journal of Southern History* 42 (November 1976):
529–56. Shalhope attributes to Taylor a change in the position of Jefferson and other Southern Republicans, once northern politics opened them
to Taylor's influence.

over persons and property, and these will beget a disso-
lution of the union."[28] How prophetic these words proved
to be Taylor could not know. But he could use the political
stature he had achieved to sound his own alarm, both to
his region and to the country at large. In his last two years
he returned to the United States Senate, and his pen was
busy to the end.

Taylor's influence as a political philosopher on subsequent spokesmen for his region is too obvious to require
much comment. And he has always had his admirers
among the friends of limited government, wherever they
lived. His present reputation is diminished in proportion
to the steady decline in their purchase upon the course
of events in our national political life.[29] But it is as thinker
and author, and not as active statesman, that Taylor's
career was most significant (as he knew was likely to
be the case). Apart from *Arator* (1813), his most popular
book, and a work of more than political implication, Taylor wrote four major studies in American politics. To
these he added several pamphlets and numerous contributions to the political press.[30] His early "Definitions of
Parties; or the Political Effects of the Paper System Considered" (1794) and "An Enquiry into the Principles and
Tendency of Certain Public Measures" (1794), along

---

[28] *Construction Construed*, p. 298.

[29] Charles A. Beard, in *Economic Origins of Jeffersonian Democracy*
(New York: Free Press, 1943), p. 323, praises Taylor as one of America's few original political philosophers. M. J. C. Vile's *Constitutionalism
and the Separation of Powers* (Oxford: Clarendon Press, 1967) praises
Taylor to the skies; see pp. 166–72.

[30] These works need to be gathered into a standard edition.

with the already mentioned *A Defence of the Measures of the Administration of Thomas Jefferson* (1804), sound many of the themes that would occupy Taylor in his later, more ambitious period: the Bank of the United States, excise taxes and tariffs, political parties as factions— *privilege* and *division*. But for years he labored in preparing his magnum opus, *An Inquiry into the Principles and Policy of the Government of the United States* (1814), a reply to John Adams' *A Defence of the Constitution of Government of the United States of America* (1787–88). For almost twenty years Taylor worked on his counterpleading against Adams' response to Turgot. And the Massachusetts statesman (for whom Taylor always entertained a genuine respect) was understandably surprised to be thus confronted in his old age with an attack on arguments which he had prepared (as Adams correctly insisted) in praise of various *state constitutions*, before a national government had been formed; an attack which treats his praise of Massachusetts, New York, and Maryland as if it were an accurate indication of his thinking on national politics. But Taylor was also correct. For it was *how* Adams defended the organization of certain states, with reference to a theory of balanced powers and a theory of "aristocracy" to be acknowledged officially in the construction of an American order, that linked to certain perennial dangers to the Republic. And with these perils, and the forms they had assumed after a quarter century of union, Taylor drew connections to Adams' theory: connections all the more meaningful in that he recognized Adams as the finest, most disinterested thinker in the Federalist camp.

Writing in competition with the best, to the judgment of the ages, Taylor probably spent too much time in completing the 656 pages of his *Inquiry*. His style, always tending toward the prolix and archaic, here often becomes completely entangled.[31] And there were tedious repetitions. But the order and organization, the logical development and use of authorities in this book mark it as a work of great penetration and careful thought. Reasoning after the fact, from history, Taylor denies that government and society are necessarily one.[32] He was no egalitarian in any of the modern senses of the word. And not too clear about the distinction between natural and conventional rights. Disparities among the ranks and conditions of men he takes to be inevitable. Even the legal rights of citizens, apart from the political, are few. But to institutionalize these distinctions (that are generally social or economic) in the form of government is to violate the genius of the organically "grown," civil-association republic, to frustrate its capacity to unite men through the unfettered operation of the *mores majorum*.[33]

The *Inquiry* is in five parts: first, of Adams and artificial aristocracy; second, of the true role of government; third, of the civil qualities of our government (i.e., changes needed in our political law); fourth, of Federalist economics; and, finally, of the good "moral principles"

---

[31] Kirk, *op. cit.*, p. 65, reminds us that John Randolph once suggested that Taylor's works be "translated" into English.

[32] "Introduction," *Inquiry*, p. xxvi.

[33] For a discussion of nonideological societies which parallels that of Oakeshott, see Frederick A. Hayek, *Law, Legislation and Liberty* (Chicago: University of Chicago Press, 1973), vol. 1, pp. 36–38.

(self-restraints) in the American system. Adams' mistake is in confusing the postfeudal English Whig regime with the American version of the agrarian republic: the English order which perfected the bad principle of economic distribution through "charters." Taylor did not rest his system on either the weakness or the virtue of men; he knew that any government would be asked by those who lived under it to provide for their various special needs. But he never allows us to forget that the power to give is the power to take; or that the only equality government can ensure is (apart from simple liberty) the equality of total subjection. Furthermore, the less government can do, the less tumult it will produce. The details of life under a strictly federal arrangement would be regulated by local law, custom, or social pressure—as in matters of religion.[34] The reason for parties, embodying a "standing interest," should disappear. Only then need we not fear the "beast, from which men flee to monarchy"—the mendacious or ideological schemes within which groups, "under the title of patriots, are, like fanaticks under the title of saints, ready to perpetrate any crimes to gratify their interest or prejudice." Otherwise, this "monster" of faction, hidden in noble rhetoric, will, as the ancients warn, return us to the situation against which we rebelled in the first place, but with one difference: we shall face tyrants by the million, instead of a single despot.[35]

Taylor's other theoretical works belong to the last few,

---

[34] Taylor believed that the church as an arm of the state spread atheism, and that true religion should flourish best in separation from the political.

[35] *Inquiry*, p. 559.

apocalyptic years of his life. For the most part, they develop, under pressure, fresh arguments for positions he has already assumed. *Construction Construed, and Constitutions Vindicated* (1820) is a philippic against the usurpations of the Supreme Court, which he perceives in the rechartering of the Bank of the United States; against a prostitution of law by interest and political theory. *Tyranny Unmasked* (1822) is a careful reply to Henry Clay's revival of Hamilton's plan to encourage trade and manufacture. *New Views of the Constitution of the United States* (1823) has as its immediate objective the adoption of certain pending amendments to the Constitution. Its theme is the original derivation of our political law and the nature of the federal power explained by that history, from 1776 forward to the moment when he writes. Madison and Marshall are Taylor's adversaries. They have distorted the record in the effort to justify a more energetic central authority.

All three books are to be valued chiefly for their insight into federal-state relations and the true nature of the Union. At this time (and for reasons detailed above) Taylor's anxiety about the continuing viability of American politics had grown apace. Therefore, these final essays were produced with dispatch and little of the elaboration which marks his *Inquiry*. They belong more to the English Augustan (and originally Ciceronian) tradition of the public or forensic essay on moral and political affairs and less to philosophy or poetry than do the productions of his unhurried deliberation. But, by reason of their usefulness to readers of *Arator* and the *Inquiry*, and also because of what they tell us about the beginnings of

a distinctively southern version of American politics, they
deserve to be reprinted and better known. For in them
speaks the senatorial voice, the republican "father" which
any educated and well-informed American of that generation would have recognized as expressing the corporate
American self—our version of *Romanitas*.

But if it is useful and instructive to compare the political writings of John Taylor of Caroline to certain clas-
sical models, to the teachings of ancient historians and
social philosophers, it is even more appropriate to connect
his most influential composition, the *Arator*, with its
specific Greek and Roman prototypes. And particularly
with the surviving production of the original of his kind,
the *De Agri Cultura* of Cato the Censor, the special hero
of the old Whigs.[36] The early Latin prose pastoral (ca.
220 B.C.) initiates a literary tradition which has its finest
flowering in Vergil's *Georgics*[37]—a tradition very much
alive in America, as witness the *Hard Scrabble* of Texas'
John Graves.[38] Like the treatises of Varro and Columella
and *The Works and Days* of Hesiod, the eighth-century

---

[36] I cite the Loeb edition (Cambridge, Mass.: Harvard University
Press, 1934), edited and translated by William Davis Hooper. For the
force of Cato as symbol in the eighteenth century, see James W. John-
son, *The Formation of English Neo-Classical Thought* (Princeton, N.J.:
Princeton University Press, 1967), pp. 95–105.

[37] See Frank O. Copley, *Latin Literature: From the Beginnings to the
Close of the Second Century*, A.D. (Ann Arbor: University of Michigan
Press, 1969), pp. 178–87; see also pp. 305–8.

[38] John Graves, *Hard Scrabble: Observations on a Patch of Land*
(New York: Alfred A. Knopf, 1974). A summary of the English portion
of the tradition appears in W. J. Keith, *The Rural Tradition* (North
Brighton, Sussex: Harvester Press, 1975).

B.C. Boeotian poet, things written in this vein mix practical agricultural advice and moral reflection.[39] All connect virtue and the proper order of human life with the disciplines of the farmer and stockman. Agriculture is a reasonable but pious dealing with mystery. It involves a prescriptive wisdom, based on experience, and embodies a practice of good manners toward the gods. Its product is the *vir bonus*, the plain good man. And the interdependence of such solid citizens, all of them capable of honor in each other's eyes, all with a share in the *patria*, is the closest we can come to the providentially provided Garden or "golden age" under the present, unpropitious dispensation: *find within, but not by virtue of, government.*

Taylor is like Cato and the other ancients of this party in treating advice on farming as a species of moral instruction. To tell a man how best to raise hogs or grow wheat or manage his servants—and to tell him that these occupations are those which the gods chose as best suited to test our stewardship—is to contribute to his moral being. Says Cato, "Our ancestors . . . when they would praise a worthy man, their praise took this form: 'good husbandman,' 'good farmer'; one so praised was thought to have received the greatest commendation."[40] And it is also in the spirit of that eldest republican to see in solid

---

[39] Varro's *Rerum Rusticarum* is printed with Cato in the Loeb edition. Columella's *De Re Rustica*, in an edition and translation by H. B. Ash, is printed in three volumes in the same series (Cambridge, Mass.: Harvard University Press, 1941). I prefer the Hesiod as translated by Richard Lattimore (Ann Arbor: University of Michigan Press, 1973).

[40] Cato, *op. cit.,* p. 3.

freemen—independent freeholders—the most important crop of a sound agriculture.[41] Rome in the Punic Wars was defended by yeoman levies, citizen-soldiers drawn up from the tribes for limited terms of service and returning to them, with dignity, once service was done. Amateurs, and without proper leadership, they avoided faction and overcame Carthage and the mighty Hannibal.[42]

Because *Arator* is about the social order of an agricultural republic, and not just about farming, Taylor includes in it materials on the relation of agriculture to the American economy, on agriculture and politics, and on the enemies of the agrarian republic—the freeloaders who would batten upon the farmer, mechanic, and small tradesman. And, on top of these seemingly extraneous asides, he also includes chapters on militia and its advantages over a hired army in a book that seems to have nothing to do with war. Earlier I described agriculture as a discipline. In hard pastoral of Cato's or Taylor's kind, the regular difficulties of agricultural life are perceived as having very positive effects in the formation of character.[43] A formidable militia is the acid test of the distribution of such character. Furthermore, republics and other constitutional orders that cannot defend themselves without a standing army are not free societies for long. Roman, British, and other histories spell out that

---

[41] The same view is reflected in Wordsworth's "Michael" and in some poetry by Robert Frost.

[42] See Livy's *History of Rome* and Arnold J. Toynbee's *Hannibal's Legacy*, 2 vols. (Oxford: Clarendon Press, 1965). Taylor knew this story.

[43] Hard pastoral, as opposed to "escapist" or Arcadian pastoral, as in Theocritus and Vergil's *Eclogues*.

lesson loud and clear. For republics survive through men who are willing to assume responsibility. The care and maintenance of personal property are the day-to-day tests of the general distribution, throughout a population, of such a wholesome spirit. In the context established by *Arator*, each duty well performed is an act of worship, the practice of those virtues "prescribed . . . as the means for the admission . . . into heaven."[44] And also a delight, an inner gratification so strong that the opinions detailed in the chapter "The Pleasures of Agriculture" are implied in the surrounding practical recommendations on the arts of husbandry.[45]

Slaves are for Taylor among the possessions which in turn possess and measure the moral stature of their owners. Or, more properly, the ultimate test of the ethics of ownership. Like Cato and other ancients in this literary tradition, he includes some practical counsel on slave use and management in his book, as well as some theoretical comment. Talking here about society, and not about the sphere of political law, he shows the "patriarchal" side of his mind. By definition, in the moment of its inception, Negro slavery was a bad idea: bad, first of all, because it was slavery; and also bad because it brought into the society of the colonies a people not likely to be accepted as citizens, if they were freed. Taylor is one with most American thinkers from Washington and Jefferson to

---

[44] *Arator; Being a Series of Agricultural Essays, Practical and Political: In Sixty-Four Numbers*, 6th ed. (Petersburg, Va.: J. M. Carter, 1818), p. 189.

[45] *Ibid.*, pp. 188–91.

Lincoln in doubting that the free Negro could ever be anything but a problem for American politics: in insisting that, once released from bondage, they would have to go somewhere else. And thus, though standing in good company, he demonstrated how little he thought of the universalist doctrine of natural rights. Unlike Jefferson, however, he saw a potentially positive moral consequence that might follow from slaveholding, as from all other stewardship of property. Hence, he denies Jefferson's argument in *Notes on the State of Virginia* that slaveholding is automatically harmful to republican virtue.[46] Jefferson and the other great statesmen of Virginia are, in their careers, proofs to the contrary.[47] The distinction which Taylor makes in all of his comment on slavery is basic to old-Whig political thought. He refuses to treat an argument from definition as if it were an argument from circumstance. Therefore, he maintains that since Negro slavery is thoroughly established, and since the law of self-preservation binds us to it, it is feckless to complain that we should not have brought in slaves at an earlier date. Writes Taylor, "Negro slavery is an evil which the United States must look in the face. To whine over it, is cowardly; to aggravate it, criminal; and to forbear to alleviate it, because it cannot be wholly cured, foolish."[48]

---

[46] Thomas Jefferson, *Notes on the State of Virginia*, ed. William Peden (Chapel Hill: University of North Carolina Press, 1955). For support of Taylor, see Edmund S. Morgan, *American Slavery, American Freedom: The Ordeal of Colonial Virginia* (New York: W. W. Norton, 1975).

[47] *Arator*, pp. 52–54.

[48] *Ibid.*, p. 93. His position assumes the homogenous republic.

The confusion between these two lines of reasoning, from definition and from circumstance, still complicates and troubles our handling of the public business, and not only where the Negro is concerned.[49]

The writer who reached toward a large audience in *Arator* is a planter's planter, the president of the Virginia Agricultural Society, lifetime member of the Philadelphia Society for Promoting Agriculture, and corresponding associate of many similar organizations. He has brought the new agronomy from England. He speaks as chief agriculturist and political counselor to the whole agrarian community. And he proposes to teach the members of that connection a little political economy and a little practical politics by preparing certain elements from each field from *within* the perspective of their rural world— with some assistance from the science and the poetry of their way of life. Such labor was for Taylor a kind of stewardship and cultivation. Scholars who would tell us that his passion for the kind of society that produced him does not inform and almost define his political thought have a hard case to make.[50] Taylor, for reasons rooted in his experience, and justified in old-Whig or agrarian republican theory, did not wish for us to develop into an urban commercial society. Like his heirs of the 1930s,

---

[49] See Lewis Simpson, *The Dispossessed Garden* (Athens: University of Georgia Press, 1975), pp. 40–43, on the link between slavery and the pastoral in Taylor. Lytle is useful on slavery in Taylor.

[50] See Lloyd, *op. cit.*, p. 287. His refusal to accept Taylor as an agrarian is surprising. It detracts from what is otherwise a useful study.

the Twelve Southerners who wrote *I'll Take My Stand,*
he saw only danger in that prospect.[51] And this open
preference for modes and orders which we have, at least
for the time, rejected may militate against his purchase
upon contemporary attention. Or perhaps it works the
other way around. For some aspects of the "enterprise-
association" republic have been obviously unfruitful.
Class struggle strains the ties that bind. The dignity of
liberty is everywhere ill understood. Under these circumstances, in the desire to recover the original genius of
American politics, the teaching of the Revolution, we are
perhaps ready to ask how we arrived at our present state
—to ask "Old Taylor," by reading him with care. And
then to appreciate the merits bespoken in the eulogy of
his colleague, Senator Thomas Hart Benton of Missouri:
". . . the ideal of a republican statesman, . . . plain and
solid, a wise counselor, a ready and vigorous debater,
acute and comprehensive, ripe in all historical and political knowledge, innately republican—modest, courteous,
benevolent, hospitable—a skillful, practical farmer, giving his time to his farm and his books, when not called
by emergency to the public service—and returning to his
books and his farm when the emergency was over."[52]

The force of Taylor's moral testimony, drawn from a
life lived according to his own firm principles, reaches us

---

[51] Twelve Southerners, *I'll Take My Stand: The South and the Agrarian Tradition* (New York: Harper & Brothers, 1930).

[52] Quoted in Jay B. Hubbell, *The South in American Literature, 1607–
1900* (Durham, N.C.: Duke University Press, 1954), pp. 219–20.

across the over one hundred fifty years since his death. And almost everything he wrote or performed tells us that Benton's praise was well deserved.

A SELECTED BIBLIOGRAPHY

Primary Sources

Taylor, John. *Arator; Being a Series of Agricultural Essays, Practical and Political: In Sixty-One Numbers.* Georgetown, D.C.: J. M. and J. B. Carter, 1813; other editions 1814, 1817, 1818 (3), and 1840.

―――. *Construction Construed, and Constitutions Vindicated.* Richmond: Shepherd and Pollard, 1820. Reprinted by Da Capo, 1970.

―――. *A Defence of the Measures of the Administration of Thomas Jefferson.* Washington, D.C.: Samuel H. Smith, 1804.

―――. *An Inquiry into the Principles and Policy of the Government of the United States.* Fredericksburg, Va.: Green and Cody, 1814. Reprinted by Yale, 1950; and by Bobbs-Merrill Co., 1969 (see below).

―――. "Letters of John Taylor of Caroline County." *John P. Branch Historical Papers of Randolph-Macon College* 2, nos. 3 and 4 (June 1908): 253–353.

―――. *New Views of the Constitution of the United States.* Washington City, D.C.: Way and Gideon, 1823.

―――. *Tyranny Unmasked.* Washington City, D.C.: Davis and Force, 1822.

Mudge (see below) contains a reasonably full bibliography of Taylor's writings; it should be supplemented by Lloyd's dissertation (also see below), especially for a catalogue of Taylor's available correspondence.

Secondary Sources

Abernethy, Thomas P. *The South in the New Nation, 1789–1819.* Baton Rouge: Louisiana State University Press, 1961.

Bailor, Keith M. "John Taylor of Caroline: Continuity, Change and Discontinuity in Virginia's Sentiments Toward Slavery, 1790–1820." *Virginia Magazine of History and Biography* 75 (July 1967): 290–304.

Baritz, Loren. *City on a Hill: A History of Ideas and Myths in America.* New York: John Wiley & Sons, 1964, pp. 159–203.

———. Introduction to John Taylor's *An Inquiry into the Principles and Policy of the Government of the United States.* Indianapolis: Bobbs-Merrill Co., 1969, pp. ix–xxxi.

Beard, Charles A. *Economic Origins of Jeffersonian Democracy.* New York: Free Press, 1943; especially chap. 12.

Bradford, M. E. "A Teaching for Republicans: Roman History and the Nation's First Identity." *Intercollegiate Review* 11 (Winter–Spring 1976): 67–81.

Craven, Avery O. "John Taylor and Southern Agriculture." *Journal of Southern History* 4 (May 1938): 137–47.

———. "John Taylor, December 19 (?), 1753–August 21, 1824, Political Writer and Agriculturist." In *Dictionary of American Biography.* New York: Charles Scribner's Sons, 1936, XVIII, pp. 331–33.

Dauer, Manning, and Hammond, Hans. "John Taylor: Democrat or Aristocrat?" *Journal of Politics* 6 (November 1944): 381–403.

Davis, Richard Beale. *Intellectual Life in Jefferson's Virginia, 1790–1830.* Chapel Hill: University of North Carolina Press, 1964, pp. 154–56.

Dodd, William. "John Taylor of Caroline, Prophet of Secession." *John P. Branch Historical Papers of Randolph-Macon College.* Vol. 2. Ashland, Va., 1908, pp. 214–52.

Drell, Bernard. "John Taylor of Caroline and the Preservation of the Old Social Order." *Virginia Magazine of History and Biography* 46 (October 1938): 285–98.

Grampp, William D. "John Taylor: Economist of Southern Agrarianism." *Southern Economic Journal* 11 (January 1945): 255–68.

Gray, Lewis Cecil. *History of Agriculture in the United States to 1860*. 2 vols. Washington: Carnegie Institution of Washington, 1933.

Keith, W. J. *The Rural Tradition: William Cobbett, Gilbert White, and Other Non-Fiction Prose Writers of the English Countryside*. North Brighton, Sussex: Harvester Press, 1975.

Lloyd, Thomas Gordon. "The Danger Not Yet Over: The Political Thought and Practice of John Taylor of Caroline." Ph.D. dissertation, Claremont Graduate School, 1973.

Lytle, Andrew Nelson. "John Taylor and the Political Economy of Agriculture," *American Review* (September, October, November 1934), III, 432–47, 630–43; IV, 84–99.

McConnell, Grant. "John Taylor and the Democratic Tradition." *Western Political Quarterly* 4 (March 1951): 17–31.

MacLean, Kenneth. *Agrarian Age: A Background for Wordsworth*. New Haven: Yale University Press, 1950.

Mudge, Eugene T. *The Social Philosophy of John Taylor of Caroline: A Study in Jeffersonian Democracy*. New York: Columbia University Press, 1939.

Nichols, Roy Franklin. Introduction to Taylor's *An Inquiry* . . . . New Haven, Yale University Press, 1950, pp. 7–29.

Risjord, Norman K. *The Old Republicans: Southern Conservatism in the Age of Jefferson*. New York: Columbia Press, 1965.

Shalhope, Robert E. "Thomas Jefferson's Republicanism and Antebellum Southern Thought." *Journal of Southern History* 42 (Fall 1976): 529–56.

Simms, Henry. *Life of John Taylor: The Story of a Brilliant Leader in the Early Virginia State Rights School*. Richmond: William Byrd Press, 1932.

Simpson, Lewis P. *The Dispossessed Garden: Pastoral and History in Southern Literature*. Athens: University of Georgia Press, 1975.

Vile, M. J. C. *Constitutionalism and the Separation of Powers*. London: Oxford University Press, 1967.

Williams, Raymond. *The Country and the City*. New York: Oxford University Press, 1973.

Wood, Gordon S. *The Creation of the American Republic, 1776–1787*. Chapel Hill: University of North Carolina Press, 1969.
Wright, Benjamin F., Jr. "The Philosopher of Jeffersonian Democracy." *American Political Science Review* 22 (November 1928): 870–92.

A NOTE ON THE TEXT

We print here the last (sixth) edition of *Arator*, seen through the press by John Taylor himself, the version of 1818. The essays in this book first appeared in 1803 in a Georgetown newspaper and were anonymously published in a book in 1813. The style of this edition was "*Arator; Being a Series of Agricultural Essays, Practical and Political: In Sixty-One Numbers. By a Citizen of Virginia.*" Taylor brought the book out in his own name in 1814, also adding to this edition the notes which are printed here and expunging certain partisan political materials as violating the genre of his composition. A new edition appeared in Baltimore in 1817. Three additional papers, unnumbered, were added to the set with this printing. A lengthy preface (also printed here) was attached to the three Petersburg, Virginia, editions of 1818, where the papers first included in 1817 are given numbers. Edmund Ruffin, one of Taylor's successors as agriculturalist and sectional spokesman, printed the last version published to this date in *Farmer's Register*, VIII (December 31, 1840), 703–71. This seventh edition contains Ruffin's fine preface.

The present edition is thus the eighth of *Arator*. Though we have chosen Taylor's last printing of the book for reproduction, the text has been prepared by examining several editions. Taylor's own list of *errata* from the sixth edition has been used to correct this text. A small number of explanatory notes have been added as a matter of editorial discretion. A complete bibliographical history of the book is very much needed, as surviving copies of the various editions are few.

I wish to thank Sister Ruth Quatman, S.S.N.D., and the other staff members of the University of Dallas Library for their assistance in obtaining Taylor materials; Dr. and Mrs. James McClellan for a Library of Congress reproduction of *Arator*; and my wife, Marie, for help and counsel in the preparation of preface and text.

M. E. Bradford

AUTHOR'S PREFACE
TO THE FOURTH EDITION
OF *ARATOR*

The essays above the signature of *Arator*, were not preceded by an explanation of the motives by which they were dictated, or of the ends designed to be effected, because they were originally published in a newspaper without any anticipation of the form they have assumed. But being now stampt by the public acceptation with some degree of value, an account of these motives and ends may extend their efficiency, and promote the examination of subjects, so important and inexhaustible.

A conviction that the prosperity of our country depended upon a competent share of agricultural and political knowledge, and that an ignorance of either, would defeat the benefits naturally flowing from a proficiency in both, produced these essays, and also a larger book, entitled *An Inquiry into the Principles and Policy of the Government of the United States** for the ends of ad-

---

* *An Inquiry into the Principles and Policy of the Government of the United States* (Fredericksburg, Va.: Green and Cady, 1814). Reissued in 1969 by Bobbs-Merrill in an edition edited by Loren Baritz.

vancing practical improvements in one science, and of preserving those we had already made in the other.

Agriculture and politics are primary causes of our wealth and liberty. Both contain internal good principles, but both are liable to practical deterioration. If one is vitiated in practice, poverty, if the other, oppression ensues. If the agriculture is good and the government bad, we may have wealth and slavery. If the government is good and the agriculture bad, liberty and poverty. To secure both wealth and liberty, an intimate knowledge of the good principles comprised in both, and a strict accordance in practice with those principles, must be indispensably necessary.

Hence results the propriety of awakening the people to the good principles of agriculture, and of keeping them awake to those of our form of government. Without commemoration, the latter might be lost, and without enquiry, the former could never be found. Both subjects are vitally important to the success of the singular experiment now making by the United States upon the theatre of the world, and contain the only means of redeeming their pledge to mankind.

Both are treated of in the two books abovementioned. *Arator* is chiefly confined to agriculture, but it contains a few political observations. The *Inquiry*, to politics; but it labours to explain the true interest of the agricultural class. The affinity between the subjects, caused them to be intermingled. But the author never imagined himself able to tear the bandage of habit from the eyes of prejudice, nor to squeeze the tincture of corruption from the heart of avarice. Without aspiring to moral heroism, or to the renown of new inventions, he only attempts to extract good agricultural practices from his own experience, and good political measures from the wise and faithful archives of revolutionary patriotism, to increase the skill of his countrymen, in making good crops and in securing them for their own benefit.

That private industry combined with political fraud, may make a nation wealthy and miserable, is exemplified in England. That one interest or class of men, may reap oppression from carrying their occupation to great perfection, appears in the state of the manufacturers of the same country. And a similar fate awaits the agricultural class of this, although it could be driven by English coercion, even up to English perfection, unless it retains the American political principles alone competent to defeat the arts, under which the productive classes of mankind are universally groaning.

Why are the agriculturists of the United States happier than those of England, under the great disadvantages of a worse system of agriculture, and of paying higher wages for labour? From the greater chastity of their political measures. The habit of drawing comparisons between our government and a foreign one, for the purposes of excusing abuses and lulling vigilance, is a treacherous delusion, and a tacit confession of an approximation towards them; but this reference is calculated to open the eyes of agriculture, to the contemplation of those foreign measures which have created reapers of its harvests, and swallowers of its profits. If such detachments of foragers and marauders from the main body of the English nation, can intercept the great crops of the best existing system of agriculture, so as to cause frequent famines among the main body itself, it evidently suggests to us the wisdom of distinguishing between those establishments necessary for good government, and such as are contrived merely "consumere fruges"; that is, to live upon the industry of others without rendering any services to the nation. To save our sorry crops from free quarter sinecures, is even more important and more urgent, than to amend our agriculture. It would secure to us comfort and happiness. By suffering frauds to pounce upon them, we cannot be made comfortable and happy, even by great crops. And the author ventures to assert, that whilst the readers of *Arator* will unanimously agree that its tendency is to improve our crops, those of the *Inquiry* belonging to the main body of society, or to those detachments, will concur in the tendency of that book, to save them from becoming a prey to political frauds; one division by commending much, the other, by commending nothing.

No body will deny that an endeavor to increase our crops is laudable, but it is a question, whether it is equally laudable to save them from the nets of political "retiarii" by teaching the plain honest yeomanry, how to avoid the mortification of starving upon them, however great. The opinion "that the more industry spends of its own earnings, and the less of them is intercepted by governments, or taken away by legal projects, the richer, the greater, and the happier will be the nation" if correct, resolves that doubt. No nation was ever oppressed ruined or enslaved by the prodigality of individuals; all nations have suffered some of these evils from the prodigality of governments. Hence a plain political maxim forces itself upon the mind, sufficient to maintain a good government, if mankind possessed prudence enough not to ramble into intricacies contrived on purpose to entrap them; namely "that national prosperity and liberty, are safe, endangered or lost, in proportion as individuals retain, or governments acquire, the investiture or disposition of the earnings of industry."

The author had another reason for uniting the subjects of agriculture and politics. He considered agriculture as the guardian of liberty, as well as the mother of wealth. So long as the principles of our government are uncorrupted, and the sovereignty of majorities remains, she must occupy the highest political station, and owe to society the most sacred political duty. It is as incumbent upon her to learn how to protect defenceless minor interests, as to defend herself. And whilst the security for her patriotism "that she cannot find any body worth plundering" exists, she should take care not to betray her wards, by suffering herself to be made poor, either by a deficiency of skill and industry, or by legal spoliations; because wealth is power. She must be rich to be powerful, and she must be powerful to discharge faithfully the sacred obligation she owes to society, by constituting the majority. If her wealth is transferred, her power will go with it, and an irresistible political influence will be acquired by a minority, which can find some body worth plundering.

The thin soil of the United States, renders political frauds particularly grievous to agriculture, from its insufficiency to bear them; and the thin population, exposes us particularly to the evils of invasion. The population, necessary to contract or prevent these evils, can never be obtained, except by enriching the soil, and the soil cannot be enriched, except by legislative cooperation with individual industry, by forbearing to transfer wealth from an application to these great national objects, to the encouragement of doubtful projects, or the diffusion of a pernicious degree of luxury. Laws shed a good or a bad influence upon all social employments, and operate most extensively upon that which is most general. Why have so many employments, expensive, useless or pernicious, flourished wonderfully in the United States, whilst the fertility of the soil has been wonderfully diminishing? Can it be ascribed to any cause but a baleful legal influence? Of what avail will be agricultural books, or societies, or individual industry, to improve the soil and strengthen the population, opposed to a system of legislation dispensing impoverishments? Of the same, experienced by societies and books for improving the representation of the British house of commons.

Legislatures must begin to notice and discuss the state of agriculture, before they can discover or remove the causes of the cadaverous countenance exhibited by the soil. These causes lie concealed in the laws. It is strenuously contended that laws are able to administer prosperity or decay to occupations of inferior utility to man, and less interesting to nations in general, and to the United States in particular, by exciting or discouraging the degree of ardour, inspired by an equal footing between the various objects of industry. Such an equipoise of justice among occupations, is in fact an equipoise of liberty among men, and constitutes the only sound test of a free government. But it is admitted that laws may both create and bestow upon particular interests wealth and power, and yet if we even exclude from the question the injuries thence resulting to other interests, it ought to be considered that they gradually suppress the idea of a government guided by the common good, and plant in its place by a succession of precedents, a system of partiality to be exercised by power without limitation, and capable of demolishing every barrier against usurpation and tyranny.

If our government however, will usurp a boundless sovereignty over the industry and property of individuals, the policy of invading the great province of agriculture, to gather spoils for enriching a number of little barren districts, is still to be questioned. If agriculture for instance, is as insignificant as banking, it has the same claim to legal favour; if less so this claim becomes stronger. From what motives have legal partialities in all countries selected their favorites? Even religion has often been converted into the spirit of folly, or the instrument of wickedness. Will they regard human occupations with more veneration? These only are left in our country exposed to the same motives which have begotten the whole tribe of legal partialities abroad, and are therefore more likely to be laid hold of with furious eagerness, and to be mangled with barbarous outrage.

Already, many members of the body politic, and even sundry excrescences which ought to be amputated, are excited up to a fever, and agriculture chilled at the heart by drafts to bestow an unnatural degree of heat upon less valuable or pernicious extremes. If our health was sound during the presidency of Washington, what must it now be? The pulsation has increased six fold in the limb of taxation; in the excrescence of banking, fifty fold; in that of protecting duties enormously; and in the patronage limb, its flutterings have become so rapid and indistinct, that congress have ordered a book to be compiled, to explain what may be called the logarithm of patronage. A healthy state of society must consist in that equable pulsation throughout all its parts, produced by an equipoise of justice, favour and protection among its several interests. Unless this is restored by amputations, retrenchments, and evacuations, agriculture cannot for ages exhibit on the soil, an equivalent degree of prosperity, which she ought in common with other interests to derive from the revolution.

Finally, if the defence of partial laws "that the sufferings they inflict on one person or class, ought to be balanced against the acquisitions they bestow on another" though false, immoral and tyrannical, are allowed to be true, virtuous, and fair, yet it ought at least to be examined by the principle it asserts. Compare then the gain from a bounty on snuff, with the loss sustained by a tax on barns. The latter in some states, owing to the deficiency of this agricultural manufacture, amounts probably upon grain only, to twenty per centum annually. Add to this loss the whole mass of agricultural suffering, arising from the whole deprivation of capital, and compare the total, with the total gain to manufacturers from protecting duties. In fact, the principle resorted to for defence by partial laws, ever was and ever will be used by governments, only to increase their power, by accumulating money at the cost of nations, to be wasted in extravagance or employed still more perniciously, in extending patronage, or spreading corruption. Under shelter of the delusion, they advance step by step towards arbitrary power, and that interest which is most productive and covers a majority, inevitably becomes its victim, unless it detects the fraud. Agriculture can never flourish, unless it applies a very different principle both to its land and its government, namely, "that renewal must constantly follow close upon the heels of decay, either to maintain fertility or to avoid oppression."

PUBLISHER'S PREFACE

The publisher of the following essays is the first who has offered to the public patronage, an experimental composition, adapted to the Soil, Climate and Agriculture of the greater portion of the United States; and so far as his knowledge extends, it is the first of the kind which this great district of country has produced. He is not qualified to judge of its merit, and can only infer from its being the work of a successful practical farmer, and not the offspring of interest or theory, that every purchaser will be reimbursed his money many fold. But however this may be, the Publisher respectfully states that rude inventions have terminated in great public good; and that the deficiency of graphical merit in the agricultural country, for which the composition was intended, is almost as strong a recommendation of this effort towards improvement, as the hieroglyphics of antiquity, were of those made for the discovery of letters. An encouragement of small improvements is the parent of perfection

in every art and science, and as agriculture is the queen of
the whole circle, the Publisher has thought it his duty to
give the public an opportunity of awakening better talents
and the greater exertions, for occupying the extensive
space between its present and a desirable condition.

The United States have been charged with a dearth of
original compositions. Their reach of European books is
the reason of the fact, so far as it extends to moral subjects; whilst the multitude, novelty and usefulness of their
mechanical inventions, repels an insinuation, that it arises
from a want of genius or industry. The strongest ground
of the charge is, the deficiency of native books upon agriculture. Whilst the country was fresh, it was natural for
the inhabitants to neglect the subject in the midst of
abundance; but its evident impoverishment, ought to
have suggested to us the necessity of native remedies for
local errours; and the incongruity of English books upon
agriculture, with the climates, soils and habits of the
United States. This incongruity by drawing ridicule upon
imitators, too often extinguishes a patriotic ardour, and
checks instead of advancing improvement.

If the book now offered to the public should have no
other good effects but those of suggesting the necessity
of writing for ourselves on the subject, and introducing
some taste for such discussions, the compensation to the
Publisher for his labour will be amply repaid. To this
taste, the agriculture of Europe in general, and of Britain
in particular, is indebted for a vast improvement within
the last century, and a similar spirit in the United States
will undoubtedly produce similar effects. Every class of
men will be benefited by it. The *Merchant* will receive

more produce, and sell more goods. The demands upon the *Manufacturer* will extend to more and finer commodities. *Lawyers* and *Physicians* will have richer clients and patients, and better fees. The *Politician* may find more resources for defending his country, maintaining her independence and rewarding patriotism. The *Printers* will sell more books and newspapers. And the *Farmer*, though the fountain from which all these benefits must flow, as receiving first the fruits of improvements, will make them subservient to his own happiness, before he diffuses them to advance the happiness of others. A tendency to shed prosperity over all these classes, has some claim to general encouragement, and whilst the Publisher respectfully solicits the public patronage on this ground, he also confidently hopes, that a considerable portion both of amusement, and information will be found in the following sheets.

ARATOR

special purpose of investigating it.* The judgment of this impartial stranger appears in the following quotations. Page 26: "Land in America affords little pleasure or profit, and appears in a progress of continually affording less." P. 31: "Virginia is in a rapid decline." P. 38: "Land in New-York, formerly producing twenty bushels to the acre, now produces only ten." P. 41: "Little profit can be found in the present mode of agriculture of this country, and I apprehend it to be a fact that it affords *a bare subsistence*." P. 45: "Virginia is the southern limit of my inquiries, because agriculture had there already arrived to its lowest state of degradation." P. 49: "The land owners in this state are, with a few exceptions, in low circumstances; the inferior rank of them wretched in the extreme." P. 52: "Decline has pervaded all the states."

These conclusions, if true, are awfully threatening to the liberty and prosperity of a country, whose hostage for both is agriculture. An order of men, *earning a bare subsistence, in low circumstances, and whose inferior rank is wretched in the extreme,* cannot possibly constitute a moral force, adequate to either object. It is therefore highly important to the agricultural class, to ascertain whether it is true, that agriculture is in a decline. A decline terminates like every progress, at the end of its tendency.

Upon reading the opinion of this disinterested foreigner, my impressions were, indignation, alarm, convic-

---

* William Strickland (of Yorkshire), *Observations on the Agriculture of the United States* (London, 1801). Reissued with *Journal of a Tour in the United States of America, 1794–1795* in an edition prepared by the Rev. J. E. Strickland (Charlottesville, Va.: University Press of Virginia, 1976).

NUMBER 1

The Present State of Agriculture

I shall consider in a succession of short essays, the present state of agriculture in the United States, its oppressions and defects, and the remedies, political and domestic,
which it needs. It is confessed, however, that the chief
knowledge of the author, as to modes of agriculture, is
confined to the states of Maryland, Virginia and North
Carolina. And therefore, whilst his remarks in relation
to its political state, will generally apply to the whole
union, those in relation to these modes, will particularly
apply to all states using slaves, or to the three enumerated
states.

Mr. Strickland, an Englishman, reputed to be sensible
and honest, published at London in the year 1801, a
pamphlet upon the agriculture of the United States, being
the result of his own observation, during a considerable
period spent in travelling through the country, for the

tion; inspired successively, by a love for my country, a fear for its welfare, and a recollection of facts.

The terrible facts, that the strongest chord which vibrates on the heart of man, cannot tie our people to the natal spot, that they view it with horror, and flee from it to new climes with joy, determine our agricultural progress, to be a progress of emigration, and not of improvement; and lead to an ultimate recoil from this exhausted resource, to an exhausted country.

NUMBER 2

The Present State of Agriculture, Continued

A patient must know that he is sick, before he will take physick. A collection of a few facts, to ascertain the ill health of agriculture, is necessary to invigorate our efforts towards a cure. One, apparent to the most superficial observer, is, that our land has diminished in fertility. Arts improve the work of nature—when they injure it, they are not arts, but barbarous customs. It is the office of agriculture, as an art, not to impoverish, but to fertilize the soil, and make it more useful than in its natural state. Such is the effect of every species of agriculture, which can aspire to the character of an art. Its object being to furnish man with articles of the first necessity, whatever defeats that object, is a crime of the first magnitude. Had men a power to obscure or brighten the light of the sun, by obscuring it, they would imitate the morality of diminishing the fertility of the earth. Is not one as criminal as the other? Yet it is a fact, that lands in their natural state, are more valuable, than those which have undergone our habit of agriculture, of which emigrations are complete proofs.

The decay of a multitude of small towns, so situated as to depend for support on unalterable districts, is another proof of the impoverishment of the soil. It is true, that a few large towns have grown up, but this is owing, not to an increased product, but to an increased pasture; whereas, in every case, where the pasture is limited, or isolated by local circumstances, small towns have sprung up, whilst the lands were fresh, and decayed, as they were worn out. I have no facts to ascertain certainly the products of agriculture at different periods relatively to the number of people; such would furnish a demonstration of its state. But I have understood, that sixty thousand hogsheads of tobacco were exported from Virginia, when it contained about one fourth of its present population. If so, had the fertility of the country remained undiminished, Virginia ought now to export two hundred and forty thousand hogsheads, or an equivalent. In this estimate, every species of export except tobacco, is excluded at one epoch, and exports of every kind included at the other: yet the latter would fall far short of exhibiting the equivalent necessary to bring itself on a footing, as to agriculture, with the former. Two hundred and forty thousand hogsheads of tobacco, which, or an equivalent, Virginia would now export, if the state of agriculture had been as flourishing as it was sixty or seventy years past, at the present value, by which all our exports are rated, would be worth above seventeen millions of dollars; and supposing Virginia to furnish one seventh part of the native agricultural exports of the United States, these

ought now to amount to one hundred and twenty millions
of dollars, had the products of agriculture kept pace with
the increase of population. If this statement is not exactly
correct, enough of it certainly is so, to demonstrate a rapid
impoverishment of the soil of the United States.

The decay of the culture of tobacco is testimony to this
unwelcome fact. It is deserted because the lands are exhausted. To conceal from ourselves a disagreeable truth,
we resort to the delusion, that tobacco requires new or
fresh land; whereas every one acquainted with the plant
knows, that its quantity and quality, as is the case with
most or all plants, are both greatly improved by manured
land, or land, the fertility of which has been artificially
increased. Whole counties, comprising large districts of
country, which once grew tobacco in great quantities, are
now too sterile to grow any of moment; and the wheat
crops substituted for tobacco, have already sunk to an
average below profit.

From the mass of facts, to prove that the fertility of
our country has been long declining, and that our agriculture is in a miserable state, I shall only select one more.
The average of our native exports, is about forty millions
of dollars annually. Some portion of this amount consists
of manufactures, the materials for which are not furnished
by agriculture; another, as is extensively the fact in the
case of flour, has passed through the hands of the manufacturer. Of the first portion he receives the whole price,
of the second a proportion. And a third portion of our
products is obtained from the sea. Of the forty millions
exported, agriculture, therefore, receives about thirty five.
The taxes of every kind, state and federal, may be esti-

mated at twenty millions of dollars, of which agriculture pays at least fifteen, leaving twenty millions of her exports for her own use. Counting all the slaves, who ought to be counted both as sources of product and expense, in estimating the state of agriculture, the people of the United States may probably amount to about seven millions, and it may be fairly assumed, that the interest or occupation of six millions of these seven, is agricultural. Of the whole surplus product of agriculture exported, after deducting the taxes it pays, there remains for each individual a few cents above three dollars. Out of this mass of profit, he is to pay for the manufactures, luxuries and necessaries he consumes, not raised by himself; and the only remaining article to be carried to the credit of agriculture, is the small gain it derives from its domestic sales, not to itself, or from sales by one of its members to another, for that does not enrich it, but to other classes, such as manufacturers and soldiers. Against the former, agriculture is to be debited with the bounties she is made by law to pay them; against the latter, she has been already debited by deducting her taxes from her exports. Neither can be a source of much wealth or profit to her, because in one case she furnishes the money by taxation, and in the other by bounties, with which her products are purchased. It is, therefore, nearly true, that the income of agriculture is only three dollars per poll, and that this income is her whole fund for supplying her wants and extending her improvements. This estimate is infinitely more correct, than one drawn from individual wealth or poverty. To infer from the first, that every body might become rich, as a defence of our agricultural regimen, would be a conclusion as fallacious, as to infer from the second, that every body must become poor, as a proof of its badness. Extraordinary talents or industry will produce extraordinary effects. Instances of happiness or wealth under a despotism, do not prove that its regimen is calculated for general wealth or happiness. A system, commercial, political or agricultural, so wretched as not to exhibit cases of individual prosperity, has never appeared, because an universal scourge would be universally abhorred. It is not from partial, but general facts, that we can draw a correct knowledge of our agriculture. Even a personal view of the country, might deceive the thoughtless, because neither the shortness of life, nor the gradual impoverishment of land, are calculated to establish a visible standard of comparison. A man must be old and possess a turn for observation from his youth, to be able to judge correctly from this source. I have known many farms for above forty years, and though I think that all of them have been greatly impoverished, yet I rely more upon the general facts I have stated, for agreeing with Strickland in opinion, "that the agriculture of the United States affords only a bare subsistence—that the fertility of our lands is gradually declining—and that the agriculture of Virginia has arrived to the lowest state of degradation."

NUMBER 3

The Political State of Agriculture

In collecting the causes which have contributed to the miserable agricultural state of the country, as it is a national calamity of the highest magnitude, we should be careful not to be blinded by partiality for our customs or institutions, nor corrupted by a disposition to flatter ourselves or others. I shall begin with those of a political nature. These are a secondary providence, which govern unseen the great interests of society; and if agriculture is bad and languishing in a country and climate, where it may be good and prosperous, no doubt remains with me, that political institutions have chiefly perpetrated the evil; just as they decide the fate of commerce.

The device of subjecting it to the payment of bounties to manufacturing, is an institution of this kind. This device is one item in every system for rendering governments too strong for nations. Such an object never was and never can be effected, except by factions legally created at the public expense. The wealth transferred from the nation to such factions, devotes them to the will of the government, by which it is bestowed. They must render the service for which it was given, or it would be taken away. It is unexceptionably given to support a government against a nation, or one faction against another. Armies, loaning, banking, and an intricate treasury system, endowing a government with the absolute power of applying public money, under the cover of nominal checks, are other devices of this kind. Whatever strength or wealth a government and its legal factions acquire by law, is taken from a nation; and whatever is taken from a nation, weakens and impoverishes that interest, which composes the majority. There, political oppression in every form must finally fall, however it may oscillate during the period of transit from a good to a bad government, so as sometimes to scratch factions. Agriculture being the interest covering a great majority of the people of the United States, every device for getting money or power, hatched by a fellow-feeling or common interest, between a government and its legal creatures, must of course weaken and impoverish it. Desertion, for the sake of reaping without labour, a share in the harvest of wealth and power, bestowed by laws at its expense, thins its ranks; an annual tribute to these legal factions, empties its purse; and poverty debilitates both its soil and understanding.

The device of protecting duties, under the pretext of encouraging manufactures, operates like its kindred, by creating a capitalist interest, which instantly seizes upon the bounty taken by law from agriculture; and instead of doing any good to the actual workers in wood, metals, cotton or other substances, it helps to rear up an aristocratical order, at the expense of the workers in earth, to unite with governments in oppressing every species of useful industry.

The products of agriculture and manufacturing, unshackled by law, would seek each for themselves, the best markets through commercial channels, but these markets would hardly ever be the same; protecting duties tie travellers together, whose business and interest lie in different directions. This ligature upon nature, will, like all unnatural ligatures, weaken or kill. The best markets of our agriculture lie in foreign countries, whilst the best markets of our manufactures are at home. Our agriculture has to cross the ocean, and encounter a competition with foreign agriculture on its own ground. Our manufactures meet at home a competition with foreign manufactures. The disadvantages of the first competition, suffice to excite all the efforts of agriculture to save her life; the advantages of the second suffice gradually to bestow a sound constitution on manufacturing. But the manufacture of an aristocratical interest, under the pretext of encouraging work of a very different nature, may reduce both manufacturers and husbandmen, as Strickland says, is already effected in the case of the latter, "to the lowest state of degradation."

This degradation could never have been seen by a friend to either, who could afterwards approve of protecting duties. Let us take the article of wheat to unfold an idea of the disadvantages which have produced it. If wheat is worth 16s. sterling in England the 70lb. the farmers sell it here at about 6s. sterling. American agriculture then meets English agriculture in a competition, compelling her to sell at little more than one third of the price obtained by her rival. But American manufactures take the field against English on very different terms. These competitors meet in the United States. The American manufactures receive first, a bounty equal to the freight, commission and English taxes, upon their English rivals; and secondly, a bounty equal to our own necessary imposts. Without protecting duties, therefore, the American manufacturer gets for the same article, about 25 per cent more, and the American agriculturist about 180 per cent less, than their English rivals. Protecting duties added to these inequalities, may raise up an order of masters for actual manufacturers, to intercept advantages too enormous to escape the vigilance of capital, impoverish husbandmen, and aid in changing a fair to a fraudulent government; but they will never make either of these intrinsically valuable classes richer, wiser or freer.

NUMBER 4

The Political State of Agriculture, Continued

In this number I shall consider a reason for protecting duties to encourage manufactures, which, if it is sound, overturns the whole argument against them. In every essay on behalf of manufactures, we are told, that by creating this class with bounties and privileges, we shall both make ourselves independent of foreign nations, and also provide a market for agricultural labour, as an aristocracy, in all its forms, is a market for labour. And the high price of wheat in England, is contrasted with its low price here, to prove the latter assertion. It would be sounder reasoning to contrast the high price of manufactures here, with the low price there, to prove that they ought to give bounties to agriculture to provide a market for manufactures. Nations and individuals are universally promised wealth by political swindlers. The English price for wheat, is coupled with the English political system. Without adopting the causes of that price, the effects springing from these causes cannot follow. The idle classes of the nobility, clergy, army, navy, bankers and national debt holders, with their servants and dependents, are the items of an aristocracy, which has reduced the agricultural class to a poor and powerless state, by the juggle of persuading it to buy high prices, by creating and maintaining these idle classes. The national debt alone maintains more people, than there are agriculturists in Britain. These do not amount to a tenth part of the nation. It is to this combination of causes, and not to manufactures singly, that the English agriculture is indebted for its high prices.

These very prices are themselves proofs of the oppression which produced them. They are the effect of the tendency which industry has to recover back some equivalent from fraud, and of the necessity of fraud to extend some encouragements to industry. But shall we oppress our agriculture, merely to demonstrate that abuses have a tendency to excite countervailing efforts, and load it with English impositions, for the sake of the inadequate reimbursement of English prices?

Let him who hopes to live to see the agricultural class of the United States, reduced by English policy to a tenth part of the nation, undertake to prove, that such a reduction would be a proof of its prosperity. If he could defend such a theory, he would at last be practically disappointed, unless our manufactures should drive the English manufactures out of the world, and occupy their place. The ingenious device of agriculture in England, in bestowing money on noble, clerical, military and chartered idlers, for the sake of selling its products to get back a part of its own, would turn out still more miserably, except for the vast addition to the manufacturing class, by foreign demands for its labour. If England only manufactured for herself, her manufactures would constitute but a wretched market for agriculture. One labourer feeds many manufacturers. One manufacturer supplies many labourers. Before the promise of English prices for bread and meat, tobacco and cotton, can be realized, from driving in manufacturing by protecting duties, we must be able to drive out manufactures by protecting fleets into every quarter of the globe; and so like some booby heirs, take up a parent's follies, at the period he is forced to lay them down.

Still more hopeless is the promise of the manufacturing mania, "that it will make us independent of foreign nations," when combined with its other promise of providing a market for agriculture. The promise of a market, as we see in the experience of England, can only be made good, by reducing the agricultural class to a tenth part of the nation, and increasing manufacturers by great manufactural exportations. This reduction can only be accomplished by driving or seducing above nine-tenths of the agricultural class, into other classes, and the increase by a brave and patriotic navy. Discontent and misery will be the fruits of the first operation, and these would constitute the most forlorn hope for success in the second. By exchanging hardy, honest and free husbandmen for the classes necessary to reduce the number of agriculturists, low enough to raise the prices of their products, shall we become more independent of foreign nations? What! Secure our independence by bankers and capitalists? Secure our independence by impoverishing, dis-

couraging and annihilating nine-tenths of our sound
yeomanry? By turning them into swindlers, and dependents on a master capitalist for daily bread.

There are two kinds of independence, real and imaginary. The first consists of the right of national self-
government; the second of individual taste or prejudice.
The yeomanry of the forest are best calculated to preserve the first, and the yeomanry of the loom are best
calculated to feed the second. A surrender of the first to
obtain the second, would be a mode of securing our independence, like England's converting her hardy tars into
barbers and tailors, in order to become independent of
French fashions.

The manufacturing mania accuses the agricultural
spirit of avarice and want of patriotism, whilst it offers
to bribe it by a prospect of better prices, whittles down
independence into cargoes of fancy goods, and proposes
to metamorphose nine-tenths of the hardy sons of the
forest into everything but heroes, for the grand end of
gratifying the avarice of a capitalist, monied or paper
interest.

Opinion is sometimes prejudice, sometimes zeal, and
often craft. These counterfeits of truth have universally
deluded the majority of nations into the strange conclusion, that it will flourish by paying bounties to undertakers for national salvation, for national wealth, and for
national independence. The first imposture is detected,
the second begins to be strongly suspected, but the third
has artfully provoked its trial, at a moment when it can
conceal the cheat under the passions excited by transitory
circumstances. Hatred of England, a pretended zeal

for national honour; and the real craft of advancing the pecuniary interest of a few capitalists; have conspired to paint a protecting duty system, into so strong a resemblance of patriotism and honesty, as to lead agriculture by a bridle made of her virtue and ignorance, towards the worship of an idol, compounded of folly and wickedness.

NUMBER 5

The Political State of Agriculture, Continued

English agriculture has completely tried the project of enriching itself, by buying markets with bounties. It has provided more of these markets, than the agriculture of any other nation. Yet it is unable to feed its own people, many of whom are indebted to foreign agriculture for daily bread. No profession in England is deficient in hands, but the agricultural, and none other a cypher in government. They have lords, bishops, officers civil and military, soldiers, sailors, bankers, loaners and capitalists in abundance, and all of them have an influence in the government. These are the markets in which the English agriculturists have successively laid out their money, in order to get good prices, and the more of these markets they buy, the less liberty and wealth they retain.

If the agriculture of the United States would only consider how it happens, that it can yet live upon six shillings sterling a bushel for wheat, when the English agriculture is perishing with sixteen, the film drawn over its eyes by the avarice with which those charge it, who design to cheat it, would fall off. The solution of the apparent wonder, lies in the delusion of buying price by bounties. The bounties are partly, but never completely reimbursed by the price. Though the payer of the bounties gets more price, he gains less profit than from the lower price, when he paid no bounties. Therefore the receivers of the bounties become rich and idle, and the receivers of the price, poor and laborious. And this effect is inevitable, because the bounties must for ever outrun the prices they create, or no body could subsist on them. If the bounty paid was equal to one shilling a bushel on wheat, and should raise the price nine pence, the receivers of the bounty would gain three pence a bushel on all the wheat of the nation, and agriculture would lose it, though it got a higher price. And this obvious fraud is precisely the result of every promise in every form made by charter and privilege to enrich or encourage agriculture.

The agriculture of the United States, found itself in the happiest situation for prosperity imaginable, at the end of the revolutionary war. It had not yet become such an egregious gudgeon* as to believe, that by giving ten millions of dollars every year to the tribe of undertakers, to make it rich, they would return it twenty; and it could avail itself of all the markets in the world, where this ridiculous notion prevailed. These were so many mines of wealth to the agriculture of the United States. The idle, clerical, military, banking, loaning, and en-

* Dupe.

nobled classes, as has been stated, do certainly have the effect of raising agricultural prices very considerably; but the agriculturists who pay and maintain these classes, still lose more by them than they gain. Now the United States, as a section of the commercial world, might have shared in the enhancement of agricultural price, produced by such unproductive orders in other countries; and paid none of the ruinous expense of wealth or liberty, which they cost. They might have reaped the good, and avoided the evil. And agriculture, for once in its life, might have done itself justice. But the wiseacre chose to reap the evil, and avoid the good; and if its situation has been occasionally tolerable, it was sorely against its will, or by accident. In the first eight years after the revolution, being the first period in the latter ages of the world, that agriculture could make laws, it legislated sundry items of the British system for buying markets or raising prices. In the next twelve, it nurtured their growth, so as to raise up some to a large, and one to a monstrous size; and also most sagaciously prohibited itself, first from sharing in the benefit of the high prices produced by aristocratical institutions in France, and secondly from sharing in those produced in the same way in England. European agriculture is gulled or oppressed by others; American, gulls or oppresses itself. The first is no longer weak enough to think, that its battalion of aristocratical items, does it any good; but it is now unable to follow its judgment; the second, though able to follow its own judgment, has adopted the exploded errors heartily repented of by the first, and far outstrips it in the celerity of its progress towards a state of absolute submission to other interests, by shutting out itself from markets enhanced at the expense of other nations; and at the same time by creating the English items of capitalists, or masters for manufacturers, bankers, lenders, armies, and navies. Our true interest was to pay nothing for markets, spurious and swindling to those who buy them, and yet to share in their enhancement of prices. We have pursued a different course, and I do not recollect a single law, state or continental, passed in favour of agriculture, nor a single good house built by it since the revolution; but I know many built before, which have fallen into decay. Our agriculture is complimented by presidents, governors, legislators and individuals; and the Turks reverence a particular order of people as being also favoured by heaven.

NUMBER 6

The Political State of Agriculture, Continued

The arguments to prove the political errors under which our agriculture is groaning, may suggest a suspicion, that I am an enemy to manufactures. The fact is otherwise. I believe that protecting duties, or whatever else shall damp agricultural effort, and impoverish the lands of our country, is the only real and fatal foe to manufactures; and that a flourishing agriculture will beget and enrich manufactures, as rich pastures multiply and fatten animals. He, who killed the goose to come at her golden eggs, was such a politician, as he who burdens our expiring agriculture, to raise bounties for our flourishing manufactures. He kills the cause of the end he looks for.

I meet such an insinuation by another argument. Protecting duties impoverish and enslave manufacturers themselves, and are so far from being intended to operate in their favour, or in favour of a nation, that their end and effect simply is to favour monied capital, which will seize upon and appropriate to itself, the whole profit of the bounty extorted from the people by protecting duties; and allow as scanty wages to its workmen, as it can. Monied capital drives industry without money out of the market, and forces it into its service, in every case where the object of contest is an enormous income. The wages it allows to industry are always regulated by the expense of subsistence, and not by the extent of its gain. Monied capitalists constitute an essential item of a government modelled after the English form. To advance this item, for the sake of strengthening the government against the people, and not for the sake of manufacturers, is the object of protecting duties. True, will say many a reader, but that is not the design here. Oh! how reverential is the logician who can prove, that an axe will cut under a monarchy, but not under a republic.

Some king, I believe, requested the mercantile class of his subjects, to ask of him a favour. The greatest, your majesty can grant us, said they, is, to let us alone. Protecting duties are such favours to manufacturers, as the pretended favours of kings are to merchants. They impoverish their customers, the agriculturists, and place over themselves an order of masters called capitalists, which intercepts the profit, destined, without legal interposition, for industry. Many other arguments might be urged to prove that protecting duties beget the poverty of manufacturers, but this is not my subject. To that I return.

The bitterest pill which the English government compelled our agriculture to swallow before the revolution, was, the protecting duty pill, or an equivalent drug, gilded with the national advantage of dealing with fellow subjects; and, after having gone through a long war to get rid of this nauseous physick, we have patiently swallowed it, gilded also by other doctors with the national advantage of dealing with fellow citizens. The power and wealth of the political doctors, who have recommended these self same political drugs, depended considerably in both cases, on their being swallowed.

I will suppose that our protecting duties do not exceed the average amount of 25 per centum, that they had expelled every article of foreign manufacture, and bestowed on our brother citizens a complete monopoly of our manufactural wants, and an ability to supply them. I will suppose too in favour of a project, which must depend on concessions to obtain the respect of examination, that the agricultural interest shall be able, after this blessed desideratum of the protecting duty system is obtained, to get at its old markets the same price for its products, and annually bring home the whole in gold or silver, for the use of our own capitalists and monopolizers. This, have said many great ministers of state, who had no knowledge of agriculture, would complete its prosperity.

It is the prosperity of giving one fourth above the market price for all the manufactures it needs. It is the boon of returning with empty ships from ports, at which the same things can be bought for one fourth less. It is the boon of a direct tax or a system of excise, to supply the revenue, which the success of the project would annihilate.

NUMBER 7

The Political State of Agriculture, Continued

The blessing of complete success in the plan of expelling foreign manufactures, by raising bounties upon agriculture, may be exhibited by figures upon data, however conjectural in amount, correct in principle. Suppose agriculture annually to bring home forty millions of dollars, she would be annually robbed of ten millions, by a protecting duty of 25 per centum, for the benefit of capitalists. Suppose her share of the taxes, state and continental, to be fifteen millions, and that out of the remaining fifteen, she has five millions to pay to bankers; ten will remain, leaving her an annual income per poll, of about $1.50 for building houses, paying expenses, and improving lands. But if we take into the account, that foreign nations neither would nor could pay our agriculturists with specie for their produce, that they would countervail upon this preposterous project, and that every countervailing act of theirs, would operate upon our agricultural products, even this $1.50 would become the victim of retaliation, and leave the farmer as fundless for purchasing manufactures, as for improving his land.

This blessed scheme of shutting up its markets, for the encouragement of agriculture, has been wonderfully over-looked as a means for encouraging manufactures. In the latter case, markets are eagerly sought for, and barter universally allowed. England takes special care not to limit the sales of her manufactures directly or indirectly to returns in specie, knowing that the attempt would destroy them. She endows them with the home monopoly, and freedom to make the best bargains in all the foreign markets they can get to. Manufacturing is her staple: agriculture is ours.

The United States hit exactly upon the same mode for the encouragement of our agriculture after the revolution, that the English did before it, for the purpose of pillaging it. Every congress has adhered to their predecessors in the same policy. The agriculturists, to get rid of it, fought England, and having evinced their power to control a great nation, are quietly submitting to this spectre of patriotism.

The English before the revolution, quartered upon our agriculture, a necessity of buying its manufactures at home, or within the empire, whilst it enjoyed the equivalents of being free from their taxation, from paying any of the interest of their paper systems, from contributions for supporting their armies, navies, bishops and pensioners, from the frauds of their treasury system, and of sharing in the enhanced prices, produced by fraud which did not reach the provinces. The same system inflicted by congress, is attended with none of these equivalents.

Agriculture pays and must forever pay most of whatever is collected by taxes, by charters, by protecting duties, by paper systems of every kind, for armies, for navies, and though last, not the least of its losses, of whatever the nation is defrauded by a treasury system operating in darkness. If the taxes are directly laid on property, agriculture pays nearly the whole of them; if on consumptions, an unequal share, because of the greater number of hands she employs than any other business, and the smaller profit derived from their labour. Had our policy, instead of assailing agriculture, with the English system of quartering upon her a legion of legal separate interests (to resist which she had spent her blood and treasure in a long war with that nation) been guided by these considerations, she would not have been subjected to the very evils, to avoid which, she had so recently and gloriously persevered through that war.

The effects of yoking agriculture to armies, navies, paper frauds, treasury frauds and protecting duty frauds since a revolution, which it laboured for, like the ox who tills the crop to be eaten by others, are visibly an increase of emigration, a decrease in the fertility of land, sales of landed estates, a decay and impoverishment both in mind and fortune of the landed gentry, and an exchange of that honest, virtuous, patriotic and bold class of men, for an order of stock-jobbers in loans, banks, manufactories, contracts, rivers, roads, houses, ships, lotteries, and an infinite number of inferior tricks to get money, calculated to instil opposite principles.

All the varieties of this order receive bounties, and agriculture pays them. They gain from six to twenty per centum profit on their capitals; agriculture seldom or never gains six, except in a few southern instances. In fact, it very rarely gains any thing, if an income, derived from an impoverishment of the land, ill deserves the name of profit.

The injustice of superadding upon agriculture these unnecessary burdens of those which are necessary, is illustrated by supposing the duties upon foreign manufactures to be only five per centum, and nearly or quite all our duties are above the supposition. To such duties are still to be added the profits of the English and American merchants, through whose hands the goods pass, and the freight. These duties, profits and freight, would alone constitute an encouragement to home manufactures of at least twenty per centum; a sum quite adequate to any encouragement which honest policy would defend, or common justice suffer. And as all the occasional calamities of commerce, are losses to agriculture, and prizes to manufactures, her fatuity in kneeling like the camel to receive burdens, under the notion that she is receiving bounties, can have no antithesis more perfect, than the species of dexterity which inflicts them.

NUMBER 8

The Political State of Agriculture, Continued

Protecting duties to enrich manufacturers, are like banks to enrich farmers, bishops to save souls, or feudal lords to defend nations. England has demonstrated the character of each member of this kindred quartumvirate. Protected by feudal lords, it was conquered almost by every invader; taught by bishops, corruption, having been distilled through all inferior ranks, deposits its essence in this reverend order of servility and selfishness; enriched by bankers, farmers flee from the cultivation of lands, which yield the highest nominal returns to agricultural labour of any in the world, until a surplus of bread is exchanged for a deficiency; and fed with the endless bounties of protecting duties, one sixth of the labouring manufacturers, constantly occupy prisons or poor houses, whilst the rest may be said to die daily upon their daily wages.

Monarchies and aristocracies, being founded in the principle of distributing wealth by law, can only subsist by frauds and deceptions to dupe ignorance into an opinion, that such distributions are intended for its benefit; but in genuine republics, founded on the principle of leaving wealth to be distributed by merit and industry, these treacheries of government are treasons against nations.

They substitute the principle which constitutes an aristocracy, for the principle which constitutes a true republic; strike with a fatal ignorance, or a sordid malignity, at the heart of the political system; and effect a fraudulent and treasonable revolution.

My fellow labourers, mechanical or agricultural, let us never be deluded into an opinion, that a distribution of wealth by the government or by law, will advance our interest. We are the least successful courtiers of any rank in society, and of course have the worst prospect of sharing in any species of wealth, bestowed by governments. It is both contrary to the experience of all mankind, and even impossible. We constitute the majority of nations. A minority administers governments and legislates. Compare the probability of its taking wealth from itself to give it to the majority to enrich itself and its partisans; and you will account for the regular current of experience. Consider, however splendidly a minority may live upon the labours of a majority, that a majority cannot subsist upon those of a minority, and you will see that it is impossible for experience in future to teach a different lesson.

Let us not flatter ourselves, that laws can be made to enable majorities to plunder these minorities, or to plunder themselves: or to fatten a man by feeding him with slices cut from his own body. If a scheme could be contrived in favour of agriculture, similar to the protecting duty scheme in favour of manufacturers, it would enslave the farmers as it does manufacturers. The utmost favour which it is possible for a government to do for us farmers and mechanics, is neither to help nor hurt us. The first it cannot do; for whom can laws strip or famish, to clothe or feed the vast majority we compose? Aware that fraud or oppression cannot permanently subsist, except by feeding on majorities, those who compose these majorities, if they are wise, never fail to see that their interest points to a republican form of government, for the very purpose of preventing the passage of laws for quartering or pasturing on them minor interests. These majorities are the pasture upon which all minor factitious interests, however denominated, fatten; and it would be as unnatural for majorities to fatten upon such legal minor interests, as for pastures to eat the herds grazing on them.

The interest of labour covers every national majority, and every legal bounty is paid by labour. This interest cannot receive legal bounties, because there cannot exist a treasury for their payment. The utmost boon with which government can endow it, is the enjoyment of that portion of its own earning, which the public good can spare. Whenever bounties are pretended to be bestowed on labour, by privileges to feudal barons to defend it, to bishops to save it, or to capitalists or bankers to enrich it, an aristocratical order is unavoidably erected to pilfer and enslave it; because though majorities cannot be enriched or ennobled by bounties or privileges, minorities

can; and these bounties or privileges must of course settle, not against, but conformably with the laws of nature, both moral and physical.

The farce of legal favour or encouragement, has been so dexterously acted in England, to delude both the agricultural and mechanical interest, the interest of labour, or the majority of the nation, as to have delivered this majority, shackled by protecting duties, bounties and prohibitions, into the hands of an inconsiderable monied aristocracy, or combination of capitalists. Into this net, woven of intricate frauds and ideal credit, the majority of the nation, the interest of labour, the agriculturists and mechanics have run, after the baits held out by protecting duties, bounties and prohibitions. From its dreams of wealth it is awakened under the fetters of a monied aristocracy, and unfortunate as Prometheus, it is destined to eternal and bitter toil to feed this political harpy, and to suffer excruciating anguish from its insatiable voraciousness. Sometimes this net has been baited to catch mechanics, at others to catch agriculturists, and perhaps it is but just, that these real brethren interests should fatten the alien tribe of stock-jobbers, as a punishment for manifesting a disposition to devour each other.

We farmers and mechanics have been political slaves in all countries, because we are political fools. We know how to convert a wilderness into a paradise, and a forest into palaces and elegant furniture; but we have been taught by those whose object is to monopolize the sweets of life, which we sweat for, that politics are without our province, and in us a ridiculous affectation; for the purpose of converting our ignorance into the screen of regular advances, which artificial interests or legal factions, are forever making in straight or zigzag lines, against the citadel of our rights and liberties. Sometimes after one of these marauding families have pillaged for a thousand years, we detect the cheat, rise in the majesty of our strength, drive away the thief, and sink again into a lethargy of intellect so gross, as to receive him next day in a new coat, as an accomplished and patriotic stranger, come to cover us with benefits. Thus we got rid of tythes, and now we clasp banks, patronage and protecting duties, to our bosoms. Ten per centum upon labour was paid to a priesthood, forming a body of men which extended knowledge, and cultivated good morals, as some compensation for forming also a legal faction, guided by the spirit of encroachment upon the rights and property of the majority. Forty per centum is now paid on our labour, to a legal faction guided by the same spirit, and pretending to no religion, to no morality, to no patriotism, except to the religion, morality and patriotism of making itself daily richer, which says it will enrich the nation, just as the self same faction has enriched England. This legal faction of capitalists, created by protecting duties, bankers and contractors, far from being satisfied with the tythe claimed by the old hierarchy, will, in the case of the mechanics, soon appropriate the whole of their labour to its use, beyond a bare subsistence; though in the case of farmers, it has yet only gotten about four times as much of theirs, as was extorted by the odious, oppressive, and fraudulent tythe system. We know death very well, when killing with one sythe, but mistake him for a deity, because he is killing with four.

NUMBER 9

The Political State of Agriculture, Continued

Prosperity, neither in manufactures, nor in paper speculations, is ever expected without a capital, and yet capital is filched from agriculture, under the pretence that it will produce her prosperity. The capital thus filched is made by laws to yield a better profit without labour, than it could with it, and becomes a premium offered by government to those who desert the labours of agriculture. Hence we see capital flying from the fields, to the legal monopolies, banking and manufacturing. The laws have established a thousand modes by which capital will produce quicker and larger profits, than when employed in the slow improvements of agriculture. These bribes offered to its deserters have already produced the most ruinous consequences. Avarice every where seizes them with avidity, and rails at agriculture, as sordid and unpatriotic, for wishing to withhold them; as the vulture might have railed at Prometheus, for wishing to keep his liver. The best informed agriculturists are driven for self-defence, or seduced by the temptations of the wealth, with which they are solicited, to sell their lands, which require labour, for the purchase of a better profit requiring none; or at least to divert to this object, whatever capital accident or industry may have thrown into their hands. And the capital thus drained from the uses of agriculture, by this irresistible and perpetual legal system, has reduced it to a skeleton for want of nourishment.

Strickland, the English farmer, who came to this country with the intention of escaping from the agricultural oppressions of his own, and returned disgusted, discovered and described this death-inflicting operation in the 52d and 53d pages of his pamphlet. "Before the revolution," says he, "the capital of the country was vested in the lands, and the landed proprietors held the first rank in the country for opulence and information, and in general received the best education which America, and not unfrequently, Europe, could afford them." Now, "the capital, as well as the government of the country has slipt out of the hands of land owners; and these new people are employed in very different, and, in the present state of things, more productive speculations than the cultivation of lands; in speculations frequently at variance with the best interests of the country. In some of the states, the gentlemen of landed property have passed into perfect oblivion: in none do they bear the sway, or even possess their due share of influence." On the eleventh day of January, 1797, a committee was raised in congress for the promotion of agriculture who reported. "That the encouragement of agriculture is an object highly worthy the public attention, as it constitutes the most useful employment for our citizens, is the basis of manufactures and commerce, and the richest source of national wealth and prosperity—and that the science of agriculture was in its infancy." One would have thought that these sentiments would have suggested the folly of starving this useful infant, to fatten the pernicious legal infant called capital; of compressing one into a dwarf and stretching the other into a giant. No such thing. It was dandled a little. A toy for its amusement called the "American society of agriculture," was talked of. This toy was found to be unconstitutional, because it would add but little to the power of the general government, and the infant was turned to graze in impoverished fields. The constitution was construed to exclude congress from the power of fostering agriculture by patents or bounties, and to give it the power of fostering banks and manufactures by patents and bounties; and a republican and agricultural people plunged into this absurdity, to advance the project of a statesman in favour of monarchy. Agriculture, in its floundering, like an ox whilst breaking, gave the statesman a tumble, and then tamely submitted to the yoke he had fashioned.

NUMBER 10

The Political State of Agriculture, Continued

As agricultural improvements cannot be made without capital; as capital will not be employed in them, if it can find more profitable employment; as the laws have created a variety of employments for capital, attracting it by bounties and premiums drawn from agriculture; and as this subtraction from one and addition to the others, have caused capital invested under such legal patronage to be more profitable than when employed in agricultural improvements; it follows, that such improvements cannot take place, whilst a policy so completely fitted to counteract them, remains. Bring before your mind some twenty or thirty modes of employing capital, and imagine that one of them produces the least profit and most toil; and further, that this one is oppressed in various ways to advance the prosperity of all the rest. Could one of the emblems of agriculture himself (mentioned in the last number) conceive, that capital would fly from all the profitable modes, to acquire comparative penury and ex-

clusive toil in the service of the profitable mode; or be
persuaded, that an utter destitution of capital can advance the prosperity of this one mode, whilst he is told
on all hands, that capital alone can advance that of every
other? This is not an imaginary, but a real case.

The project of creating a race of capitalists, as an en-
gine to endow the government with more power, seems
to me to be unfavourable to all the callings and interests
of society, save to the calling of governing, and the calling of capitalists. Whilst agriculture is more particularly impoverished by it, that impoverishment contains a
resulting blow for every thing which a fertile country and
a flourishing agriculture nurtures; and the bounty of
protecting duties will inflict upon the manufacturers
themselves, or real workmen, in lieu of comfort and competence, which a multitude of them would gain by free
industry, an impossibility of obtaining either, with the
consolatory prospect of the vast wealth of their masters,
the capitalists.

Under the same system, England, the most fertile
country in the world, wants bread. Arthur Young* states,
that a portion of that country, sufficing, if cultivated, to

---

* Arthur Young (1741–1820) was the most influential of English champions of the new agriculture during Colonel Taylor's lifetime. In 1792 he
was appointed secretary to the Board of Agriculture. The forty-six
volumes of the *Annals of Agriculture* which he edited between 1784 and
1815 contain evidence of a revolution in the science. His writings were
voluminous. Taylor clearly knew them well. On this era of great cultivators see Kenneth MacLean's *Agrarian Age: A Background for Wordsworth* (New Haven, Ct.: Yale University Press, 1950). Young had a
major responsibility in the development of local agricultural societies
throughout England and America. George Washington contributed to the
Annals. Also King George III.

make England a great exporter of bread stuff, lies un-cultivated. The average crop of wheat in England is about 35 bushels an acre, and the average price about 15s. a bushel sterling. Yet capital finds better employment under this system there, than in agriculture. This exor-bitant price is therefore an insufficient equivalent for the oppression it suffers from the system. The average crop of wheat in some states is as low as five, in none above ten bushels to the acre, and the average price about five shillings sterling. Will one seventh or one fourth of the crops, and one third of the price here, enable agriculture to bear a system, under which, with a product and price, ten or twenty fold better, it is not enabled to supply a nation with bread? An acre of wheat in England pro-duces to the farmer 26*l.* 5s. sterling; here in some states 1*l.* 10s., in others 3*l.* sterling. And here the profits of money-jobbing, or capitalists, are as great as in England. If agriculture with such products and prices, is so bad a business there, compared with credit-jobbing, as to be unable to raise bread for the nation, what fate do our products and prices pronounce upon it here?

A material difference between the landed interest of the United States and of England, is the funeral dirge of the former. There it is distinct from agriculture, and asociated with the aristocracy of capitalists. Here it is united with agriculture, and fated without equivalent to feed that aristocracy. There it is a landlord, here it is a tenant. There its rents supply it with capital to embark in the legal money sponges for absorbing the earnings of labour; here it is labour itself whose earnings these money sponges absorb. There it is fed with the most delicious

morsels of royal patronage, afforded by a system for
pilfering not landlords, but labour; here, but a few of
these morsels fall to its share, and these have been previously carved from its own carcase. There the interest of
idleness legislates, and it legislates in favour of idleness.
Here the interest of labour legislates, and it also legislates
in favour of idleness.

NUMBER 11

The Political State of Agriculture, Continued

The political evils which bear upon agriculture, are a providence which will unalterably determine its fate, unless they are removed, and therefore the only remedy, which can avert this fate is to remove them. I shall quote Strickland but once more, because his veracity is insufferable. I have selected hitherto his softest passages, for he asserts, that our soil is nearly a caput mortuum; that our landed property is no longer an object of profit or pleasure; that few good houses are building in the country, or improvements of any kind taking place; and that the opulent are quitting it for the towns. But when he says, page 55, "the mass of those we should call planters or farmers, are ignorant, uneducated, poor and indolent," his veracity becomes insolent. Has Mr. Strickland forgotten, that we agriculturists had the sagacity to discover, that the English system of creating an order of capitalists, was levelled directly at our prosperity, and the magnanimous perseverance to get rid of its authors? Let him remember this achievement, and forget what has become of the system itself; and then he will certainly retract his severe censure upon our understandings and perseverance.

I would further ask Mr. Strickland, whether it is a very uncommon thing, even in his enlightened England, for the people to mistake the shadow for the substance, or to follow their passions in pursuit of the oppressor, rather than their reason in pursuit of the oppression. In short, are not the pages of history replete with instances of destroying the tyrant and retaining the tyranny? And why should we agriculturists be called ignorant and indolent, when we are only gulled, just as mankind in general, the enlightened citizens of Europe, and his own fellow subjects are gulled? Why should the good sense and constancy of regarding the principle rather than the agent, be exclusively expected of us?

It is, however, certainly true, that nothing can flourish under oppression. Neither agriculture nor civil liberty can exist in declamations, or be toasted into prosperity. Our struggles, to resuscitate dying agriculture, must, like those of Sisyphus, yield to a stronger depressing power. The plough can have very little success, until the laws are altered which obstruct it. Societies for improving the breed of sheep or the form of ploughs, will be as likely to produce a good system of agriculture, under depressing laws, as societies for improving the English form of government under their depressing system of corruption. A good pen may produce a very bad treatise.

Agricultural societies, to take a chance for success, must begin with efforts to elect into the general and state legislatures, a genuine agricultural interest, uncorrupted by stock-jobbing, by a view of office, or by odious personal vices; taking care to combine talents with this genuine character. Wise agricultural elections, constitute the only chance for abrogating a policy, which is the ruin of agricultural prosperity.

The bounties, frauds and useless expenses, which strengthen the government and corrupt the nation, and are drawing a vast annual capital from agriculture, would then be applied to the invigoration of the militia. Such a measure would return to manufactures and agriculture their own capital, and improve both the national soil and the national spirit. The nation would exchange ineffectual armaments for an irresistible ardour; an impoverishing, for an improving soil; disrespect for itself and its native haunts, for national pride and love of country; and a school of stock-jobbers and contractors, for a school of patriots. But agriculture and the militia receive abundance of praise and an abundance of oppression and neglect, nor can a mode of encouraging either by law, be discovered, whilst no difficulty is felt in rearing up mercenary armies, and more mercenary capitalists for the same reason. It is impossible by law to encourage agriculture and the militia, and also capitalists and standing armies.

The remedy of construing the constitution honestly is a simple one. It certainly intended to bestow as little power to tax agriculture, in order to raise a bounty for manufactures and credit corporations, as it does to tax manufactures, in order to raise a bounty for agriculture. Let the imposts be regulated by their constitutional intention, and agriculture will cease to be oppressed by bounties bestowed by statesmen out of her purse, to advance their own designs. The words and the spirit of the constitution are so entirely adverse to the idea of enabling congress to exercise a partiality equivalent to the ruin or opulence of states, relying distinctly upon agricultural or manufactural staples of commerce, that the unconstitutionality of the power, ought to render the policy of its exercise an unnecessary inquiry. It is further unnecessary, because however favourable it may be to capitalists, it is subjugation even to manufacturers, and must impoverish a vast majority of the people in every state of the union to enrich a few, neither the necessity or advantage of which is suggested by the constitution.

It is easy to withhold future charters for establishing corporations to fleece agriculture and manufactures; it will be harder to repeal those already granted. Yet there is no point upon which the liberty of the nation more certainly depends, than the subversion of the doctrine of a judicial power, to turn laws into contracts, and render them irrepealable, under a line of the constitution, which uses the identical words "law and contract" in different senses. To try this doctrine, by which charters, once the vehicles of liberty, are ingeniously converted into vehicles of slavery, I wish that congress would grant to a corporation of capitalists, the exclusive privilege of furnishing the country with manufactures for one thousand years, with a stipulation for protecting duties, equal to an exclusion, for the same term. It would bring this momentous question to a fair decision whilst we have power to consider it.

The last, though not the least political oppression upon agriculture, which I have selected, for this short consideration of its political state, is our treasury system, copied from the English, and of course liable to the same abuses. It is so utterly destitute of any security for the honest application of public money, that no congress, committee of congress, or member of congress has ever examined the accounts of a single year, or been able to form a conjecture on the subject. The detail of checks is a detail of dependence and subserviency, and a tissue of ineffectual formality. The money passes in gross sums into the hands of a host of sub-treasurers. The system fell at once into the grossest of those corruptions which contaminate the British policy, that of losing sight of money after its appropriation, and considering it as constitutionally gone, however small a proportion of its object was obtained: so that an army upon paper, costs the same sum as an army in the field. This subject is however too long and intricate to follow away from that I am pursuing. This abuse in both countries endeavors to shrink from public view, behind screens called sinking funds, for applying a surplus of revenue to the payment of debt. These screens cover pecuniary abuses against those annual critical examinations of the items of public expenditure, so wholesomely practised by state legislatures. Such annual examinations by congress would probably leave with agriculture a considerable amount of capital annually taken from her, to enrich knaves; for no other description of men can get a shilling from the omission of an annual examination of the public accounts. From the loan of money in Holland to put the United States Bank in motion, to this day, every minority has testified to great pecuniary abuses; and none when converted into a majority, has ever provided a remedy against them.

The only remedy in this case, as in others, is to elect into congress a genuine agricultural interest, uncorrupted by a mixture with stock-jobbing, by a view of office, or by odious personal vices, and combined with good talents.

NUMBER 12

The Political State of Agriculture, Continued

The political causes which oppress agriculture have been considered, before the domestic habits which vitiate it, to guard against the error of an opinion, that the latter may be removed, whilst the former continue. So long as the laws make it more profitable to invest capital in speculations without labour, than in agriculture with labour; and so long as the liberty of pursuing one's own interest exist; the two strongest human propensities, a love of wealth, and a love of ease, will render it impossible. The reason why agriculture is better managed in Europe than in the United States, is the coercion of necessity upon the labourers to improve it to the utmost. The landed interest there and here, as was before observed, entirely differ. The tenants or agriculturists are a species of slaves, goaded into ingenuity, labour and economy, without possessing any political importance, or the least share in the government. They are lashed into a good system of agriculture in the same way that good discipline is produced in an army; and this good system of agriculture is also for the benefit of their landlords and legislators, just as the good discipline of an army is for the benefit of its generals and other officers. It is more out of the power of English tenants or agriculturists, to become landlords, capitalists or manufacturers, or to escape the coercion which forces them to stretch the mind and the muscles after improvement, than of soldiers to desert. However they may move from place to place, like horses transferred from owner to owner, they are doomed to the same fate. Oppression which causes agricultural improvements in England, will prevent it in the United States, because it cannot seize and hold fast the agriculturist. There, he can only soften oppression by superior skill or industry. Here, he can flee from it into a wilderness, or into a charter, and gain greater profit with less labour. We copy the English frauds upon the agriculturists, forgetting that the English power over him does not exist here. That instead of being able to lash him into excellence for the benefit of others, we can only solicit him by his own interest and happiness; and that this solicitation is an insult upon his understanding, if it honestly tells him, that government will establish the policy of scattering bounties at his expense, and of bestowing more profit and ease upon paper capital or fraudulent credit, than he can derive from solid land and honest labour. Being free, if he is wise, he will prefer a share of profit and ease, to a share of loss and toil. The cunning declaimers in praise of those who choose the yoke of evils, for the sake of getting the yoke of blessings for themselves, only deceive fools, so that wisdom as well as wealth is flying from the agricultural interest, and taking up her residence with the policy of making capital employed under charters, in credit shops and in manufacturing, more profitable than capital employed in agriculture. This union of wisdom and wealth, will in time reduce agriculture to the European regimen, and the agriculturists to the grade of tenants to a system for fostering dealers in money and credit, at the expense of the makers of bread, meat and cloth. This system, however slowly, certainly creates a class of rich and wise, and a class of poor and ignorant, and terminates of course in some European form of government.

I have heard it said that the weight of talents in Congress, has already appeared very visibly against the agriculturists. Let us not deceive ourselves by ascribing this to popular folly in elections. It is owing to the transit of wealth, and of course wisdom, from agriculture to its natural enemies, charter and privilege. This constant process diminishes daily the chance for elections to hit on agricultural talents, and will soon destroy the power to obtain them. If the fact exists as to a deficiency of these talents in Congress, it proves the existence of a moral system which begets that fact, and discloses the inevitable fate of the agricultural interest.

To the force of this baleful system, as well as to the brevity proper for an essayist, some of the defects sprinkled throughout the view I have taken of the political state of agriculture, ought in justice to be ascribed; and if it fails to excite the agriculturists in and out of Congress to look into their solution, it will only prove that the system has already had its effect on the author or his readers.

Chartered knowledge is kept alive by its associations, and chartered interests advanced by frequent and mature consultations.* An imitation of this example is the only mode of reviving agricultural knowledge, and of obtaining justice for agricultural interest. And if the suggestion of establishing agricultural societies in each Congressional district, for the purpose of considering and explaining respectfully to Congress, what does it good, and what does it harm, in imitation of other interests, should be adopted by agriculture, it may at least acquire the capacity of distinguishing between good and evil. (Note A.)

---

* "Charter" in this context signifies legal privilege or sanction—as with a "chartered" bank. Legal monopolies, patents and bounties are associated phenomena. The term is part of Taylor's protest against the promotion by government of one economic interest or element of the population at the expense of another.

NUMBER 13

Slavery

Negro slavery is a misfortune to agriculture, incapable of removal, and only within the reach of palliation. The state legislatures, hopeless of removing all its inconveniences, have been led by their despair to suffer all; and among them, one of a magnitude sufficient to affect deeply the prosperity of agriculture, and threaten awfully the safety of the country; I allude to the policy of introducing by law into society, a race, or nation of people between the masters and slaves, having rights extremely different from either, called free negroes and mulattoes. It is not my intention to consider the peril to which this policy exposes the safety of the country, by the excitement to insurrection, with which it perpetually goads the slaves, the channels for communication it affords, and the reservoir for recruits it provides. I shall only observe, that it was this very policy, which first doomed the whites, and then the mulattoes themselves, to the fate suffered by both in St. Domingo; and which contributes greatly to an apprehension so often exhibited.* Being defined by experience in that country, and by expectation in this, it is unnecessary for me to consider the political consequences of this policy.

My present object is to notice its influence on agriculture. This so entirely depends on slaves in a great proportion of the union, that it must be deeply affected by whatever shall indispose them to labour, render them intractable, or entice them into a multitude of crimes and irregularities. A free negro and mulatto class is exactly calculated to effect all these ends. They live upon agriculture as agents or brokers for disposing of stolen products, and diminish its capital, both to the extent of these stolen products, and also to the amount of the labour lost in carrying on the trade.

They wound agriculture in the two modes of being an unproductive class living upon it, like a stock-jobber or capitalist class, and of diminishing the utility of the slaves. This latter mode might be extended to a multitude of particulars, among which rendering the slaves less happy, compelling masters to use more strictness, disgusting them with agriculture itself, and greatly diminishing their ability to increase the comforts, and of course

---

* Santo Domingo, a French colony in the Caribbean, was, in 1791, the site of the greatest of all successful slave uprisings. The Republic of Haiti (1804) is a lasting consequence of this eruption. Another was an antiabolitionist "backlash" throughout Europe and the New World. The doctrines of the French Revolution, in their impact on free mulattoes, provoked the uprising. It was a datum for Southern thought on slavery and emancipation until 1878—and perhaps even later. Between 1791 and 1804 thousands fled the island for North America. They brought with them a tale of horror.

the utility of slaves, would be items deeply trenching upon its prosperity. It is however unnecessary to prove what every agriculturist in the slave states experimentally knows, namely, that his operations are greatly embarrassed, and his efforts retarded, by circumstances having the class of free negroes for their cause.

The only remedy is to get rid of it. This measure ought to be settled by considerations of a practical moral nature, and not by a moral hypothesis, resembling several mechanical inventions incarcerated at Washington, beautiful and ingenious, but useless. It is substantial, not balloon morality, by which the questions ought to be considered; whether a severance of the free negro class from the whites and slaves, will benefit or injure either of the three classes; or whether it will benefit or injure a majority of them as constituting one body? The situation of the free negro class is exactly calculated to force it into every species of vice. Cut off from most of the rights of citizens, and from all the allowances of slaves, it is driven into every species of crime for subsistence; and destined to a life of idleness, anxiety and guilt. The slaves more widely share in its guilt, than in its fraudulent acquisitions. They owe to it the perpetual pain of repining at their own condition by having an object of comparison before their eyes, magnified by its idleness and thefts with impunity, into a temptation the most alluring to slaves; and will eventually owe to it the consequences of their insurrections. The whites will reap also a harvest of consequences from the free negro class, and throughout all their degrees of rank suffer much in their morals from the two kinds of intercourse maintained with it. If vice is misery, this middle class is undoubtedly placed in a state of misery itself, and contributes greatly to that of the other two. The interest of virtue, therefore, as well as sound policy, is allied with the interest of agriculture, in recommending the proposed severance. If it should not benefit every individual of the three classes, as is probable, no doubt can exist of its benefiting a majority of each, and a very great majority of the whole. No injury, but much good to the whites and slaves is perceivable in the measure. And relief from the disadvantages of inferior rights, from the necessity of living in a settled course of vice, and from the dangers portended by it to a commotion among the slaves, promises great benefits to the free negro class itself from a severance.

It may be easily effected by purchasing of Congress lands sufficient for their subsistence in states where slavery is not allowed, and giving them the option of removing to those lands, or emigrating wherever they please. Perhaps both the national safety and prosperity would justify a harsher measure. To advance both by bestowing rewards, cannot be severe, unjust or illiberal.

At least it will be admitted by those acquainted with the subject, that the prosperity of agriculture is considerably influenced by the circumstances alluded to in this number.

NUMBER 14

Slavery, Continued

Societies are instituted to control and diminish the imperfections of human nature, because without them it generates ignorance, savageness and depravity of manners. Those best constituted, cannot however cure it of a disposition to command, and to live by the labour of others; it is eternally forming sub-societies for acquiring power and wealth, and to these perfidious, ambitious, avaricious or unconstitutional sub-societies, the liberty and property of the rest of the body politic has universally fallen a prey. They are of a civil or military complexion, or of both, as the circumstances of the case may require fraud or force. Anciently, the general ignorance of mankind, caused the frauds of superstition to suffice for working the ends of traiterous sub-societies. As these became exploded, the more intricate pecuniary frauds were resorted to. Now, on account of the increasing knowledge and more prying temper of mankind, military force is united with pecuniary frauds. And hitherto the most perfect society for the public good, has never been able to defend itself against sub-societies in some form for advancing the wealth or power of a faction or a particular interest. Combine with this universal experience, that it is impossible to conceive a form of society better calculated to excite and foster factions or sub-societies, than one constituted of distinct colours, incurable prejudices, and inimicable interests, and the inferences are unavoidable. If the badges of foolish names can drive men into phrenzy without cause, will not those which powerfully assail both reason and the senses, create deadly factions.

The attempt will undoubtedly terminate according to the nature of man, as it has once already terminated; but its catastrophe ought rather to be courted than avoided if the author of the notes on Virginia* is right in the following quotations. "The whole commerce between master and slave," says he, "is a perpetual exercise of the most boisterous passions, the most unremitting despotism on one part, and degrading submissions on the other. The parent storms, the child looks on, catches the lineaments of wrath, puts on the same airs in the circle of smaller slaves, gives a loose to his worst of passions, and thus nursed, educated and daily exercised in tyranny, cannot but be stamped by it with odious peculiarities. The man must be a prodigy who can retain his manners and morals

* *Notes on the State of Virginia* was first published in Paris in 1785 and then, in an authorized English edition, in 1787. The first American printing was in Philadelphia in 1788. The modern text, edited by William Peden, was published in 1955 by the University of North Carolina Press. Query XVIII, "Manners," is the subject of Taylor's reply.

undepraved by such circumstances. The Almighty has no attribute which can take side with us in such a contest." Such is the picture exhibited in the Notes on Virginia of "the manners" of the people, without a single palliating circumstance; and Winterbotham in his history of America has quoted and varnished it anew.

No man has been less accustomed than the author of the Notes on Virginia to paint his opinions, for the same reason that an Indian paints his body; and yet from reading the whole chapter on the manners of that state, a stranger would hardly form a more correct idea of them, than a stranger to Indians would of their colour, on seeing one painted coal black. Circumstances affect the mind, as weather does beer, and frequently produces a sort of moral fermentation, which throws up bubbles of prismatic splendor, whilst they are played upon by the rays of some temporary effervescence, but destined to burst when the fermentation ceases. The Notes on Virginia were written in the heat of a war for liberty; the human mind was made still hotter by the French revolution; and let those who were insensible of the mental fermentations and moral bubbles generated by these causes, censure Mr. Jefferson. I should be unjust to do it.

If Mr. Jefferson's assertions are correct, it is better to run the risque of national extinction, by liberating and fighting the blacks, than to live abhorred of God, and consequently hated of man. If they are erroneous, they ought not to be admitted as arguments for the emancipating policy. The considerations, which this chapter of impassioned censure of slave holders, inspire, are too extensive for a hasty essay, but a few of them may be

noticed. I shall pass over the enlistment of the Deity in
the question with an humble hope, that his justice and
mercy do not require the whites and blacks to be placed
in such a relative situation, as that one colour must ex-
tinguish the other; and as inclining to think the enrol-
ment of his name on the side of the slaves, somewhat like
a charge of inattention to his own attributes, apparently
siding with masters throughout all ages and among most
nations hitherto, the liberating St. Domingo masters excepted; and not a little tinged with impiety. Slavery was
carried farther among the Greeks and Romans than
among ourselves, and yet these two nations produced
more great and good patriots and citizens, than, probably, all the rest of the world.* In the United States it
is also probable that the public and private character of
individuals is as good, as in the countries where loco-
motive liberty and slavery to a faction, exist; nor do the
slave states seem less productive of characters in whom
the nation is willing to confide than the others. Even
the author of the quotation himself may be fairly adduced
as an instance which refutes every syllable of his chapter
on Virginia manners, unless indeed this refutation, and
an abundance of others like it, can be evaded by forming the best citizens into a class of prodigies or monsters,
to evade the force of eminent virtues towards the refutation of erroneous assertions.

These facts are referred to the consideration of the

* The possibility that slaveholding may have had the kind of positive
effects on a republican society that Taylor believes it often did has been
reconsidered recently by Edmund S. Morgan. See his *American Slavery,
American Freedom* (New York: W. W. Norton & Co., 1975).

physiologist. To me it seems, that slaves are too far below, and too much in the power of the master, to inspire furious passions; that such are nearly as rare and disgraceful towards slaves as towards horses; that slaves are more frequently the objects of benevolence than of rage; that children from their nature are inclined to soothe, and hardly ever suffered to tyrannize over them; that they open instead of shut the sluices of benevolence in tender minds; and that fewer good public or private characters have been raised in countries enslaved by some faction or particular interest, than in those where personal slavery existed.

I conjecture the cause of this to be, that vicious and mean qualities become despicable in the eyes of freemen from their association with the character of slaves. Character, like condition is contrasted, and as one contrast causes us to love liberty better, so the other causes us to love virtue better. Qualities odious in themselves, become more contemptible, when united with the most degraded class of men, than when seen in our equals; and pride steps in to aid the struggles of virtue. Instead therefore of fearing that children should imbibe the qualities of slaves, it is probable, that the circumstance of seeing bad qualities in slaves will contribute to their virtue.

For the same reason the submission and flattery of slaves will be despised, and cause us rather to hate servility than to imbibe a dictatorial arrogance; and only inspire the same passion with the submission and flattery of a spaniel. It is the submission and flattery of equals, which fills men with the impudent and wicked wish to

dictate, and an impatience of free opinion and fair discussion. This reprehensible temper is a sound objection
against any species of human policy, which generates it,
and applies most forcibly against that conferring on an
individual a power, so to dispense money and honours, as
to procure submission and flattery from the highest ranks
and conditions in society, a thousand times more genial to
pride, than the submission and flattery of a poor slave;
and ten thousand times more pernicious to nations.

Virtue and vice are naturally and unavoidably coexis-
tent in the moral world, as beauty and deformity are in
the animal; one is the only mirror in which the other can
be seen, and therefore, in the present state of man, one
cannot be destroyed without the other. It may be thus
that personal slavery has constantly reflected the strongest rays of civil liberty and patriotism. Perhaps it is
suffered by the Deity to perform an office without which
these rays are gradually obscured and finally obliterated
by charters and partial laws. Perhaps the sight of slavery
and its vices may inspire the mind with an affection for
liberty and virtue, just as the climates and deserts of
Arabia, would make it think Italy a paradise.

Let it not be supposed that I approve of slavery because I do not aggravate its evils, or prefer a policy which
must terminate in a war of extermination. The chapter
on the manners of slave-holders before quoted, concludes
with an intimation, that the consent of the masters to a
general emancipation, or their own extirpation, were the
alternatives between which they had to choose. Such a
hint from a profound mind is awful. It admits an ability
in the blacks, though shackled by slavery, to extirpate

the whites, and proposes to increase this ability by knocking off their shackles. Such a hint adds force to the recommendation in the previous essay for separating the enslaved and free blacks, as some security against the prognosticated extirpation. And after such a hint, "with what execration should the statesman be loaded" who thus forewarned, should produce the destruction of the most civilized portion of society, and re-people half the world with savages. If England and America would erect and foster a settlement of free negroes in some fertile part of Africa, it would soon subsist by its own energies. Slavery might then be gradually re-exported, and philanthropy gratified by a slow reanimation of the virtue, religion and liberty of the negroes, instead of being again afflicted with the effects of her own rash attempts suddenly to change human nature. (Note B.)

NUMBER 15

Overseers

So far from having a system of agriculture among us, very few have even taken the trouble to discover or provide any basis for one. Had Archimedes proposed to move the earth without any thing for himself or his mechanism to stand on, or an architect to erect a city without a foundation, such projects would have been equivalent to ours for erecting a system of agriculture upon the basis of the impoverishment of the land. Of what avail is any rotation of crops, the best contrived implements of husbandry, or the most perfect use of those implements, applied to a barren soil? Could a physician correctly call the regular administration of a slow poison a system of medicine, because he used the best constructed lancets, caudle cups, syringes and clyster pipes in killing his patient?

It is absurd to talk of a system of agriculture, without having discovered, that every such system good for any thing, must be bottomed upon fertility. Before, therefore, we launch into any system, we must learn how to enrich our lands. The soil of the United States upon the Atlantic Ocean is naturally thin, and exceedingly impoverished. It produces, however, good crops, when made rich, almost under any species of cultivation. To make it rich therefore ought to be the first object of our efforts, as without effecting this, all other agricultural objects, beneficial to ourselves or our country, must fail. Instead of this, for one acre enriched, at least twenty are impoverished.

The disposition of our soil and climate to reward husbandry bountifully, is disclosed in the great returns bestowed upon bad culture, by the very moderate degree of natural fertility, possessed by the former. The climate is beyond our power, but the productiveness of the soil without the help of art, is an encouragement for us to recollect how impiously we have neglected the cultivation of a Deity so propitious. But this Deity has a rival demon called ignorance, for whose worship the slave states have erected an established church, with a ministry, entitled overseers, fed, clothed and paid to suppress every effort for introducing the worship of its divine adversary. This necessary class of men are bribed by agriculturists, not to improve, but to impoverish their land, by a share of the crop for one year; an ingenious contrivance for placing the lands in these states, under an annual rack rent, and a removing tenant. The farm, from several gradations to an unlimited extent, is surrendered to the transient overseer, whose salary is increased in proportion as he can impoverish the land. The greatest annual crop, and not the most judicious culture, advances his interest, and establishes his character; and the fees of these land doctors are much higher for killing than for curing. It is common for an industrious overseer, after a very few years, to quit a farm on account of the barrenness, occasioned by his own industry; and frequent changes of these itinerant managers of agriculture, each striving to extract the remnant of fertility left by his predecessor, combines with our agricultural ignorance, to form the completest system of impoverishment, of which any other country can boast.

I mean not to speak disrespectfully of overseers; they are as good as other people; nor is it their fault if their employers have made their wealth and subsistence to depend on the impoverishment of half a continent. The most which the land can yield, and seldom or never, improvement with a view to future profit, is a point of common consent and mutual need between the agriculturist and his overseer; and they generally unite in emptying the cup of fertility to the dregs.

It is discovered in England from experience, that short leases were the worst enemies to agriculture. Those of twenty one years are found by experience to be too short for improvement. Must the practice of hiring a man for one year by a share of the crop, to lay out all his skill and industry in killing land, and as little as possible in improving it, suggested by the circumstances and necessities of settling a wilderness among hostile savages, be kept up to commemorate the pious learning of man to his primitive state of ignorance and barbarity?

Unless this custom is abolished, the attempt to fertilize our lands, is needless. Under the frequent emigrations of owners from state to state, and of overseers from plantation to plantation, it cannot be accomplished. Impoverishment will proceed, distress will follow, and famine will close the scene. It is a custom which injures both employers and overseers, by gradually diminishing the income of the one, and of course the wages of the other. Wages in money would on the contrary, correspond with a system of gradual improvement, by which the condition of both parties would be annually bettered, and skill in improving, not a murderous industry in destroying land, would soon become a recommendation to business, and a thermometer of compensation.

NUMBER 16

Inclosing

The modes of fertilizing land form a system, wholly unfit, as we shall see upon enumerating a few of its constituents, to be enforced by an itinerant order, bribed to counteract most or all of them. The most effectual is found, when we have found the most copious fund of manure. Manures are mineral, vegetable or atmospherical. Perhaps the two last may be resolvable into one. Mineral manures are local and hard of access. But the earth swims in atmosphere and inhales its refreshments. The vegetable world covers the earth, and is the visible agent, to which its surface is indebted for fertility. If the vast ocean of atmosphere is the treasury of vegetable food, vegetable manure is obviously inexhaustible. The vegetable world takes its stand upon our earth to extract the riches of this treasury, larger than the earth itself, and to elaborate them into a proper form for fertilizing its surface. The experiment of the willow, planted a slip, in a box containing 200 pounds of earth, and at the end of a few years, exhibiting a tree of 200 pounds weight, without having diminished the earth in which it grew, demonstrates the power of the vegetable world to extract and to elaborate the atmospherical manure. This 200 pound weight of willow, was a prodigious donation of manure, by the atmosphere, to the 200 pound weight of earth in which it grew. It was so much atmosphere condensed by the vegetable process, into a form capable of being received and held by the earth, and of being reduced to vegetable food, during its struggles to return to its own principle, through the passes of putridity and evaporation. Vegetables, like animals, feed on each other. Inclosing for the sake of rearing vegetables to enrich the earth, is the mode by which the greatest quantity of atmospherical manure can be infused into it with the least labour. It is prepared and spread without expense. Cross fences, those drawbacks of man's folly from divine benevolence, are saved by inclosing to fertilize; and if the laws for confining land under inclosures, for permitting animals to prowl at large, and for punishing landholders for the trespasses committed by these marauders on their land, were made more comfortable to justice, common sense and common interest, the supplies of manure from the vegetable world, would become combined with a vast diminution of labour. Thus the two primary objects of agriculture (to fertilize the land, and save labour) would be both attained to a measureless extent. Vegetables would collect from the atmosphere, an inexhaustible supply of manure, and spread it on land; fencing and timber to great extent would be saved, and agriculture would soon aspire to her most elegant ornament and useful improvement, live fences.

But alas! we persist in the opinion, that lands trespass

on cattle, and not cattle on land. Out of emulation I suppose of an ancient doctrine, which the bayonet only could confute, that it was better to fasten the plough to the tail than to the shoulder.

It is yet a question, whether the earth is enriched by any species of manure, except the vegetable or atmospherical, and experiments have hitherto leaned towards the negative. Without new accessions of vegetable matter, successive heavy dressings with lime, gypsum and even marle, have been frequently found to terminate in impoverishment. Hence it is inferred, that minerals operate as an excitement only to the manure furnished by the atmosphere. From this fact results the impossibility of renovating an exhausted soil, by resorting to fossils, which will expel the poor remnant of life, and indeed it is hardly probable that divine wisdom has lodged in the bowels of the earth, the manure necessary for its surface.

However this question may be determined, the impossibility of obtaining mineral manure in quantities sufficient to enrich an impoverished country, leaves us no alternative; whilst the spasmodic efforts it excites in the agony of death, are better calculated to accelerate the evil, and to aggravate national distress by inspiring false hopes, than to remedy the impoverishment of excessive culture.

If vegetable matter is either the only manure, or the only attainable manure, capable of renovating our country, let us cast our eyes upon its surface, and discover the demand, by computing the impoverishment. We want as much as we have expelled, to get back to the state from

which we set out. We must retrieve, before we can improve. The nation never dies; it is the yoke fellow of
the earth; these associates must thrive or starve together;
if the nation pursues a system of lessening the food of
the earth, the earth in justice or revenge will starve the
nation. The inclosing system provides the most food for
the earth, and of course enables the earth to supply most
food to man. It is time working on space.

NUMBER 17

Inclosing, Continued

Let us boldly face the fact. Our country is nearly ruined. We have certainly drawn out of the earth three fourths of the vegetable matter it contained, within reach of the plough. Vegetable matter is its only vehicle for conveying food to us. If we suck our mother to death we must die ourselves. Though she is reduced to a skeleton, let us not despair. She is indulgent, and if we return to the duties revealed by the consequences of their infraction, to be prescribed by God, and demonstrated by the same consequences to comport with our interest, she will yet yield us milk.

We must restore to the earth its vegetable matter, before it can restore to us its bountiful crops. In three or four years, as well as I remember, the willow drew from the atmosphere, and bestowed two hundred weight of vegetable matter, on two hundred weight of earth, exclusive of the leaves it shed each year. Had it been cut up and used as a manure, how vastly would it have enriched the two hundred weight of earth it grew on? The fact demonstrates that by the use of vegetables, we may collect manure from the atmosphere, with a rapidity, and in an abundance, far exceeding that of which we have robbed the earth. And it is a fact of high encouragement; for though it would be our interest, and conducive to our happiness, to retrace our steps, should it even take us two hundred years to recover the state of fertility found here by the first emigrants from Europe; and though religion and patriotism both plead for it, yet there might be found some minds weak or wicked enough, to prefer the murder of the little life left in our lands, to a slow process of resuscitation.

Forbear, oh forbear matricide, not for futurity, not for God's sake, but for your own sake. The labour necessary to kill the remnant of life in your lands, will suffice to revive them. Employed to kill, it produces want and misery to yourself. Employed to revive, it gives you plenty and happiness. It is a matter of regret to be compelled to rob the liberal mind of the sublime pleasure, bestowed by a consciousness of having done its utmost for future ages, by demonstrating that the most sordid will do the utmost for gratifying its own appetites, by fertilizing the earth; that the process is not slow, but rapid; the returns not distant, but near; and the gain not small, but great.

Inclosing is a single channel for drawing manure from the atmosphere and bestowing it on the earth. Though it is the great canal, there are a multitude of feeders. These are not lost in admiration of the most powerful mode for fertilizing the earth, and will be subsequently remembered.

At present it is necessary to consider the best mode of

practicing the inclosing theory. It is one which can only succeed in combination with a great number of agricultural practices, at enmity with those which at present prevail.

It is at enmity with the practice of summer fallowing for wheat. Being founded in the doctrine, that vegetables extract the principles of fertility from the atmosphere, and elaborate them into a manure for the earth, it is inconsistent with the doctrine that the earth will be improved by keeping it bare. If vegetables do not feed upon, and consume earth, but upon the atmospherical manure, which may have been introduced into, or is floating around it, then a naked fallow by increasing evaporation, will impoverish the earth, and waste at each ploughing a portion of this fleeting fertility, without its being arrested by a crop.

It accords with the doctrine of turning in a clover lay, or a bed of any other vegetable matter, for a crop speedily sown or planted thereon, without disturbing this new bed of vegetables, by which the previous stock of atmospherical manure in the earth is vastly increased, and the least loss by evaporation sustained.

It is at enmity with shallow ploughing, because it admits atmospherical manure into the earth by water and air, to a less depth, and loses it sooner by evaporation, and the more rapid escape of water from its fluidity.

It accords with deep ploughing, because it enables the earth to absorb more atmospherical manure through the two great vehicles, air and water; and because it buries deeper the manure deposited on the earth in a vegetable form; in one case inhaling more, and in both exhaling less.

It is at enmity with the custom of exposing a flat surface to the sun, and accords with an opposite one; because by the first the force of its rays in promoting evaporation is increased, and by the second diminished. These cases are selected to suggest to the reader, that the theory of fertilizing the earth by atmospherical or vegetable manure, is one, which, if correct, will reach and influence nearly the whole circle of our agricultural modes of managing the earth.

NUMBER 18

Inclosing, Continued

If plants feed on earth, why do they perish by drought? If they did not feed on atmospherical manure, why do they instantly revive from rain? And why do we see them considerably revived even without rain, when the air becomes condensed, after having been greatly rarified, if the food it affords them was not too thin in one case, and more substantial in the other?

Drought becomes far less pernicious to crops, in proportion to the stock of atmospherical manure with which the earth has been stored to meet it, and the obstacles opposed to its loss.

To avoid a frequent reference to experience as a voucher for the doctrines advanced in these essays, I shall once for all observe, that they are always drawn from that source, except when the contrary is expressed. But it would be tiresome to the reader to wade through a list of experiments made with more industry than scientific skill, for a long course of time, and suggested, not by a love of fame, but by necessity. Besides we must acquire principles before we descend to details.

Let us return to the case of drought. Its effects are greatly diminished by burying with the plough a copious supply of vegetable matter, and by opposing an uneven surface to evaporation. It is because this vegetable matter or atmospherical manure, elaborated into a solid form, is the food of plants; and this food is retained longer by deep ploughing and an uneven surface, than by shallow ploughing and a level surface. And if these latter practices are not combined with a good stock of vegetable food, the effects of drought appear sooner, and are more fatal.

The sudden benefit of rain to plants, demonstrates that it is loaded with their food; and its transitory effect equally demonstrates that this food rapidly evaporates. There is no manure the effects of which are more sudden or less permanent. As they disappear from drought, the loss must be attributed to evaporation. Checks upon evaporation are of course auxiliaries to the inclosing system.

The shade to the earth is a check it naturally produces, and a consequence of this check is, that the atmospherical manure carried by air or rain into the earth, being longer retained, is imbibed in greater quantity by the vegetable cover, and elaborated into a manure more permanent, than when deposited in these vehicles.

Wood, and all the vegetables of softer texture, are exposed to the effects of putrefaction and evaporation, in a degree so far below water, that a complete dressing of atmospherical manure, conveyed in the vegetable vehicle, will discover its benefit for years, whilst one conveyed in rain will disappear in a few weeks. It follows that the nearer the vegetable vehicle of manure from the atmosphere, approaches to wood, the longer it will last, and that the nearer it approaches to water, the shorter it will last.

If this principle is sound, a point of great importance to the inclosing system is settled; whether it is better to plough in vegetables in a succulent or dry state? Every experiment I have ever made, decides in favour of the latter, and these decisions correspond with the requisitions of our theory. By ploughing in the vegetables succulent, we stop the process for extracting, elaborating and condensing atmospherical manure, and chiefly bury water, liable to the laws of evaporation, demonstrated in the case of rain, the richest, but the most short lived of every species of manure. The rapidity with which the water of vegetables in a succulent state evaporates, is demonstrated in curing grass for hay; and the loss is probably greater when the vegetable is never reduced at all to a dry and hard state. On the contrary, by suffering the vegetable to acquire its most solid form, it will extract more manure from the atmosphere, and this manure will be retained vastly longer by the earth; so long indeed, that a good farmer will accumulate fresh supplies upon a remaining stock from time to time, so as to replenish his land at a compound ratio. And by suffering the vegetable cover, whatever it is, to gain its hardest form, it affords longer shade to the surface of the earth, whilst it is also making daily extracts from the atmosphere, during its whole succulent existence, to be deposited within its bowels.

NUMBER 19

Inclosing, Continued

To draw from the atmosphere the greatest quantity of manure, to check the loss the earth sustains from evaporation during the process by shade, to give the manure the most lasting form, and to deposit it in the most beneficial manner, are primary objects of the inclosing system.

The best agent known to us for effecting the three first, is the red clover. Its growth is rapid; its quantity exceeds the product of any other grass; it throws up a succession of stems in the same summer; and these stems are more solid and lasting than those of other grasses. These successive growths constitute so many distinct drafts from the great treasure of atmospherical manure in one year. Whilst these drafts are repeated, the clover is daily securing the treasure, in a form able long to elude the robber evaporation, whom it also opposes by shade. To its extracting from the atmosphere the greatest quantity of manure, and elaborating it into a lasting form the most suddenly of any other vegetable cover, clover lays for wheat are indebted for their fame. Their success has been attributed to the portion of the vegetable in a succulent state, whilst it was owing to the greater portion which had arrived to maturity previous to the fallow. To ascertain this fact, let one moiety of a clover field be turned in as soon as its first crop flowers, and the other after the stem of the last crop is hard, and the whole sown on one day in wheat.

The peculiar propensity of clover to be improved by a top dressing of the gypsum, is another striking circumstance of its affinity to the system for fertilizing land by its own cover. As its growth is suddenly and vastly increased by this top dressing, it furnishes reason to believe, that the effect flows from a disposition communicated by the gypsum to the clover, for imbibing atmospherical food by its external parts; and so much as it thus gains, affords to the earth a double benefit. One, that this food not being extracted from the stock of atmospherical manure, possessed by the earth, does not impoverish it; the other, that being bestowed upon the earth from whence it was not taken, it adds to its fertility.

The tap root of the clover also advances the intention of the inclosing system in several respects. By piercing the earth to a considerable depth, apertures or pores are created for imbibing and sinking deeper a greater quantity of atmospherical manure: so well defended by the shade of the top; and the friability thus communicated to the soil, affords a most happy facility to the plough, for turning in its vast bed of vegetable matter.

In commemorating the value of clover as an agent for

transferring a portion of the inexhaustible wealth of the atmosphere to the earth, we must not forget that every member of the vegetable world, contributes to the same purpose; and that these auxiliaries to clover will powerfully second its efforts, and may be successfully substituted for it, where circumstances deny its use. In the exhausted lands, sandy soil and dry climate of the country below the mountains, clover will not live. Recourse must therefore be had to other means of improving the land to endow it, with a capacity of resorting to its use. It is eminently endowed with this capacity by a certain degree of fertility, and thenceforth good management will retain and increase it.

In the mean time, the best substitute for clover should be sought for by experience. The bird-foot clover, as it is called, is one of considerable promise; it will flourish in a sandy soil, is equally improved by the gypsum, affords early and good shade, makes a multitude of seed, and may by a small degree of skill, be kept up without being sown. Though it perishes early in the summer, it yet leaves a great cover of dry vegetable matter on the earth, which defies evaporation, until the plough can turn it in. And its dead coat is frequently pierced by other grasses, and sometimes by luxuriant growths of weeds, before unknown to the soil, which seem to come forward as witnesses to the fact of its fertilizing the land. This grass is an enemy to wheat on account of its early and rapid growth, and of course ought only to be used to fertilize land in which wheat ought not to be sown. And as wheat cannot be beneficially sown in land unable to produce red clover, the bird-foot clover seems designed to take up the care of the soil, at the point of impoverishment, where the red lays it down. As red clover is the best associate of wheat, for the purpose of saving and improving a good soil, bird-foot is the best associate of Indian corn, for rendering the same services to a bad one.

Individuals of the vegetable world are quoted, not to insinuate that their powers for the object proposed are extremely peculiar, but to illustrate my hypothesis. The entire vegetable creation must contribute towards sustaining this hypothesis, or it must fall. If it is supported by this spacious foundation, there are few systems better supported. Therefore, after having deduced the benefit resulting to land by inclosing, from the hypothesis that vegetables draw, retain, and bestow on the earth the atmospherical manure in great abundance, I shall proceed to consider other modes of manuring it, chiefly founded in the same hypothesis.

NUMBER 20

Manuring

It is not my design to advance any thing strange or new, or to recommend expensive, difficult, or uncommon modes of improving land. Brilliant projects for improvement, in the present state of agriculture, would be like diamonds set in lead. My utmost design is to point out a few improvements which even ignorance can understand, and poverty practice; yet such as may not be beneath the regard of knowledge, nor the interest of wealth.

The most abundant sources for artificial manure in the most exhausted district of our country, are the offal of Indian corn, the straw of small grain, and the dung of animals. We find in the two first, proofs of the value of dry vegetables as a manure. If these few means of fertilizing the country, were skilfully used, they would of themselves suffice to change its state from sterility to fruitfulness. But they are so egregiously neglected or mismanaged, that we hardly reap a tythe of their value.

There is no farinaceous plant which furnishes so rich

and so plentiful a crop as the Indian corn. It yields food in abundance for man, beast and land. By the litter of Indian corn, and of small grain, and by penning cattle, managed with only an inferior degree of skill, in union with inclosing, I will venture to affirm, that a farm may in ten years be made to double its produce, and in twenty to quadruple it; the ratio of its increased value is of course still greater.

There is no other secret in the business than that none of these manures be wasted. The agriculturist who expects to reap good crops from neglecting his manures, is equally a fanatic with the religionist, who expects heaven from neglecting his morals.

Details, however unentertaining, may not be useless; therefore I shall often resort to them. The stalks of corn should constitute the chief litter and part of the food, both of the stable and farm pen yard, during the winter. The sooner they are used after the corn is gathered, the more saccharum remains to bestow value on them as food, and the more manure they will yield, as evaporation diminishes both; and this proceeds far more rapidly whilst standing single, subject to the vicissitudes of weather, than when immersed in the steady moisture and cold climate of the farm yard. As a food, they are better for horses than for cattle, because of the superior masticating power of the former; whereas cattle are able to eat but little of the stalk itself, and chiefly confine themselves to picking an inferior food attached to it. Stalks carried morning and evening in loads, into the farm pen and stable yard, furnish both to cattle and horses much food, but to the latter early in the winter, they are a species of fodder the most beneficial I have ever tried; and besides the manure they furnish, will amply recompense the farmer, by enabling him to spare his hay and corn blades, to be used when the labour of his team becomes harder. They enable him also to relieve his land from the tax of pasturing horses, by the preservation of hay and blades for the summer's use, and are in that way eminently subservient to the inclosing system.

To the stalks are to be added the blades, tops, shucks and cobs of the Indian corn, all in some degree a food, and a plentiful litter. The value of the cob as a food is highly spoken of, but has not been ascertained by me; as a manure, by depositing them in deep furrows two or three feet apart, barely covering them with a plough, and bringing the land two years afterwards into tilth, I have found them excellent. In every view they illustrate the vegetable power of elaborating atmosphere into hard and enriching substances.

The great object in making and applying the manure arising from litter of every kind, and the dung of animals, is to avoid the loss by evaporation. In obedience to the old English authorities, I have in various ways compounded dunghills, kept them through the summer, and covered with earth and with bushes, the manure of the farm pen; and the loss has been regularly graduated by the fermentation produced, from a moiety to three fourths, being invariably greater, the better the litter was rotted, or the greater the degree of fermentation. As a farther experiment to ascertain the same fact, I have several times penned the same cattle on the same space for the same period, ploughing up one portion as soon as the pen was removed, and leaving the other unploughed for eight or ten weeks. On putting both at one time in the same crop, the result has uniformly been, a vast inferiority to a line, of that left exposed to the effects of evaporation.

NUMBER 21

Manuring, Continued

An effervescence which shall become so intense, as to produce a visible evaporation or smoke, is said to be an effect of ploughing in a cover of green vegetables, and this effect is stated as an argument of fertilizing consequences to the earth. If an escaping torrent of manure is calculated to impart lasting fertility to the earth, then the hypothesis which considers evaporation as a channel for impoverishing, and not for fertilizing the earth, is an error. Then also the ancient English habit of making manure by contriving every means of promoting evaporation is correct, and the modern notion that this habit wastes manure by restoring it to the atmosphere, is incorrect. The heat of the sun will sometimes make wet earth smoke, but instead of enriching, it thereby extracts the manure contained in water. The evaporation of green vegetables in a perceptible smoke, must have a similar effect. The idea that this smoking of the earth was a proof that we were making a great quantity of manure of green vegetables, may have been borrowed from inferring the same thing from the smoke of dunghills compounded of dry; and whilst the latter opinion is exploded by the common instances of the vast loss of manure it produces in these dunghills, the former may have continued, though founded in the same principle, for want of familiar experiments to disprove it.

The system of husbandry for fertilizing the earth, by increasing its friability, for the sake of enabling it more copiously to inhale the atmospherical manure, has the great defect of not providing against the effects of exhalation. Inhaled atmosphere being as rare and as light as inhaled water, is as liable to the laws of evaporation, and its benefit to the land must of course be as transient. Against this defect, the permanency of atmospherical manure, in the form of hardened vegetables, so much less exposed to these laws, provides.

To support the details of manuring, it is necessary to advert occasionally to principles. Tull's husbandry* is the remedy recommended for the erroneous opinion, that ten cultivated acres will not produce the means of manuring above one. This error is founded on the inhaling, without considering the exhaling quality of the earth; and to supply the want of manure, we are advised to expose our lands to evaporation in the greatest possible degree, by naked fallows.

On the contrary, I am convinced, that if we will watch

* Jethro Tull (1674–1741) of Prosperous Farm was the father of English scientific agriculture. His most famous work is *Horse-hoing Husbandry, or an Essay on the Principles of Tillage and Vegetation* (London, 1733).

and arrest the thief evaporation, whether stealing our means for raising manure, or sweating the earth as a Jew sweats gold, we shall discover modes of fertilizing land infinitely beyond our most sanguine hopes, both by additions of manure, and obstructions to evaporation.

Twenty-five years ago, I found more difficulty in manuring one acre for five labourers, including women and boys, owing to a waste of my means for raising manure, and an ignorance of applying it, than I do now in manuring two acres for each. By manuring two acres for each labourer, with the three resources only common to every bread stuff farm, it follows that we may manure about one seventh of the land we annually put in tilth, if, as I suppose we can seldom plough more than fourteen acres for each labourer, including women and boys. This is at once attaining to the summit of European exertion, without the aid of lime, marle, soot, the sweepings of cities, and several other resources for improving land, which contribute greatly towards conducting European farmers to the same stage of improvement; and without the vast benefit of inclosing. Two reasons exist for an event apparently so unlikely; the Indian corn furnishes a fund of litter for raising manure, infinitely exceeding any of theirs, and their waste of manure by evaporation is avoided.

NUMBER 22

Manuring, Continued

This subject compels me to revert to a use of Indian corn, before the mode of its culture is considered. Its blade makes the finest fodder, and if well saved furnishes but little litter, because it is all eaten. Being the best hay, it ought to be saved for the hottest and most laborious season of the year, which occurs immediately after the green clover fails. The first part of the Indian corn which should be used as food, is the stalk, because it is harder to keep sound through the winter, than any other fodder, and its saccharum is continually wasting. The tops should be devoted to covering a farm pen of rails, in the form of three sides of a square, closed to the ground on the outside, and open within, and to a house for pumpkins and turnips stacked in the common form. Some loss will accrue from the evaporation of a cover, whether composed of straw or corn tops, and tops make infinitely the best. And some annual cover of a winter's farm pen for cattle, is indispensible, as being a vast saving upon the

European custom of stationary cow houses. Arthur Young is, I think, of opinion, that 1,200 acres is that size for a farm best adapted for the economy of labour. Suppose two hundred and fifty acres of this farm to be annually ploughed, and fifty to be annually manured: If this manuring is commenced around a station for raising manure, in four years the station is isolated in the midst of two hundred acres of manured land, leaving it about six hundred yards from the nearest of the manured land, which distance increases, as the manuring is extended, from that minimum, to its maximum, namely, the distance from the centre to the verge of an area of one thousand two hundred acres. Hence the expense of carrying in the litter, and carrying out the manure, will presently become so enormous, as to drive the farmer into the ancient ruinous and abandoned custom of infield and outfield, or that of highly improving a spot around his house, and highly impoverishing the rest of his farm.

An ambulatory cow house is the remedy for this disastrous mode of management. The sheep and cattle should be employed in manuring abroad, and the horses at home. The farm pens of the farmer should be placed in the field for cultivation, with an eye to convenience or saving of labour, both in receiving the stalks from the shift of the preceding year, and also in distributing the manure in that to be cultivated. It is far better to make a lane of great length to conduct the cattle to water, than to omit this management.

The greatest assiduity should be used in conveying the corn stalks to these farm pens, and the stable yard as early as possible, reserving the shucks, the straw, the tops, the blades, and the hay for later periods; because the injury to the stalks standing single and exposed to the vicissitude of weather, is infinitely greater from evaporation, than to these other articles of food and litter. Some small quantities of straw and shucks should however be used with them, to produce compactness as a defence against evaporation, and to treat the cattle with a variety of food, so grateful to animals. The straw and the shucks, after the stalks are all in, will bestow a cover on them, impenetrable to drought, and secure against evaporation; the several kinds of litter are beneficially mingled, and the tops which covered the cow house are the last food of its inhabitants.

The ground to be manured, should be fallowed in the winter, since the more friable its state, the better it commixes with the unrotted contents of the farm pens, and the better these contents are covered with the plough. If this is neglected, the want of a thorough commixture, and the exposure of manure on the surface, both of which will happen in a degree when the long litter of the farm pen is carried on unploughed ground, generally causes the loss of one half of the manure, and one half of the crop.

NUMBER 23

Manuring, Continued

The winter's fallow, to receive the spring manure, is a business capable of some improvement, and economy of labour. This fallow, when the manure is for Indian corn, as it ought to be where that grain is cultivated, should be made by three furrows, forming a ridge five feet and a half wide. Two of these furrows are made by a large plough, calculated to cut deep and wide, and to turn the sod completely over; and the third by a plough called a trowel-hoe, made one third larger than usual, with a coulter on the point, and a mould board on each side. If the field has been left in such ridges at its last cultivation, the large plough cuts a furrow on the ridge on each side of its summit, making the sod it turns up to meet thereon, and leaving under that sod all the earth it can cover, unbroken; these two furrows will leave the old water furrow between them, or an equivalent space, which the described trowel-hoe-plough, with its two large mould boards, will break up, throwing the sod on each side. Both these ploughs should be drawn by four horses, leaving the furrow made by the trowel-hoe uncommonly deep and wide. In this state the ground lies through the winter. Its vegetable cover is buried so as to escape some loss by evaporation, the unbroken space is so mellowed by the cover of the sod, as to become soft and friable by the spring, and the bottom of the large open furrow, commonly a dead clay, is invigorated by a winter's exposure to the atmosphere.

The manure ought to be devoted to Indian corn, because a crop of great value is thereby gained, whilst it is going through the process, supposed in England to be necessary to reduce it to vegetable food. Complete putrefaction is there considered as necessary, for this end. Whereas, by planting the Indian corn, as soon as the unrotted manure of the farm pen is carried out and ploughed in, its growth is greatly nourished and finally perfected, by the time the putrefaction is completed. It catches the evaporation produced by the moderate fermentation of the rotting vegetable matter of which the manure is compounded, and exactly that portion of manure which is lost, by the custom of rotting it before it is used, becomes the parent of a great crop. By the fall the manure is reduced to a fit pabulum for wheat, and even more of it is saved for this end, mingled in the earth, and subject to a moderate fermentation, than if it had been retained in hot dunghills through the summer, exposed to a violent effervescence, and then exclusively devoted to this crop upon a naked fallow. The area manured would not be at most above half the extent, and the degree of enrichment nearly the same.

Indian corn thrives better with unrotted manure, than any other crop, and is precisely the crop, and almost the solitary one, ready to associate with coarse litter, the first growing weather which occurs after it is *applied*. Potatoes and tobacco may possibly possess the same quality. The former certainly associate well with coarse manure, but neither are profitable as a crop; one is not adapted to the climate favourable to Indian corn, and the other is not admissible into any good system of agriculture.

NUMBER 24

Manuring, Continued

Manure from the litter of a farm, ought to be chiefly made in the cool portion of the year, to avoid the enormous loss produced by a combination of heat, moisture and vegetable matter. If a considerable portion of this litter is reserved for the summer's use, a considerable loss is unavoidable. A small part of it only may be kept for the stable, more for the sake of the horses than for the object of manure. It is better for that object to exhaust the litter in the winter season, than to reserve any of it for summer, if the opinions that vegetables extract manure from the atmosphere, and that manures are gradually evaporated back to their origin, be true; because litter is exposed to a far greater loss from evaporation, by a commixture with moist dung in summer, than if it had been spread on the farm yards in winter, and ploughed into the earth in spring, before any considerable fermentation occurs. Hence, as the dung of animals, constitutes but a small portion of the manure which ought to be raised on a well managed farm, it would be a loss to sacrifice a considerable mass of vegetable manure, for this object of inferior value. The American custom of penning cattle during the night in the summer season, properly attended to, is therefore a far more thrifty one, for the object of manuring, than the English custom of mingling moist dung and vegetable litter during that season. By ours, both these kinds of manure escape much of the loss from evaporation; by theirs, this loss is increased as to both, by an excessive effervescence.

Yet the dung of animals during the summer season is an item of great moment for enriching lands, if it is saved without subtracting from the more valuable item of the winter's farm yards. The most beneficial mode of its application within the scope of my observation, is penning cattle and sheep, graduating the size of these pens by observation, until the designed quantity of manure shall be deposited within two weeks at most, and ploughing it in on the day the pen is removed invariably. The loss from evaporation is so great that a pen ought never to remain above two weeks. I have frequently seen cow pens continued in one spot, until the daily loss balanced the daily accession of manure; and the richness of the land with these daily accessions, became stationary. By a regular course of removing these pens, and immediately ploughing in the manure, the farmer will be agreeably surprised to find, that the improved area will infinitely exceed his hopes; for his ground will be equally enriched by far less dung, on account of these precautions against evaporation, and the cattle will, of course, go over a far greater space.

The land thus manured by the tenth of August, may be sown in turnips, at one pint of seed to an acre, broadcast. After that period, the pens which had stood from fourteen down to ten days (for the time should be diminished as the cattle fatten) should be removed every seven days, because no draft will be made from the land by a turnip crop, the quantity of the manure is increased, the evaporation is diminished by the length of the nights, and the cattle have improved in plight.

One hundred head of small and ordinary cattle, of the ages common when raised on the farm, and as many sheep, will in this way manure eighteen acres annually, sufficiently to produce fine crops of Indian corn and wheat, and a good growth of red clover after them, with the aid of gypsum; and the clover when preserved by the system of inclosing, will by two years' crops, left to fall on the land, restore it to the plough, richer than the manuring made it. About eight of these acres will also have yielded a crop of turnips, good or bad, according to the season and the soil.

But horses cannot be comprised in this mode of management, because of the inadequacy of their nature to its exposure and hardships. Whatever they are fed on, furnishes some litter, some must be saved to help it out, the manure they make in the summer should be used as late as possible in the spring, and as early as possible in the fall, and the litter saved should only be contemplated to last, until a new supply from the crop of wheat can come in. These precautions against evaporation, with placing the summer cleanings under cover, or at least where it may be trodden hard, may be resorted to without a great sacrifice of litter or vegetable manure.

NUMBER 25

Manuring, Continued

Infinitely the most abundant source of artificial manure within the reach of a bread stuff farmer, is that raised in farm pens during the winter. Skill and industry in this single point, would as suddenly, but more permanently improve the face of our country, as paint does that of a wrinkled hag.

Of these pens, each with a shelter, there should be at least five, or equivalent divisions for cattle, beeves, sheep, and calves, muttons, and hogs. A disposition of them ought to be made upon a calculation of economy, as to the combined objects of collecting the litter, carrying out the manure and feeding the animals. After the Indian corn crop is planted, that portion of it excepted, .for which the manure of the farm yards is intended, these animals should be placed on their summer's establishment; every other species of labour on the farm should cease, until the harvest of manure is secured, and its security against evaporation should be an object of as much solicitude, as the security of hay against rain. On making a breach in the body of manure, the olfactory nerves will advise you of the necessity of precautions against this loss. These are, to remove the manure in regular divisions, and not by wounding and mangling it in different places, create channels for the escape of its richest qualities. To deposit it in straight rows, and at regular distances across the whole field to be manured, that the manure first carried out, may be immediately spread and ploughed in after one row is finished. And to spread and plough in well each row, without waiting for a succeeding one. The object is to secure the manure against evaporation as soon as possible after it is exposed to it.

My general rule is to deposit the loads, consisting of as much as four common oxen can draw, in squares at ten yards distant from each other, so that the extreme distance in spreading it, will be five from the centre of each heap. But this general rule admits of important exceptions. If the land fluctuates in fertility, the loads may be deposited at twelve yards distance, which is a good dressing; and if it is accompanied with gypsum, the quantity to an acre may be diminished one fifth, in consideration of its aid.

For some years I have used gypsum with the coarse manure of the farm yards, and I think it the most beneficial mode of using it. The manure carried out each day is ploughed in, before which one bushel of gypsum to the acre, ground fine, is sown on it, after it is spread.

The reader will recollect that the ground to be manured has been fallowed into high ridges, five feet and a half wide, having a deep and wide water furrow between each ridge. Over this uneven surface, the coarse manure being spread as equally as possible, and sown with gypsum, the ridge is to be reserved by the same three furrows and the same two ploughs with which it was formed, each drawn by four horses. On both sides of the deep furrow, with the mould board towards it, a deep and wide furrow is to be run by a large plough, cutting on its right side with one share, so as to throw the earth it raises by its mould board into this old deep furrow, and to form precisely in it, a neat ridge or list on which to plant the corn. And the large trowel-hoe-plough with its two mould boards, splits the summit of the fallow ridge, and throws its earth and manure into the two furrows made on each side by the preceding plough. If these ploughs are of the proper kinds, and the operation is well performed, the manure is secured in the best manner against evaporation, the ground is secured in fine tilth, and unless it is of a very unyielding texture, shallow culture thereafter, will secure a crop, equal to the capacity of the land.

A considerable saving of labour may be made by a very simple instrument for raising the manure into the carts, and scattering the heaps; and by dividing and balancing the labourers so judiciously, that loading, carting, spreading and ploughing may proceed, without having too few labourers at one work, and too many at another. The instrument is precisely a hilling-hoe, except that three strong square iron prongs are substituted for the blade. These sink from the usual elevation of a hand-hoe by their own weight, into the bed of coarse farm yard manure, easily rend from its edge or its surface, a mass of manure equal to the strength of the labourer, hold it

well in raising, and by a small jolt, from the helve's falling on the top of the cart, drop it therein with certainty.
In scattering the heaps, they take up the manure, and
hold it sufficiently to aid the action of throwing it two or
three yards. Over edged instruments, their advantages
are infinite, as coarse manure must be cut and chopt to
pieces with great labour, before these will raise or scat-
ter it; as several strokes are often necessary to obtain a
hoe or spade full; and as their contents often fall off in
being raised. And over the pitchfork with a horizontal
handle, their pre-eminence is little less, as they save the
labour of stooping, and possess in a far greater degree
the powers of a lever. These pronged hoes are only unfit
to scrape together and raise the small quantity of fine
manure, which falls to the bottom as the coarse is removed. Hoes and spades collect this as usual. This very
simple instrument, a three pronged hoe, helved in the
same angle as a common hilling hoe, and having its
prongs as long as the blade of the hilling hoe, has I think,
enabled me for some years to carry out and spread my
farm yard manure in half the time it had previously occupied. For many purposes it is also an excellent garden hoe.

Some time may be saved, and some skill exerted, even
in the simple object of laying off the ground to receive
the loads of manure. Being ridged, these ridges and furrows must be the course of the rows of manure, to avoid
the inconvenience of crossing them. The person dividing the ground for receiving manure follows one, beginning five yards from the edge of his field, if his rows are to
be ten apart, and measuring by the step, which he must
by experiments have reduced to considerable accuracy;

he digs a hole as he proceeds at one stroke with a hoe, at each spot on which a load is to be deposited. At the same time he watches the quality of the land, and lessens or extends the distances between his holes, according to that criterion.

NUMBER 26

Manuring, Continued

It is unnecessary to consider whether the animal and vegetable manure I have been treating of, ought to be ranked among the auxiliaries of the atmospherical, or the atmospherical degraded into an auxiliary of theirs. For my part, if I was driven to the alternative of rejecting one, I should not hesitate to cling to the atmospherical, as the matrix of all; or rather to that portion of it within our reach, by other channels than those of farm yards and animals. I would even prefer a confinement to the single mode of extracting manure from the atmosphere by vegetables, and applying these vegetables to the enrichment of the earth they grow on, by inclosing, to every other mode of manuring land, excluding this. It works so widely, so constantly, and at so small an expense of labour, that properly used, it insures an annual improvement; and a constant progress towards fertility, however slow, must terminate at it. Human life is said to be short, compared with what we know and conjecture of time. Within one fourth of one of these short cycles, I have known a fourfold increase of product from the same fields, produced chiefly by the inclosing mode of manuring. Without however insisting on its title to pre-eminence, it surely deserves to be considered as a powerful auxiliary of the valuable modes of manuring land, recently treated of.

To make room for this invaluable article in a system for improving our country, it is necessary to explode and banish a scheme of tillage, founded in the massacre of the earth, and terminating in its murder. It is called the three shift system. Its course is, Indian corn, wheat, pasture. Under it, the great body of the farm receives no manure, and no rest; and the result is, that the phrase "the land is killed and must be turned out," has become common over a great portion of the United States. This system, the most execrable within the scope of imagination, under which the richest country on earth could not live; being called an improved mode of agriculture at its introduction, was blindly received under that character, and our eyes cannot even be opened by the sound of our own melancholy confessions, "that our lands are killed." As a system for extorting crops from the earth, it is precisely similar to the rack for extorting truth from the sufferer; it stretches, tortures, mangles, obtains but little of its object, and half or quite kills its victim.

The system of inclosing, to manure the earth by its own coat of vegetables, is at open war with this murdering three shift system, upon the suppositions, that the matter of these vegetables being chiefly extracted from the atmosphere, must be some accession of fertility to the earth, and that any such accession is better than a perpetual exhaustion. It will probably be conceded by every reader, that both Indian corn and wheat are exhausting crops; there can of course remain no doubt, but that this system impoverishes the land two years in three. The only question then is, whether this loss will be compensated, by grazing the field bare during the third year. From whence is the recompense to come? Soft from recent tillage, and unprotected by a strong sward, the land is exposed to all the injury the hoof can inflict. Thinly sprinkled with an insufficient food, the restlessness of perpetual hunger produces unabating industry in the cattle, to tread it into a naked arena, closing its pores like a road against refreshments from the atmosphere, and exposing its flat and naked surface to heat, an agent of evaporation, able to pierce and expel from stone itself. This three shift system has only one merit; honesty. In theory it promises to kill our lands; in practice it fulfills its promise.

The inclosing system requires four shifts, to succeed tolerably well without manure, and extremely well with it. From a long course of experiments, my result is, that a three shift system is far inferior to four shifts, without grazing either; and that one fourth of a farm, properly managed in the latter way, after having been worried by the old rotation of corn, wheat and grazing, may in fifteen years be made to produce more than the whole would previously do. I have kept a farm in three and in four shifts for years, and the result is extremely in favour of the latter, though its land was at first of inferior quality. To this article for manuring our lands, objections are made, among which, the want of pasturage, and the want of space for our labour, should we reduce the size of our fields, are the most serious. Answers to these objections, will be more apposite in considering the subjects of stocks, pasturage and labour, should these essays ever get so far, than in the midst of our present subject. That is, manuring, and the object of this paper, is to confront the inclosing four shift system, with the grazing three shift system, as modes of manuring or improving land.

To illustrate the theory "that vegetables extract their matter chiefly from the atmosphere, and are of course a powerful vehicle for fixing and bestowing atmospherical manure on the earth," the following fact is circumstantially related, on account of its complete application, and to expose it to investigation. Some years ago, a locust tree at colonel Larkin Smith's, in the county of King and Queen, and State of Virginia, received an injury which made it necessary to cut away entirely the bark around its body for eight or ten inches, so that its bark above and below was wholly separated, without a cortical vein between. The wound was entirely covered with a close bandage of some other bark, which lapped beyond the edges of the wounded bark, above and below. And the tree was left to its fate. The plaster bark never grew to the tree, but the edges of the wounded bark, gradually approached each other under its shelter, and after several years met and united. By the time the wound was healed, the body of the tree above, had become one third larger than its body below it. And though several years have elapsed, the latter has not been able to overtake the former. The upper part of the tree, rooted in the air, vastly outgrew the under, rooted in the earth. There-

fore it must have drawn either its whole or chief sustenance from the atmosphere. Indeed, between the bark and
the wood of most trees, and of the locust particularly, we
find the chief channel of their juices; and the communication of these juices was utterly cut off, so that neither portion of the tree could supply the other. If the part of the
tree fed from its roots, extracted from the earth, the food,
which the earth had previously extracted from the atmosphere; and if the earth was reimbursed gradually by the
atmosphere, what it lost in feeding this part of the tree,
then even the small acquisition of the tree below the in-
terdict to communications, as well as the great one above,
is to be considered as wholly obtained from the atmosphere, and might on that supposition be considered as
probable evidence in favour of the theory, that vegetables
get from the air and give to the earth. But probable testimony is superfluous, when the superior growth above so
clearly evinces, that they do extract food from the atmosphere.

I might quote the fertile state of new ungrazed countries; their abatement in fertility if grazed, though un-
cleared; the improvement of worn out lands by suffering
them to grow up in trees; their greater improvement if
these trees are cut down and suffered to rot on the surface, as further proofs that the earth cannot bear a constant drain of vegetable matter, and that this matter in
any form enriches it, to evince both the ruinous effects of
the three shift system, and that inclosing is the remedy;
but the intelligent reader will advert to these and many
other considerations, and I only add, that the fact of the

earth's surface being the depository of its fertility, proves that this fertility is owing to atmospherical or vegetable matter, and alone determines the efficacy of the inclosing theory.

NUMBER 27

Manuring, Continued

Though we have passed the best, all the resources within our power for manuring land, are not exhausted. Whether gypsum is a manure, or a medium for drawing manure from the atmosphere by increasing the growth of vegetables, is an unimporant inquiry. Within the last ten years, I have expended between two and three hundred tons of it in a variety of experiments, which have produced the conclusion that it increases very considerably the product of vegetable matter in almost all forms. Now if most or all of the matter of vegetables, is drawn from the atmosphere, and if gypsum increases these drafts, we have only to realize this unexpected treasure, by turning it into the earth. It increases like compound interest, and in a few years, land worth only one pound an acre, will become worth five. Thus by the help of inclosing, gypsum and vegetables, we may enable ourselves to fit, survey, divide, sell or bestow on our children, atmosphere to a great value. Let us therefore at least admit it into the catalogue of manures, when used in combination with inclosing.

It would be tedious to recite a multitude of experiments in the rapid excursions of an essayist, through the agricultural kingdom, with very little regard to method; and therefore I shall only trouble the public with the results deemed most useful. Except when sown on clover, which it benefits almost at all seasons, I have found gypsum succeeds best when covered. I would even prefer harrowing it in with oats and clover, to sowing it on the surface after they are up. The best modes of using it, according to my experience, are sowing it on and ploughing it in with coarse litter; sowing it just in advance of the plough, when fallowing for corn, on land well covered with vegetable matter from having been inclosed, so as to bury it with the litter; this is in fact the same experiment with the last, except that the gypsum has less vegetable manure to work upon in the second than in the first case; bestowing on clover annually a top dressing, giving the preference to the youngest, if there should be a deficiency of the gypsum; and rolling both wheat and corn with it, when sown or planted, bushel to bushel. This has been the settled course for a farm for three or four years, and within no equal term has it equally improved. The wheat crop is less benefitted immediately than any other, but this rolling of the wheat facilitates the vegetation of the clover sown on its surface in the spring, and strengthens it against summer drought, so frequently fatal to it in coarse soils; and by thus improving the fertility of the land, considerably augments succeeding crops. Intervals of twelve yards wide, quite across large fields,

sown with unplastered wheat, whilst the rest was plastered by mingling a bushel of one, with a bushel of the
other, exhibited to a line on each side by the natural
growth, an inferiority of strength from the cutting of the
wheat throughout the whole period of rest.

The immediate benefit of gypsum to Indian corn, is
vastly greater than to any other crop, clover excepted,
whilst its benefit to the land is equally great. Unplastered
spaces left across large fields of clover, have in sundry
instances produced a third or fourth only of the adjoining
plastered cover. Unplastered spaces across large fields
of corn, have been frequently visible during the whole
crop, producing not an equal, but a considerable difference. Gypsum, clover, and inclosing, working in conjunc-
tion, have within my own knowledge doubled, trebled,
and in a very favourable soil quadrupled the value of
land, in the space of twelve or fifteen years; whilst the
land regularly produced two exhausting crops, those of
corn and wheat in every four years of the period, and
these crops were continually increasing.

Of lime and marle we have an abundance, but experience does not entitle me to say any thing of either.
About a family, a variety of manures may be thrown
together, and form a small store for gardens and lots.
Among these, ashes deserve particular attention. Like
other manures they suffer by the exposure and evaporation, but less, because water is a menstruum which will
convey much of their salts into the earth, if they are
spread; the same menstruum conveys most of these
salts out of the ashes, if they are exposed to it before
they are applied as a manure. Hence when ashes have not

been reduced by water in richness, they are to be used as a manure more sparingly, and when they have, more copiously. In their unreduced state, just from the chimney, when sprinkled an inch thick on the long litter and dung from a recently cleansed stable, they constitute the best manure I have ever tried for asparagus. The beds are well forked up in the fall, covered two or three inches deep with the unrotted stable manure, on which the fresh ashes are placed, and so remain until they are thrown into proper order in the spring. (Note C.)

NUMBER 28

Labour

Perhaps this subject ought to have preceded that of manuring, as it is idle even to think of a good system of agriculture in any point of view, if the labour on which it depends is convulsed by infusions the most inimical to its utility; and if those who direct it, are to live in a constant dread of its loss, and a doubt of their own safety. Such a state of uncertainty is painful to the parties, unfriendly to improvement, and productive of extravagance and idleness in all their varieties. Yet those who keep it alive, persuade themselves that they are complying with the principles of religion, patriotism and morality. Into such fatal errors is human nature liable to fall, by its deliriums for acquiring unattainable perfection.

One would think that the circles of ethics and logic could not furnish less doubtful questions than these. Were the whites of St. Domingo morally bound to bring on themselves the massacre produced by the liberation of their slaves? Is such a sacrifice of freemen to make freemen of slaves, virtuous or wicked? Will it advance or destroy the principles of morality, religion and civil liberty? Is it wise or foolish?

The history of parties in its utmost malignity is but a feint mirror for reflecting the consequences of a white and a black party. If badges and names have been able to madden men in all ages, up to robbery and murder in their most atrocious forms, no doubt can exist of the consequences of placing two nations of distinct colours and features on the same theatre, to contend, not about sounds and signs, but for wealth and power.

And yet an amiable and peaceful religious sect, have been long labouring with some success, to plunge three fourths of the union, into a civil war of a complexion so inveterate, as to admit of no issue, but the extermination of one entire party. Suppose the extermination shall fall on the blacks, the ferocity acquired by the whites during the contest, and the destruction of the labour in three fourths of the union, will not endow the remaining fourth with wealth or happiness. If the whites should be the victims of this enthusiastic philanthropy, and our northern brethren should succeed in overwhelming the southern states with the large negro patriotism and civilization, what will they have done for the benefit of the liberty, virtue or happiness of mankind? The French revolution, bottomed upon as correct abstract principles and sounder practical hopes, turned out to be a foolish and mischievous speculation; what then can be expected from making republicans of negro slaves, and conquerors of ignorant infuriated barbarians? What can those who are doing the greatest mischiefs from the best motives, to their fellow-citizens, to themselves and to their country, expect from such preachers of the gospel, such champions of liberty, and such neighbouring possessors of a territory larger than their own.

But what will not enthusiasm attempt? It attempted to make freemen of the people of France; the experiment pronounced that they were incapable of liberty. It attempted to compound a free nation of black and white people in St. Domingo. The experiment pronounced that one colour must perish. And now rendered blinder by experience, it proposes to renew the last experiment, though it impressed truth by sanctions of inconceivable horror; and again to create a body politic, as monstrous and unnatural as a mongrel half white man and half negro.

Do these hasty, or in the language of exact truth, fanatic philosophers, patriots or christians, suppose that the negroes could be made free, and yet kept from property and equal civil rights; or that both or either of these avenues to power could be opened to them, and yet that some precept or incantation could prevent their entrance? As rivals for rule with the whites, the collision would be immediate, and the catastrophe speedy. Divested of equal civil rights and wealth to prevent this rivalship, but endowed with personal liberty, they would constitute the most complete instrument for invasion or ambition, hitherto forged throughout the entire circle of human folly.

For what virtuous purpose are the southern runaway negroes countenanced in the northern states? Do these states wish the southern to try the St. Domingo experiment? If not, why do they keep alive the St. Domingo spirit? War is the match which will in the course of time be put to such a spirit, and an explosion might follow, which would shake our nation from the centre to its extremities. Is it humanity, wisdom or religion, or some adversary of all three, which prepares the stock of combustibles for this explosion?

Suppose France was about to invade the United States, and should ask Congress previously to admit a million of her most desperate people into the southern states, ready to join and aid her armies; could the northern members of the union find any motive drawn from policy, religion, morality or self interest, for agreeing to the proposal? And yet in case of such an invasion, a million of negroes, either slaves, but artificially filled with a violent impatience of their condition, and deadly hatred of their masters; or free men, but excluded from wealth and power, would hardly be less ferocious, merciless or dangerous, than a million of desperate French people.

A policy which weakens or renders incapable of self-defence at least three-fourths of the union must also be excessively injurious to the remaining fourth, whose wealth and security must increase or diminish by increasing or diminishing the wealth and security of the larger portion. Nor does the least present gain, afford to the northern states a temptation for incurring so dreadful an evil. Their manners will neither be improved, nor their happiness advanced, by sprinkling their cities with a yearly emigration of thieves, murderers and villains of every degree, though recommended by the training of slavery, a black skin, a woolly body, and an African contour.

And yet even the northern news-papers are continually dealing out fraternity to this race, and to this moral character, and opprobrium to their white masters, with as little justice in the last case, as taste in the first. What had the present generation to do with the dilemma in which it is involved? How few even of its ancestors were concerned in stealing and transporting negroes from Africa? If some remnants of such monsters exist, they are not to be found in the southern quarters of this union. And if self preservation shall force the slave holders into stricter measures of precaution than they have hitherto adopted, those who shall have driven them into these measures, by continually exciting their negroes to cut their throats, will accuse them of tyranny with as little reason, as the prosecutors of the slave trade accuses them of negro stealing.

The fact is, that negro slavery is an evil which the United States must look in the face. To whine over it, is cowardly; to aggravate it, criminal; and to forbear to alleviate it, because it cannot be wholly cured, foolish. Rewards and punishments, the sanctions of the best government, and the origin of love and fear, are rendered useless by the ideas excited in the French revolution; by the example of St. Domingo; by the lure of free negroes mingled with slaves; and by the reproaches to masters and sympathies for slaves, breathed forth from the northern states. Sympathies, such as if the negroes should transfer their affections from their own species to the baboons. Under impressions derived from such sources, the justest punishment will be felt as the infliction of tyranny, and the most liberal rewards, as a niggardly portion of greater rights. For where will the rights of black sansculottes stop?

Such a state of things is the most unfavourable imaginable to the happiness of both master and slave. It tends to diminish the humanity of one class, and increase the malignity of the other, and in contemplating its utter destitution of good, our admiration is equally excited, by the error of those who produce, and the folly of those who suffer it.

NUMBER 29

Labour, Continued

Slaves are docile, useful and happy, if they are well managed; and if their docility, utility and happiness are not obstructed by the circumstances adverted to in the last number. Knowledge manages ignorance with great ease, whenever ignorance is not used as an instrument by knowledge against itself. But our religious and philosophical Quixotes have undertaken to make ignorance independent of knowledge. They propose to bestow a capacity for liberty and rule on an extreme degree of ignorance, when the whole history of mankind announces, that far less degrees possess no such capacity. One would suspect, except for the integrity of these divines and philosophers, that they were impostors disguised in the garb of religion and philosophy, striving to disengage a mass of ignorance from those who now direct it, for the purpose of appropriating it to themselves. Free it cannot be. It must become the slave of superstition, cunning or ambition, in some form. And what is still worse, when thrown upon the great national theatre to be scrambled for, that interest which shall gain the prize, will use it to oppress other branches of knowledge. In its hands the blacks will be more enslaved than they are at present; and the whites, in pursuit of an ideal freedom for them, will create some vortex for ingulphing the remnant of liberty left in the world, and obtain real slavery for themselves.

Under their present masters the negroes would enjoy more happiness, and even more liberty, than under a conqueror or a hierarchy. Slavery to an individual is preferable to slavery to an interest or faction. The individual is restrained by his property in the slave, and susceptible of humanity. An interest or faction is incapable of both. Did a hierarchy or a paper system ever shed tears over its oppressions, or feel compunction for its exactions? On the contrary, joy swells with the fruit of guilt; and the very conscience, which abhors the secret guillotine, used to cut out a neighbour's purse, and transfer it to its own pocket, without difficulty retains the contents. Thus men imagine that they have discovered a way to elude the justice of God, whose denunciations have overlooked chartered corporations, and are only levelled against individuals. The crime, they suppose, is committed by a body politic, and scripture having exhibited no instance of one of these artificial bodies being consigned to the region of punishment, their oppressions, however atrocious, are considered as a *casus omissus*, and as affording a mode for fattening the body with crimes and frauds, without hurting the soul.

It is otherwise with the personal owner of slaves. Religion assails him both with her blandishments and terrors. It indissolubly binds his, and his slave's happiness or misery together. These associates he cannot dissever; he chooses the alternative indeed for both, but he must choose the same.

If an interest or a combination of men is the worst species of master, and if this black mass of ignorance turned at large and defined by the plainest marks, must naturally fall under the dominion of some interest or combination, the miseries inflicted both on their owners and themselves, by the perpetual excitements to insurrection, and those to be expected from the experiment whenever it is made, are attended with no compensating counterpoise whatsoever to either of the parties, even in hope. Should these fruitless attempts be forborne, and should the slave states take measures for abolishing these excitements to general disquietude and calamity, some system for the management of slaves, beneficial to themselves and their owners, is so closely connected with agriculture, that the next number will be devoted to that subject.

NUMBER 30

Labour, Continued

Animal labour is brought to its utmost value, by being completely supplied with the necessaries and comforts required by its nature. These comforts have more force to attach the reasonable than the brute creation to a place, and yet the attachments of the latter from this cause, are often strong. The addition of comfort to mere necessaries, is a price paid by the master, for the advantages he will derive from binding his slave to his service, by a ligament stronger than chains, far beneath their value in a pecuniary point of view; and he will moreover gain a stream of agreeable reflections throughout life, which will cost him nothing.

A project towards an object so desirable, may possibly contain a hint which some one will improve. Let the houses of the slaves be of brick walls, able to withstand hard usage, and remain tight, built in one connected line, with partitions, making each a room sixteen or eighteen feet square; let there be a brick chimney in the centre between each two rooms, affording a fire place to each, and two warm chasms, one on each side of the fire place for beds. A square window with a wooden shutter, to be opposite the door of each room, and three panes of glass above each door. No joists or loft, but to be lathed on the rafters and their couplings, nearly to the top of the roof, and the whole inside to be plastered. Hence, though the house should be low, the pitch of the rooms will be high; and salubrity will be consulted with a precaution against fire, amounting to a certainty within the house, as there will be no inside fuel, the floor being of earth. The roof will be a mere shell plastered within, and if the chimneys are sufficiently high, the absence of interior combustibles, combined with the lowness of the house, will form a great security against fire, so frequently fatal to the houses of slaves, and sometimes to the inhabitants.

A regular supply of a winter's coat, jacket and breeches, with the latter and the sleeves of the former lined, two oznaburg shirts, a good hat and blanket every other year, two pair of stockings annually, a pair of shoes, a pair of summer overalls, and a great coat every third year, will constitute a warm clothing for careful slaves, and the acquisitions they make from their usual permissions, will supply them with finery.

The best source for securing their happiness, their honesty and their usefulness, is their food; and yet it is seldom considered as a means for advancing either. If the happiness of an idle epicure is deeply affected by food, what must be its influence upon labour and hunger? In the article of food, the force of rewards and punishments may be happily combined to unite the whole body of slaves into conservators, instead of being pilferers of the moveables on a farm. It may be made both a ligament to tie the slave to its service, and enable him to perform that service better. A scheme for producing these ends has been found so successful in practice, and coincides so entirely with the subject of agriculture by slaves, that it is chosen to terminate this subject. Bread alone, ought never to be considered as a sufficient diet for slaves, except as a punishment; and at one meal each day they should have salt meat boiled into a soup with peas, beans, potatoes, turnips, cabbages, cimblins or pumpkins. At other meals, salt fish, milk or butter-milk. Vegetables are raised in great abundance at little expense, and at all seasons a supply of some species should be allowed to the slaves without stint. We shall be astonished upon trial to discover that this great comfort to them, is a profit to the master, in its single effect of contributing to their health, without estimating the benefits arising from a cheerful acquiescence in their condition. One great value of establishing a comfortable diet for slaves, is its conveniency as an instrument of reward and punishment, so powerful as almost to abolish the thefts, which often diminish considerably the owner's ability to provide for them. These can seldom or never be committed without being known to the other slaves, but they are under no interest to restrain them. It is the interest of all to steal, by which they occasionally get some addition to bread, if this addition cannot be procured by honesty. But if thefts are punished by placing the whole on that diet, all will have an interest to prevent and forbear theft, provided a diet much more comfortable is thereby secured. Nor is in-

volving all in the punishment a hardship, because all
share in the benefit, which nothing but this system for
preventing the waste of theft can produce; and because a
knowledge of the criminal is usually general. It is this
unavoidable knowledge, which makes the innocent com-
rades, who will not surrender their own daily comforts,
that another may occasionally steal luxuries, a solid check
upon theft. The better the diet of negroes, the more effectual will such a system become. It should be executed
rigidly, so as to produce a loss of food additional to bread,
of double value to the thing stolen, except the guilty person is detected, who ought in that case to sustain the
whole punishment, which must either be corporal, or a
sale to some distant place. The latter, combined with
the enjoyments provided for slaves by this system, will
soon become an object of terror; and as many buyers care
little for moral character, it is unexceptionable, provided
the seller states it fairly, and records it in the bill of sale,
as he ought to do, for his own honour and security.

A daily allowance of cyder will extend the success of
this system for the management of slaves, and particularly its effect of diminishing corporal punishments. But
the reader is warned, that a stern authority, strict discipline, and complete subordination, must be combined
with it, to gain any success at all; and that so long as white
soldiers cannot be kept in order, or rendered useful, without all three, he is not to expect that black slaves can
without either; nor that those can be governed by the
finest threads of the human heart who possess only the
coarsest.

NUMBER 31

Labour, Continued

Those tied by habit to the rotation of corn, wheat and pasture, or the three shift system, object to the inclosing and four shift system, "that having labour adequate to the tilling one third of their arable land, a portion of it would be unemployed, by restricting this labour to the cultivation of a fourth only." The rotation of corn, wheat and clover for two years, without being cut or grazed, need only be confronted with its rival course, to satisfy the reader, that under the latter system, the fourth will soon overtake the third in product, and at length infinitely exceed it. The profit of making greater crops from less land, is visible at once. The same crop from a fourth may produce profit, and yet a loss from a third. If 120 acres of poor land produce 120 barrels of corn, and the expenses of cultivation amount to a barrel an acre, there is no profit; but if 90 acres of the same land are improved by inclosing, so as to produce 120 barrels, there will be a profit of 30 barrels. This principle equally applies to every case of an existing profit under the three shift system, because whatever it may be, it is greatly increased by obtaining an equal crop by cultivating less land.

The error of making the mode of cultivation subservient to fluctuating labour, instead of adapting the labour to permanent land, however egregious, cannot properly be termed vulgar, because it is common to men of the best, as well as to those of the meanest understandings. However glaring it is, it really constitutes the most stubborn argument in favour of using labour to kill rather than to improve land; and though some readers may think it idle to controvert a mistake, apparently not within the scope of human weakness to commit, the greater number will, I fear, consider the application of labour to the improvement rather than to the impoverishment of land, as far more ridiculous. The collision between these opinions, will excuse the matter of this number, though it may seem trite to some, and visionary to others.

An application of labour to land, which daily diminishes the fertility of the land, considered in a national light, is obviously a national evil; and a habit from which such boundless or wide ruin and depopulation must ensue, supposing it to be general, seems incapable of deserving the approbation of virtue, or the concurrence of selfishness. If the employment of labour in the course of corn, wheat and pasture, produces a regular impoverishment of the soil, the practice falls within the scope of this observation.

It is equally at enmity with the purest devotion of self-interest, which ever chilled the human heart. This devotion pants for compound or increasing, not for decreasing interest; and beholds with horror a diminution of principal. Our three shift system gradually destroys the principal, land, and gradually diminishes the interest, crop. If the labour increases as in the case of slaves, the effect is not to enrich, but to impoverish the owner.

Flight is his resource against the poverty he derives from the increase of his slaves. If the application of labour to the impoverishment of land, was universal, an emigration to another world, would be the only remedy; if national, it must amount to an abjuration of our country and form of government; if state, to a banishment from our native soil and relations. But this miserable remedy itself will ere long be exhausted, and after an internal struggle for the best birth in a bed of thorns, the discovery will be made, that an endeavour in each to feather his own nest, is the only way to procure comfort for all; and that the prosperity of the nation and the happiness of individuals, depend on the improvement of land by a proper application of labour.

But what shall we do with our surplus labour, is repeated, if we cease to employ it in killing land? One would think that this doubt could never be entertained, except by a fatalist, who believed that such was the end for which labour was created. The effects of labour are the same in agriculture as in architecture; far more is necessary to build than to destroy; shall we thence also infer, that labour is destined to destroy houses? Where is the difference between destroying houses and destroying the means by which houses are rendered comfortable? The early Kentucky settlers contended, that unless the sugar makers killed the sugar trees, it threw a portion of their labour out of employment, and therefore inferred, that it was one of nature's wise laws, that labour should kill the sources of sugar. Did they borrow this opinion from our querist, who thinks it wise and natural to employ it in killing the source of bread? If an abundance of labour caused a land killing agricultural system, and its scarcity the reverse, Flanders should be a wilderness and Virginia a garden. A great recommendation of the inclosing and four shift system, is the saving of labour it creates in fencing, and in renouncing the culture of exhausted lands, to be applied to improvement. When we come to consider a project for the management of a bread stuff farm, we shall discover full employment for this surplus labour, which the three shift system fears would be idle, if not employed as a land executioner. The raising of manure, covering with clover every spot of land which will bear it, and converting all moist land into meadow, would alone be sponsors for the futility of the apprehension. And yet many other objects of labour must be combined with the four shift and inclosing system, to accelerate and augment the rewards it will bestow. Hay in abundance must be made, crops will be augmented, modes of tillage must be improved, transportation will increase with litter, manure and crops, and gypsum if resorted to, is by no means niggardly in providing employment for labour. If these observations have not removed the apprehension of ruin, seriously and generally entertained by the disciples of corn, wheat and pasture rotation, should they change the application of their labour from impoverishing to improving their land, it will still be removed by their own superior reflections, if they will be pleased to reflect. They will certainly discover that the danger of wanting employment for their labour, lurks, not in improving but in impoverishing their lands, and that whilst they shudder at an apparition, they are embracing an assassin.

NUMBER 32

Indian Corn

It was very improbable that one who has often joined
in the execration of Indian corn, should have been destined to write its eulogy. Had we designed to transfer
from ourselves to an innocent plant the heavy charge of
murdering our land, its acquittal before a jury whose
own condemnation would be the consequence, could not
be expected; but as nothing is more certain than that the
exclamations against corn and tobacco (and for the last
thirty years wheat ought to have been placed at the head
of the triumvirate) for killing our lands, have proceeded
from conviction, without a suspicion that we ourselves
were the perpetrators of the act; I shall venture to bring
Indian corn to trial before the real criminals, and its
mistaken accusers.

Arthur Young, in his travels through France and Spain,*
observes that the regions of maize exhibited plenty and

---

* *Travels in France* (London, 1792), 2 volumes.

affluence, compared with those where other crops were cultivated. As a faithful agricultural annalist, he records the fact; being but little acquainted with the plant, he could not satisfactorily account for it. Even a nation which has lived with it, and almost upon it for two hundred years, so far from correctly estimating its value, have only learnt to eat it, but not to avail themselves of half its properties. Those for killing land, they have turned to the utmost account; those for improving it, they have wholly neglected. The first capacity is common to all crops; the last is possessed by few. Indian corn produces more food for man, beast and the earth, than any other farinaceous plant. If the food it produces for the two first was wasted, and men and beasts should thence become poor and perish, ought their poverty or death to be ascribed to the plant which produced the food, or to those who wasted it? Is Indian corn justly chargeable with the impoverishment of the earth, if the food it provides for that is not applied?

If the theory which supposes that plants extract most or all of their matter from the atmosphere, and that the whole of this matter is manure, be true, then that plant which produces most vegetable offal must be the most improving crop, and it will hardly be denied that Indian corn is entitled to this pre-eminence.

Let us compare it with wheat. Suppose that the same land will produce as much grain of the one as of the other, which in its use will make equal returns to the earth. Here the equality ends, if indeed it exists even in this point. The corn stalks infinitely exceed the wheat straw in bulk, weight, and a capacity for making food for the earth. If any attentive man who converts both his stalks and straw into manure, will compare their product in April, when he may distinguish one from the other, he will find of the former a vast superiority in quantity. The English farmers consider wheat straw as their most abundant resource for manure, and corn stalks are far more abundant; corn therefore is a less impoverishing, because a more compensating crop to the earth, credited only for its stalks, than any in England. In comparing crops, to ascertain their relative product, and operation on the earth, we must contrast farinaceous crops with each other; and consider the litter or offal they produce, not as wasted, but as judiciously applied to the compensation of the land. At the threshold of the comparison, corn exhibits a return from the same land of more offal or litter in its stalks alone, than wheat does altogether. But to the stalks of corn, its blades, tops, shucks and cobs remain to be added, each of which will nearly balance the litter bestowed on the land by wheat. Not only the quantity of the vegetable matter produced by corn, is far greater than the quantity produced by wheat, but the quality is better, and the risque of loss from evaporation less. The straw of wheat after it is ripening or ripe, standing or lying out on the ground, is vastly diminished in weight by moisture, and injured after it is cut, even by dews. I think I have known it thus lose two thirds of its weight. Among the several kinds of litter furnished by corn, the shucks and cobs lose nothing of their value by evaporation; the rind of the stalks seems intended by nature to resist it, that the farmer may have time to save them both as food and litter; from the same rind the top derives some security, and the fodder is only exposed to it as grass is in being made into hay. But the quality of every part of the corn offal is better as manure than the wheat offal. The cob is said to be a valuable food, reduced to meal; if so it probably contains an oil. The stalk abounds in salts far beyond wheat straw. The tops and blades cured green, save from evaporation, salts lost by straw. And even shucks, being more nutricious as food, must be allowed some degree of richness beyond the straw. The whole of the corn offal is better food than wheat straw, but its blades and tops are so greatly superior, that cattle prefer them to hay, and will fatten on them as well. The corn offal can therefore maintain a fat herd, furnishing abundantly that which forms a compound with vegetable matter, of the richest consistence. To this object the straw is incompetent.

Let us now compare corn and wheat as farinaceous food only. Corn in a proper climate for it, produces more farinaceous matter than wheat to the acre, from the richest down to the poorest soil; and hence also results a greater return to the earth. The highest product of corn I have heard of in the United States is 125 bushels to the acre, of wheat 60, a difference somewhat diminished by the difference of weight. Fifty bushels of corn to the acre, are almost invariably produced by land well manured and well cultivated, whereas even half that crop of wheat is extremely rare. And in districts where the average crop of wheat is five, that of corn is usually about fifteen bushels an acre. Besides, corn both growing and gathered, is less liable to misfortunes than wheat.

Indian corn may be correctly called meal, meadow and

manure. To its right to the first title, almost every tongue in the largest portion of the United States can testify; to the second, an exclusive reliance on it for fodder or hay, in a great district of country during two centuries, gives conclusive evidence; but the rueful countenance of this same district, either disproves its claim to the third, or disallows any pretension of the inhabitants to industry or agricultural knowledge.

In Europe no husbandman expects a tolerable crop of any kind, except the land has been well manured within seven years at most; here we have obtained for two centuries from Indian corn, bread, meat and fodder, without giving it, generally speaking, a dust of manure, or allowing any rest to the land which produces it. Is there any country in Europe, able to bear this draft for such a period, without exhibiting the cadaverous aspect of the corn district of the United States?

But not content with bestowing on other crops, the meagre modicum of manure, which happened to lie unavoidably in the way of ignorance, whilst the maintenance of every thing was required of corn, without allowing it any, we have suffered the manure provided by corn itself to waste and perish; and having both withheld from it foreign aids, and transferred to other plants the small portion of its own resources for manure, which accident may have saved, and permitted the residue to be lost, we charge it with being an exhausting and killing crop.

Such is the experimental process hitherto pursued, but it must be reversed, before the question can be tolerably understood or fairly determined. It will be reversed by

converting every dust of its offal into manure, and manuring highly for corn. With good cultivation, an acre
of well manured corn, seldom produces less than fifty
bushels. This crop furnishes also other food equivalent
to a tolerable crop of hay, and such an abundance of
means for raising manure, that I have no doubt if properly applied, it would be a resource for our even shorten-
ing the English manuring rotation, which embraces the
whole farm every seven years at most. Hence I conclude that corn, besides being the most productive of any
farinaceous crop, is also the least impoverishing, and
even an improving crop aided by inclosing.

The brevity I have prescribed to myself, induces me to
pass over several inferior superiorities of Indian corn,
and to conclude its encomium with one of peculiar value.
As a fallow crop, it is unrivalled, if as fallow crops ought
constantly to do, it receives the manure. Arthur Young
proves the vast superiority of a fallow crop over a naked
fallow in England, where a crop greatly inferior to corn in
value, is necessarily used. This is usually peas or beans.
It is less productive, less valuable as bread stuff, less
fraught with fodder, almost wholly destitute of litter for
raising manure, more precarious, more liable to disaster
after it is gathered, more chargeable in point of seed, and
requires more skill, trouble and expense in its cultivation.
Under all these disadvantages, a fallow crop in England
is preferable to a naked fallow. Under all the advantages
of using corn as such, it becomes a brilliant object in
America, if attended with a complete manuring, as fallow
crops in England invariably are. In that case, fifty bushels
of corn and thirty of wheat may be expected from cul-

ture. No value is produced in England by the fallow crop and the fallowing wheat, equal to eight bushels of bread grain. But credit to corn the savings and additional produce arising from the above enumerated considerations, and it certainly promises to the American farmer, far greater benefits from a good system of husbandry, than any crop within the reach of an English farmer.

NUMBER 33

Indian Corn, Continued

The plant which contributes in the greatest degree to national subsistence, best deserves the patronage of skill and industry; and yet the cultivation of maize remains as it was borrowed from the aboriginal farmers of America, except, that if product is the test of science, they must be allowed to have been more accomplished husbandmen than their imitators. As the Indians certainly made better crops to the acre, and preserved the earth in better heart, than we do, we may at least hope to accomplish a degree of perfection, which from their success we know to be attainable, however deterring may be the prospect of our ability to improve upon it. If indeed we could be persuaded to relinquish what we have retained of this indigenous system, and to draw one from scientific principles and European experience, perhaps we might recover the palm in the cultivation of maize, from those to whom we have ourselves assigned it by special cognomination.

Neither in theory or practice, in Europe or elsewhere, did we ever hear of condemning land perpetually to severe crops, two years out of three, without aiding it by any species of manure. But if we add to this system the two items with which it is usually attended, one, close grazing the year of rest, as it is called (a rest like that enjoyed by a man first stunned with blows and then trampled to death), the other, frequent ploughings of two or three inches deep to let in sun and keep out atmosphere as much as possible, it would be viewed as the most complete agricultural caricature hitherto sketched by the finest fancy for the ridiculous.

In England, a thorough manuring, universally attends a fallow crop, the effect of which is a medium product of wheat, of about thirty bushels to the acre. Let manuring attend maize as a fallow crop, and we follow this example. To come up to it, however, we must get our land into equal heart with theirs, when it receives this manuring; and then we should be able fairly to estimate the value of Indian corn. In its cultivation, the first improvement required, is therefore to manure it at the usual rate of other fallow crops.

The second is to plough vastly deeper than we plough at present. In our dry and hot climate, the preservation of the moisture, and the inhalation of the atmosphere, are sufficient reasons for this. To these are to be added, the deepening of the soil, and an increase of pasture for the plant. The maize is a little tree, and possessing roots corresponding to its size, these roots will of course strike deeper, both to procure nourishment, and to strengthen this small tree against severe winds. It follows with a great degree of probability, that this large plant requires deeper ploughing than a smaller one. Yet we plough shallower in its cultivation than the people of Europe do in cultivating wheat.

I shall here endeavor to prove the truth of a pair of paradoxes. One, that shallow ploughing increases; the other, that deep ploughing diminishes labour. A single observation almost suffices to sustain both. By shallow ploughing, the seeds of grass and weeds, are kept near the surface throughout the year, locked up by frost, drought or immersion, ready to sprout up on the occurrence of every genial season, when they appear in millions, and instantly require the plough, however recently used; by deep, if skilfully done, these seeds, which abound most near the surface, are deposited below a depth of earth, which they penetrate slowly and in small numbers, so that the repetition of ploughing is far less necessary.

One or two deep ploughings, according to the nature of the soil, will, with the subsequent use of the skimmer or the harrow, serve to make the crop of corn; in place of which at least four or five shallow ploughings, with the same aid, will often destroy it.

To demonstrate the difference in point of labour, I will describe the tillage of corn as I practice it to some extent, and leave the reader to make the comparison in his own mind with the usual mode of cultivation.

The rows are never ploughed but in one direction, cross ploughing being wholly abandoned. Their width is five and a half feet. The field being once thrown into the position of ridges and furrows, never requires to be laid off again. The furrow is left as deep as possible, and when the field comes again into tillage, the list or ridge is made upon this furrow, so that there is a regular alternity between ridges and furrows. If the soil is of a friable nature, a large plough drawn by four horses, and cutting a sod about twelve inches wide and eight deep, is run on each side of this old furrow, and raises a ridge in its center, on which to plant the corn. The old ridge is split by a large trowel-hoe-plough, having a coulter on the point, two mould boards, drawn by four horses, and cutting ten inches deep. If the soil is stiff or tough with turf, the first plough with four horses, ridges or lists on the old water furrow, with four furrows of the same depth and width. On the summit of this ridge or list, a deep and wide furrow is run with a trowel-hoe-plough and two mould boards, in which the corn is planted and covered between two and three inches deep, with the foot. The planting is guided by a string carried across the ridges, with coloured marks at the distance apart intended for the corn. This furrow is a complete weeding of the ridge previous to planting, which it should barely precede. The corn receives no more ploughing until it is thinned and hand-hoed along the rows, about two feet wide. After this a deep furrow is run on each side of it by a large plough, drawn by two horses, with a mould-board, causing the earth thrown out of it to meet at the corn, though the furrow is a foot from it. Thenceforth the tillage consists of a streak or furrow of a mere weeding plough called a skimmer, cutting with two wings twenty-four inches—drawn by one horse; and of a central, deep and wide furrow, made with a trowel-hoe and two mould boards, drawn by two horses, to be repeated when necessary. The whole to be concluded with a narrow weeding or hand-hoeing along the slip in the direction of the row, not yet kept completely clean by the skimmer.

NUMBER 34

Indian Corn, Continued

The judicious reader will discern, that the effects of high ridges and deep furrows, in cultivating corn, are numerous. The corn is planted immediately over the furrow of the preceding crop, and by completing the reversal of the ridge early in its culture, it grows upon a depth of tilth three or four times exceeding what is attained by planting and cross ploughing in the usual mode. Its roots are never cut in one direction, and this great depth of tilth thus early obtained, by superseding the occasion for deep ploughing in the latter period of its growth, saves them in the other. The preservation of the roots, and their deeper pasture, enables the corn much longer to resist drought. The litter of inclosed grounds, thrown into the deep furrow upon which the corn list is made, is a reservoir of manure, far removed from evaporation; within reach of the roots, which will follow it along the furrow; and calculated for feeding the plant in droughts. The dead earth brought up by the plough from the deep furrow is deposited on each side of it, without hurting the crop on the ridge, and with the bottom of the furrow remains four years to be fructified by the atmosphere, so as to escape the present loss, sometimes accruing from mingling too much dead earth with the soil by deep flat ploughing, and yet to mellow and deepen it more rapidly. And much labour is saved in planting the crop, whether the hoe is used after a string, or the string is carried across furrows previously made on the ridge.

In all lands unable to produce forty bushels of corn to the acre, the considerations of produce and saving labour united, have determined the proper distance to be five and a half feet square, with two or three stalks at each station, except in poor spots where one will suffice. If it can produce that crop or more, I have planted it at the distance of five feet six inches, by two feet nine, leaving two stalks in sandy, and three in stiff lands. Deep ploughing in one direction, by shielding the corn against drought, and saving its roots, allows it to be planted thicker than usual.

Young's experiments have ascertained that fallow crops are more profitable than naked fallows. Several superiorities of Indian corn over the fallow crops used in England, have been noticed. The following are, I believe, omitted. The high ridges produced by the mode of cultivation I have adopted, double the surface exposed to the atmosphere, and lessen by one half that exposed to the sun, so as to increase inhalation and diminish exhalation very considerably. No other fallow crop will enable us to obtain these benefits by the agency of the plough, because none of them will admit of being drilled sufficiently wide apart, nor admit of an equal use of the plough.

Corn is a fallow crop, peculiarly adapted to co-operate with the system of inclosing; whereas a fallow for wheat, by which an ungrazed lay of grass, weeds, or even of red clover is turned under, frequently defeats the hopes of the farmer. Hence he is seduced into the ruinous practice of feeding off his clover before he commences his fallow; a practice under which very rich land only will improve; whereas the heaviest cover, turned under by a large plough and four horses, is a pledge for good crops both of corn and wheat, owing to the quality of the former of thriving upon the food yielded by coarse litter, and the time gained during its growth, for reducing this litter to proper food for the latter.

The winter's manure, like this litter, is also made more extensively beneficial to a crop of wheat, than if it had been exposed to putrefaction throughout the summer, because whatever escapes into the atmosphere, during a violent summer's fermentation, is lost both to the earth and to the crop of wheat; whereas the fermentation is less violent, when this litter is mingled with the earth, which catches a portion of its fertilizing qualities as the slow putrefaction proceeds, and less of the manure is lost when the wheat is sown, than if rotted in a body, whereas much of it is dissipated in the atmosphere; a dissipation which corn partly prevents, and partly saves.

The manure made on the winter's farm pen, remains wet, cold, and unrotted until the month of April, and when composed of corn stalks is of a rough and hard nature. Yet land covered with fifty loads and sown with one bushel of gypsum to an acre, will produce three-fold more corn than in its natural state; and this crop is made in five months; a space just sufficient to reduce the coarse litter to a pabulum proper for wheat. The better this coarse litter and the earth are divided and mingled, the less will be the fermentation, and the greater the crop. The sudden growth of the corn, demonstrates the vast benefit to be derived from litter as coarse and hard as corn stalks, whilst their degree of the putrefaction is inconsiderable, and consequently the vast loss sustained by completing this putrefaction, without gaining a valuable crop from its process. After the process of fermentation and putrefaction is finished in the earth, the residuum is the same, as if it had been finished out of the earth; besides this residuum, supposed by the old theory of compounding, stirring and rotting dunghills, to contain all the fertilizing qualities of vegetable matter, Indian corn enables us to reap a rich harvest of bread stuff from the process towards it.

The same property of Indian corn presents us also with a vast addition to our vegetable matter for manure. The crop of offal as well as that of food, is augmented three fold by the matter separated from coarse litter in reducing it to manure proper for wheat. This of itself exhibits the vast preference of corn as a fallow crop, to the application of rotted manure to a naked fallow for wheat. No two crops can be exactly fitted for advancing a good system of agriculture. The coarse organs of the one, relishes the food rejected by the delicate organs of the other, and by the economy of saving what would otherwise be lost, not only enable us to obtain an additional crop, but by increasing our means for raising manure in a three fold ratio, must have the effect of increasing the crops of wheat themselves, far beyond the confines to which they are limited by naked fallows.

NUMBER 35

Indian Corn, Continued

The reader will remember, that Indian corn is to be planted on a high ridge, and that cross ploughing is excluded. These ridges should run North and South, to equalize both the benefits and injuries derived from the sun. The injury suffered by a flat surface from its excessive heat, would be rather increased than diminished, by exposing one face of the ridge to the South, whilst the Northern aspect would lose the benefit of its genial warmth. These high ridges have another important effect. However steep the declivity, we never see the roots of trees, shrubs or grasses, penetrating through the ground into the atmosphere. It is of course evident that they recoil from one element, and bend towards their food in the other, whenever it is to be found. By the position of the corn on high ridges from its infancy, the roots on approaching the declivity on each side, are trained to run lengthways of the ridge, and thus escape the injury they would otherwise sustain by getting into the range of the deep middle furrow.

As it would be unreasonable to expect the reader to recollect observations made in considering the subject of manuring, I shall remind him, that the ground intended to be manured for Indian corn is fallowed in the winter; that before or after the rest of the crop is planted, this manure is carried out, ploughed in, and the corn to be benefited by it, planted; and that before it receives any ploughing, the corn is to be thinned and wed or hand-hoed. This process will bring us into June, and allow an interval for recruiting the teams, when clover is in its best state for that end. By this time the corn is from eight to twenty-four inches high. At this juncture the deep furrow before mentioned on each side of it being run, narrows the ridge for about eight days, until it is again widened by the middle furrow; and that space will suffice to give to the corn roots, the longitudinal direction which shields them against all injury; this furrow being the only deep one received by the corn after it is planted (the water furrow excepted, out of the way of which the roots are thus trained), being bestowed on it whilst it is young and its roots short, and being run near a foot from it, the roots of the corn, by this mode of culture, wholly escapes injury, and the effects of drought on the plant being thus diminished, its product is increased.

The first ploughing which is to answer the end both of a fallow, and a list or ridge on which to plant the corn, is by far the most material part of the system, and indeed the only good security for its success. The furrow must be deep and wide, so as to overturn into the old water furrow, a considerable mass of the litter produced by inclosing, whether weeds or clover. This mass, in addition to its being a reservoir of food, gradually supplying the corn during the summer as it putrefies, operates powerfully in preserving the friability and mellowness of the earth, by the passage of the air perpetually escaping from it, through its tegument, in its congenial element. By this process, the propensity of hard and cold soils to run and bake, is removed or diminished; a propensity which is encouraged in the highest degree by shallow ploughing on naked or grazed fields. And by the same process, the inconveniences of a mass of dry litter, on enclosed fields, combined with shallow ploughing are also avoided; because it is so well buried, that the corn is planted above it, and sprouts in a bed of clean earth.

The accidents to which Indian corn is liable, are far inferior to those of any other farinaceous plant, and less remediless. It comes up better; it may be re-planted, and at last it may be transplanted. This last precaution for insuring a crop, is executed with little labour by planting a portion of it very early, in the quarter of the field where it will vegetate and grow quickest, somewhat thicker, to furnish plants; and by transplanting those drawn out in thinning in moist weather, or after a season, as the tobacco-makers say. The corn plants will live better than those of tobacco or any other herb I have ever tried, and may be transplanted until they are eighteen inches high. The large plants will be equal to the smaller and later planted corn. Indeed I often fill up vacancies by setting the plants of the same field as it is thinned, and always thin as I set to avoid a double perambulation. A pointed stick both aids in thinning and in setting the corn, which is done nearly as rapidly as tobacco is planted.

I repeat a fact which most people know, to remove an objection against the very deep ploughing recommended as the basis of the corn crop, arising from an erroneous opinion in a few, that the roots of corn and most other herbaceous plants, seek their food only near the surface; whereas the roots of wheat will penetrate four feet of tilth, and those of corn will strike still deeper. An objection that the roots of the latter will not reach the reservoir of food provided for them in the deep covered litter of an enclosed field, would therefore be erroneous.

No grain exhibits so many varieties, or is so liable to change as the maize; the preferred species can only be preserved or improved by selecting the seed at the time of shucking; this will also prevent its exposure to a sweat, and produce its better vegetation; and it increases the crop, which is deeply influenced by the length of the grain. (Note D.)

NUMBER 36

Ploughing

This subject has been unavoidably anticipated by its connexion with others, but yet it is not wholly exhausted.

I utterly deny the truth of the theory which asserts that ploughing is a substitute for manure; for though I admit, that the atmosphere is the matrix of manures in all forms, and that deep ploughing will cause the earth to inhale and retain atmospherical manure better than shallow, yet atmosphere being more subtile than water, must be more fleeting; and its properties must of course be elaborated into more permanency than when merely caught by the earth's power of absorption, to perfect their efficacy. Even rain though richer and grosser, is quickly wasted by evaporation; and atmosphere, a diet too thin for the exclusive sustenance of plants, as is seen in droughts and on all poor soils, cannot be fixed by ploughing, because earth has not the power like vegetables of elaborating it into a lasting form. Plants speedily die in atmosphere and live long in rain or water.

We must avoid the plausible error, that if the atmosphere is the matrix of manure, its inhalation may permanently enrich the earth, and supercede the slow process necessary for its elaboration into the vegetable form for that end. We know that marle possesses the property of permanently enriching itself by fixing the atmospherical fertilizing qualities; but we know also, that such is not the nature of other earths. This natural difference is the reason prescribing different modes for fertilizing marle and such earths, and exploding Tull's exclusive reliance upon the mode by which marle is enriched, for enriching earths of different properties. But yet deep ploughing ought not to be rejected, because although it does not enable earths generally to extract from the atmosphere, a sufficiency of its fertilizing qualities to make them rich; yet the portion they do extract, if even as transitory as rain, may still retain a high value among the several agents, necessary for producing the most perfect effects of good husbandry.

Lime and gypsum repeatedly applied to land kept in constant culture, without the intervention of vegetable matter, will finally render it barren; but if ploughing was a sufficient substitute for manuring, by absorbing and fixing atmosphere, it would have provided a sufficient quantity of pabulum for these exciters to exercise their power upon, and effectually have prevented the imbecility arising from reiterated exertions, by reiterated supplies.

Plants perish by an overdose of dung or rain, but not by one of atmosphere, because it is sparely sprinkled with their food, and this food must be collected, condensed and rendered operative, by some process more effectual than the inhalation of atmosphere by the earth; which, alone, will hardly produce more sensible effects than its inhalation by a man as a substitute for a dose of nitre.

The degrees of value in manure, probably rise with its permanency, and may be marked, simple atmosphere 1. Rain 2. Green herbs 3. Dung 4. Dry herbs 5. Wood 6. If the reader should place a large decaying trunk of a tree mostly under ground, and manure a spot of earth with a different substance of equal weight, he would discover which would longest preserve the land in heart.

Tull's theory, "culture without manure," has hitherto been the practice of the Southern states, with this difference, that he ploughed deep, they shallow; but yet the complete destruction of a soil originally good, which it has effected, ought after two hundred years experience, to explode so much of it, as excludes the necessity of manure. The same shallow ploughing which produced good crops, whilst the land was naturally rich, would produce good crops if it was made artificially rich. The good crops obtained by bad culture from rich land, demonstrate that fertility is the first object to be effected. But whilst this is admitted, the effects of uniting fine tillage with a fertile soil, ought not to be forgotten, by any who possess a taste for excellence or for wealth.

Hence, deep ploughing has been often recommended in these essays, and to these recommendations are added the following remarks.

Deep ploughing upon a naked and poor soil, by which a caput mortuum is brought to the surface, has frequently proved pernicious. This has been owing to a variety of causes, but among them, the preservation of a flat surface, though least suspected, has probably been the most operative. The simple process of burying under a sterile tegument, the little strength of the land, neither promises nor performs much; but the disappointment of hopes really forlorn, frequently causes us to abandon effort, and embrace despair.

By the system of these essays, inclosing, manuring, and high narrow ridges, are combined with deep ploughing. The two first replenish the earth with large stock of vegetable matter, and the last has the effect of collecting the existing soil in the centre of the ridge, and depositing the sterile on its two sides, there to remain for above three years, exposed to the action of the atmosphere. Thus all the bad effects of deep ploughing are avoided. Instead of a naked surface, it is applied to one largely replenished with vegetable matter. Instead of forcing the soil and substratum into a topsey-turvey position, it collects and doubles the first for a present crop, and provides for the amelioration of the other, for a future one. It deepens and fructifies the soil, whilst it makes the best provision for present profit. For the reader is to observe that I am speaking of poor lands, whose soils require doubling, for present subsistence, and improving for future comfort; and not of those whose soils cannot be pierced by the plough.

Deep ploughing (by which I always mean the best to be performed by four good horses in a plough) combined with inclosing, by turning under a good coat of dry vegetable matter, creates a covered drain, and thus vastly obstructs the formation of gullies in hilly lands, even if fallowed with a level surface. But such lands will admit of narrow ridges as well as level, by a degree of skill and attention so easily attainable that I observe it to have existed in Scotland above a century past, under a state of agriculture otherwise execrable, and among the ignorant highlanders. It is effected by carrying the ridges horizontally in such inflections as the hillyness of the ground may require, curved or zig-zag, preserving their breadth. The preservation of the soil is hardly more valuable than that of the rain water in the successive reservoirs thus produced to refresh the thirsty hill sides, instead of its rushing to and poisoning the vallies. This classic system of agriculture has been introduced into Virginia by a gentleman of Albemarle, in a style completely adapted to the nature of the country, and which will be copied by those who shall not be discouraged by its perfection. His ridges, however, are wide, whereas in the maize country, they ought not to exceed five or six feet.

If inclosing, manuring, deep and horizontal ploughing were unattended by any other advantages, that of preventing the land from washing away would in many views be a sufficient recommendation of such a system. The disaster is not terminated by the destruction of the soil, the impoverishment of individuals, and transmission of a curse to futurity. Navigation itself is becoming its victim, and in many parts of the United States, our agriculture has arrived to the insurpassible state of imperfection, of applying its best soil to the removal of the worst farther from market.

The alternation once every four years between deep furrows and high ridges, according to the recommended mode of cultivating corn, and the deep ploughing, by burying one portion of the garlick very deep, and exposing another to frost, will probably destroy it; a conjecture founded upon its considerable diminution in grounds thus treated.

NUMBER 37

Culmiferous Crops

Among these, wheat is the most valuable, and is exposed to most calamities. These calamities are sometimes the effect of climate, at others of bad tillage, and gradually diminish, as the climate becomes less favourable for Indian corn; for which inconvenience, the additional compensation according to the same thermometer is bestowed, of a greater suitableness for rye, oats and barley. In the climate and soil proper for maize (I speak generally without regard to exceptions) rye and barley seldom succeed, oats are light and precarious, and wheat is preferable, both on the score of value and risque, to either. There are two calamities only common to wheat, which may not be avoided with certainty; those of the Hessian fly and rust. As to the weavil they are certainly avoided by getting it out early; a habit which will prevail, so soon as it is discovered, that wheat may be severed from the straw by treading or a machine, with the labour necessary to secure it in stacks or barns. The

facility with which the grain then comes out, has enabled
me in a dry harvest, to tread an entire considerable crop,
almost by the time the harvest ended; and I generally
pursue the practice as far as the weather will permit, so
as to leave a remnant only in stooks capable of being
gotten out so soon after harvest as to avoid this calamity.
The best bread and seed wheat, is invariably that gotten
out and cleaned within a day or two after it is cut, and
deposited dry, in a dry place, in barrels, hogsheads, or
chests opened or closed.

The Hessian fly is so little understood, as to have become an excuse for the loss of crops proceeding from bad
tillage. Lands are tired by shallow and incessant culture,
or by being prevented from invigorating themselves with
vegetable substances. Even the richest bottom lands are
subject to weariness, and sometimes are said to have
grown lousy, so that they will cease at length to yield
good corn; and the crop has the appearance of being infested by insects. To such causes are owing, I think,
most of the charges brought against the Hessian fly.
They would be removed by manuring, covering the land
with good clover lays, and by deep ploughing, in the
cultivation of the maize fallow crop or of any other,
according to the foregoing system; or by managing naked
fallows in the same way. And moreover, a probability
exists that the two deep ploughings, one in the winter
and the other early in June, recommended by the same
system, might destroy the fly itself in some form, and
other insects, to great extent. At least my experience has
never furnished me with a single instance, in which a
crop has suffered by any insect, when the land was in

heart and well covered with dry vegetable matter, when
that matter was turned under as deep as four horses in
a plough could do it, when the land had received a second
good ploughing by two horses in a plough, and when the
wheat was seeded on high and narrow ridges, with a
clean furrow.

The rust, as it is called, may be better understood,
because it may be certainly produced, by a due combination of heat, moisture, shallow ploughing, and a flat
surface. By this process we shall never fail of obtaining
it on a stiff soil, from which the rain water cannot escape,
just as by dosing a man with arsenic, we are sure of
poisoning him at last. Of course we should no more
prescribe this system of agriculture to the wheat, than
arsenic to the man, if we do not wish to poison it, although its diet, like that of a man, may disagree with it
occasionally, in spite of art and caution. Deep ploughing, high ridging, and deep wide water furrows, constitute a model of culture the reverse of that which
inevitably afflicts wheat with the calamity called the rust,
and hence may sometimes prevent, and generally diminish it. The draining of the ridges and the flues, for
the transmission of air through the wheat, created by the
deep wide furrows, will diminish the heat and moisture,
which appear to be the chief causes of the disease; and
vigorous roots in a deep tilth, may add to the capacity of
the plant to resist the malady.

Plastering, by an equal measure of gypsum mixed with
it, and moistened, has benefited wheat in sundry experiments to the conjectured extent of ten per centum, when
it has been free from what is called the bird foot clover;

and injured it thrice as much, when infested with that grass, owing to the effect of gypsum on its growth, which is such, that this species of clover among the plastered wheat will be three or four fold more luxuriant, than among the adjoining unplastered. But the land is so considerably benefited by this plastering of wheat, that in several instances, I have seen intervals of ten yards wide across large fields, where it was omitted for experiments, exhibiting for several years afterwards a decided inferiority of soil. Besides it produces the highly valuable effects of causing the clover seed sown on the surface of the wheat to sprout, grow and stand drought better, and of doubling or trebling its crop the year succeeding the wheat, either for cutting, or for the more beneficial purpose of falling on the land.

To preserve or improve any species of wheat, a selection by hand must be annually made, with which to commence a new stock of seed.

NUMBER 38

Succulent Crops

The trials I have made of this family, have resulted in the rejection of the whole, an individual excepted, as possessing but little value except for culinary purposes; and the remarks I may make, denying them to be objects otherwise valuable, are to be understood, as admitting their high usefulness as food for man, in respect to his comfort, to his health and economy. But, pumpkins excepted, none of them have in my experience produced profit, used in any other mode. I have long and patiently persevered in trials of the turnip and potatoe, according to every mode I could collect from European books. The former are extremely precarious, sown broadcast, and extremely troublesome, drilled, thinned, ploughed and twice hand hoed; a process necessary to obtain a tolerable chance for a great crop. They are a food so little nutritious, that some animals die confined to them, none fatten without an additional food, and all eat an enormous quantity, so as seriously to enhance the labour of feeding. They are great exhausters of land, perhaps the greatest; and so far have I failed in preventing this effect, by taking up the turnips in the fall, that it was quite visible in lands similarly manured adjoining the turnips, both in straight and crooked lines. Nor have I discovered the great benefit said to be experienced in Europe, of feeding the turnips on the ground by sheep in folds removable every twenty-four or forty-eight hours.

The potatoe is by no means so precarious nor exhausting a crop as the turnip, although it participates in no very small degree of both qualities. The objections to it are the great quantity of seed to an acre necessary to be preserved through the winter, and used in the spring; the tediousness of planting and gathering; and the poorness of the food. Before I had seen Young's experiments, I had found that hogs would die on them, raw or boiled, and ascribed it to the inability of the climate to bring them to perfection; but he proves the fact in England to be the same.* It is true that horned cattle will thrive well on a liberal allowance of potatoes, attended plentifully with good hay; but they would thrive on the hay alone, nor do my experiments prove that the potatoe is the cheapest additional food.

The pumpkin on the contrary, in several respects, seems to me to be preferable to it. The expenses of seed, of planting and of gathering, are very wide apart. The labour of cultivation is nearly the same. The pumpkin crop is less uncertain, and far heavier to an acre. Probably a pound of pumpkin may afford less nutriment than so much potatoe, but it is invariably healthier, and sel-

---

* Young wrote extensively on hogs—particularly in his *Essay on the Management of Hogs* (London, 1770).

dom fails in combination with Indian corn, to dispose all animals to fatten kindly, and to aid in advancing this end, so as greatly to diminish the expense. It entirely answers the end of fodder or hay in the fall season, in fattening cattle and sheep, and enables the farmer to spare his stock of both; a circumstance highly beneficial to one, who does not abound in those articles, by enabling him to feed his teams better, and to save a sufficiency to allow them enough, from the failure of the clover, until the new crop of hay or fodder comes in. Perhaps no circumstance has contributed more to the impoverishment of several of the United States, than the negligence to provide dry forage for summer, producing the evils of a loss of labour, of weakening the teams, and of ruinous grazing. The pumpkin, with the daily addition of a few corn stalks thrown into the pens, is preferable to the best hay or fodder I ever tried; and it appears to me to be much less of an impoverishment than the potatoe; arising, I suppose, from its entirely covering the ground about the last of June, if properly cultivated.

My mode of cultivating it is this. I select the intended number of acres in the proposed corn field of the ensuing year; where the land is infested with some plant, proposed to be destroyed by culture for two successive years, and by the impenetrable shade of the pumpkin vine during the first. In the winter the ridges are cleaned by four furrows run as deep as four horses can manage a large plough, throwing the moiety of each into the old water furrow; and I make a new water furrow wide and deep where the centre of the ridge lay. In the latter end of March, as much manure as will make the land rich is spread on, and the ridges are restored by similar

four furrows to the first position, agreeing with that of
those for the ensuing year's corn field. If the land is
stiff, a second ploughing with a small plough may be
necessary to pulverize it. The pumpkins are planted in
the mode of planting corn, at five feet and a half distance in the direction of the ridges, and two feet nine
inches across them. They receive one deep ploughing,
the ridges are raised high and the water furrows made
deep and wide; the plants whilst tender are defended
against a small bug; and the ground is kept clean until
the vines begin to overspread it. One plant only is left
in a place.

The custom of sprinkling pumpkins over corn fields,
scatters the crop so, that the labour of its collection
exceeds its value. By giving them more room, the fruit
will be larger, but the product less. As soon as they begin to ripen, their use should commence near their residence, to save the labour of a distant removal. In this
use they may be made considerably subservient to manuring, by penning the animals fed on them. The remnant must be gathered before frost, and deposited about
three feet high in a stack made of corn tops in the common form, convenient to the pumpkins, open at both
ends, and their use rapidly continued to avoid risque.

Indian corn, dry or boiled alternately, is the best food
to be united with the pumpkins which I have tried. The
pumpkins are fed raw, chopped by broad hatchets in
troughs, and eaten ravenously. They produce a great saving of grain, and an entire saving of dry forage, a considerable addition to the meat, milk, and butter, and some
increase of manure.

NUMBER 39

Leguminous Crops

Indian corn must be recognised as the prince of this family, if it belongs to it. No individual of the whole tribe can compare with it for meal, malt, fodder, and litter. In England, where sundry of its cognominal relatives are highly celebrated as fallow crops, their chief merit consists in preparing the ground for wheat, or for some other culmiferous crop. It was never imagined, that the least competition as to value existed between the fallow crop and its successor; and the great doubt has been, whether a naked fallow or a fallow crop ought to be preferred. Young decides for the latter, on account of the profit resulting from the succulents or legumes used as fallow crops there; and his arguments are tripled in weight, by the triple value of Indian corn used as a fallow crop here.

It results that I reject the succulent and legumes resorted to in England as fallow crops, and I prefer the maize for that purpose; wherefore in the previous chapter, the first have not been considered in that character, nor will the latter be so in this.

But I shall advert to legumes as a valuable food for man, not sufficiently attended to, whilst I admit that in every other view, including the danger of destruction from accident, they are inferior to maize; and that even in this, they are rather to be considered as its coadjutor than rival.

Among them, the pea is selected as covering most individuals, and most fitted to our climate. Four gallons of dry peas annually, will add inconceivably to the health, strength and comfort of a labourer, if prepared by good boiling with salt meat of any kind. The ruinous state of our country affords but too much space to raise peas without much expense of skill or labour. In the shifts of most of our farms there is no scarcity of poor land. Such ought never to be sown with wheat or any other culmiferous grain, because they will produce no profit, and because severe exhausters as they are, must be excluded from land already exhausted, under any system of agriculture which meditates its improvement. A portion of such land may be selected, sufficient to produce four gallons of dry peas for each resident on the farm of all ages, exclusive of what they may gather and use at their will in a green state, to be planted among corn at the distance of five feet and a half square, the distance also of the corn. Of this, one stalk only is left in each hill. The ground is ridged, ploughed but one way, and both crops are planted in the direction of the ridges. It remains without producing any other crop (these two excepted growing together) enclosed, ungrazed, in deep furrows and high ridges running North and South, until the revolution of the course of culture, which consists of four years, is completed; and is very much improved. It is more so if aided by a bushel of gypsum to the acre. The poor land thus treated, is rendered more productive than as usually managed, and the object of its improvement is accelerated by such a culture beyond what would be obtained by a state of perfect idleness.

If circumstances prevent this course, the peas are raised in the same mode with pumpkins on a portion of the intended corn field of the following year, where noxious plants are to be eradicated, equally enriched, and similarly cultivated; except that the labour is very much lessened by the use of a weeding plough called a skimmer. They are drilled by the hand as thick as the common garden pea, in a shallow furrow on the summit of the ridges, and covered with the hand hoe. If the land is rich, they will cover the whole ground, so that little is lost by the distance, required in reference to the succeeding corn crop; and a small spot of land will produce the necessary quantity.

The best kind of pea for the end in view (which is extremely important to a well managed farm), known to me, is white with black eyes. But as there are many peas which answer this description, besides a great number of others, the reader must be referred to his own experience or inquiries for the necessary selection.

NUMBER 40

Live Stock

Among the queries proposed by the Richmond Society to awaken the dormant science of agriculture, the eighth is so propounded as to admit that which I deny, "that keeping a large stock, and inclosing to improve land by excluding stock, are rival and incompatible systems." I shall therefore consider this admission as a prevalent opinion, which powerfully combats, and extensively retards a system upon which the regeneration of our lands possibly depends.

It must be admitted that keeping a stock, equal at least to the whole grass, produced both by the arable and meadow grounds of the farm, and not the inclosing system, has generally prevailed: and therefore as such a stock is not only a large one, but the largest capable of being kept, it follows, that one of the experiments of the proposed comparison, has been completely tried in Virginia.

And what is the result? It is found by computing the

consequences reaped by Virginia, from her system of keeping these enormous stocks; enormous in proportion to their food. She exports neither meat, butter nor cheese. She is unable to raise as much of either as she consumes. She cannot breed a sufficiency of draft animals, for her own use. And after having ruined her lands by grazing, so far from deriving a profit from it, she is obliged to deduct annually a considerable sum from the profits of her agriculture, wretched as it is, to supply the deficiencies of her more wretched system of grazing. If it is a fact, that lands will sink under a system of oppressive taxation by crops, is it not conceivable that they will also sink under excessive grazing? And if by cropping them less, more bread can be raised, may it not follow, that more meat may also be raised by grazing them less? Fertility is as necessary a requisite for raising stocks as for raising bread, and whatever will produce it, is a harbinger of both; a system of grazing therefore, which impoverishes a country, is as likely to terminate in large stocks, as a system of culture having the same effect, in large crops.

The opinion "that by calling in the aid of inclosing to recover the lost fertility of the country, we must sacrifice our stocks," defeats its own objects; stocks depend as intimately upon this recovery, as bread stuff, and are in fact unattainable without it, except by a vast depopulation of the country, to make up the loss of food for stocks, occasioned by the impoverishment of the land, by extending the space of their range.

It was hardly to be expected, that a good system of grazing would have been found in union with an execrable system of agriculture, and therefore, instead of inquiring whether we ought to sacrifice our mode of tillage to raising stock, or our mode of raising stock to our mode of tillage; the true question probably is, whether we ought not to abandon both, because both modes obviously impoverish our lands, and gradually diminish both crops and stocks.

In Britain, generally, arable lands are not grazed, though grazing is pursued probably to an injurious excess. There, meadows, natural or artificial, and well turfed standing pastures, are prepared and used for grazing; and if these precautions are useful to a moist climate and a rich soil, they cannot be dispensed with by a dry climate and a poor soil.

To raise large stocks, we must first raise large meadows and rich pastures, defended by a sod both sufficient to withstand the hoof and the tooth, and capable of becoming richer under their attacks. If any local difficulties in effecting this are discerned, they point directly to another view of the subject. Supposing that raising large stocks and inclosing arable lands against grazing, were really incompatible objects, our attention is of course turned towards our climate and soil, for the purpose of making the election; and it is very obvious that a warm dry climate and a sandy soil, ought not to make the same choice, with a climate cool and moist, and a clay soil.

Still those who have to struggle with natural disadvantages in raising stocks, will not find them insurmountable, so far as it is their interest to surmount them, if they will resort to the very system for fertilizing their lands, supposed to obstruct the object. The system itself requires strong teams, meat for labourers, and stock sufficient to consume the offal of all the crops. Inclosing is only a coadjutor to manuring, and had it excluded the means for the latter, it would have excluded a more valuable object than itself. So far from it, that it vastly advances those means, by a regular, and ultimately a great increase of crops, and consequently of litter, offal, and stocks.

Suppose a farm under the system recommended in these essays, to have trebled its crops on the same fields in twelve years—if the whole additional crop thus gained was devoted to stocks, is it not certain that it would support far greater, than the same farm could do in its grazed state? Is it not obvious, that the offal of this treble crop, will support a stock three times as large through the winter, as the offal of one third of it; and that the three fold crop of grain, will admit of large drafts for the still farther increase of stocks, whilst one third of such a crop, might admit of no such contribution? The supposition is a fact. It may be farther discerned, that as the crops by the acre increase, the space cultivated may be gradually diminished, so as to release a portion of the labour for the purposes of draining, manuring, and raising artificial grasses; and in that view constituting a different mode of providing for stocks, from that of grazing exhausted arable lands. A glance of intellect decides between the two modes.

NUMBER 41

Live Stock, Continued

The grazier and the ploughman are characters so different, and their occupations are so distinct, that had
these essays related to a system of grazing, "Pecuarius"
ought to have been their signature. What stronger proof
can exist of our agricultural ignorance, than a notion of
succeeding in both lines at the same time, by respectively
violating the first principles of both. To succeed in grazing, it is necessary to cover the land with a strong and
rich turf; to succeed in agriculture, this turf must be
destroyed. Having destroyed the turf by the plough, we
endeavour to prevent its renovation by assailing it with
the tooth and the hoof, the instant it germinates; and
propose to raise large stocks without grass, and large
crops on land too poor to produce it. In England, the
ideas of promoting crops by treading and grazing, and
grazing by ploughing up pastures and meadows, would
excite great admiration; and the general prohibition in
leases against the latter, discloses the disapprobation of

the system of reaping corn and stocks annually from the same land. The question, whether the business of grazing or of tillage, is the most profitable, frequently occurs; but whether the same land ought or ought not to be exposed both to tillage and grazing, is one never made by good husbandmen. In many parts of the United States, the distinction between tillage and grazing is well understood, and their separation beneficially practiced; but in most, sundry circumstances not necessary to be adduced, have united these occupations; a union indispensably necessary to a certain extent for tillage, and incapable of being dispensed with. It is therefore necessary for me to prove, that the system of enclosing arable lands, for the purpose of excluding grazing, is not inconsistent with the stocks necessary for meat, labour and manure, beyond which, the occupation of tillage forbids their extension.

If meadows and well turfed pastures, are best for grazing, and if by excluding grazing from arable lands, its product is vastly increased, it follows, that we can effect this union not only without injury to either of the objects, but so as to advance the interest of both, by allotting proper portions of the farm to each, and managing such portions according to the principles indispensably dictated by the ends intended to be produced. Whereas, the principles necessary to produce stocks or grain, being not only different, but exactly opposed, since we must produce grass for one end, and destroy it for the other, by applying both to the same land, a warfare ensues which cripples, and finally kills both the combatants.

By thus appropriating particular portions of a farm, we may manage each portion according to the principles necessary to make it more productive; and the productiveness of each, will advance that of the other. The better crops of grain we raise, the more offal is produced, and this offal, by furnishing litter and food for stocks, raises stocks sufficient to reduce it to manure; the chief means for improving our pasture, meadow and arable land. An increase of stocks must follow an increase of manure, because it begets an increase of their food and litter, just as their decrease is an inevitable consequence of the diminution of manure.

We see that some of the states, Virginia for instance, can no longer raise meat, cheese or teams sufficient for home consumption, and the cause of this phenomenon will illustrate my reasoning. No state, and probably no agricultural country, ever went more thoroughly into the plan of grazing arable land, of neglecting meadows and permanent pastures, and of endowing their stocks with the privilege of unlimited grazing; and the end is ruin to the stocks themselves, as a consolation for ruin to the lands. The indiscriminate grazing is the very cause, which is impoverishing both the husbandman and grazier, and the greedy project of succeeding in both characters, by extorting from the earth a double contribution, has defeated our success in either.

Such a project is as fatal to a country, whose climate and soil are not naturally adapted to the production of grass, as an obstinate culture of rice and cotton, would be to the state of Massachusetts. If therefore we are to be brought to the proposed computation, the election between tillage and stocks is settled by the consideration of soil and climate, as they may be favourable to grass, bread

stuff or other products, because, however we may sometimes be able to force nature, her spontaneous efforts on
our side are the best sureties for success.

Let any gentleman, for instance, of the bread stuff
country of the United States, compare the profit he would
derive from doubling his crops of grain, with that he gains
by keeping the largest stocks within his power. He will
discern, that such an accession of annual income, will
generally even exceed the whole value of his stocks, instead of their profit; and if the enclosing system, aided
by the means heretofore explained, will rapidly double
his crops of grain, the preference between that and its
rival is determined; and the object of grazing at the expense of tillage in an impoverished country, ought to be
abandoned.

NUMBER 42

Live Stock, Continued

If we impoverish our land by grazing or tillage, both stocks and crops, whatever they be, will gradually diminish; gradually become less profitable; and finally, insufficient to afford a maintenance. It is true that some bottom lands exist, so rich, as to bear, and even improve under tillage and grazing, if red clover is the grass used, and if it is suffered to get well in flower before the stocks are turned on it. But this is owing to the extreme fatness of the soil, its ability to cover itself with a luxuriant coat of clover, the accession of vegetable matter by a great portion being trodden on and rejected by the cattle, and the entire acquisition of its tap root, containing from the size it acquires in such land, no inconsiderable quantity of the same matter. Besides, land of this quality is so rare, as to constitute an anomaly entirely foreign to any system of agriculture proper for the United States. Very few of us have ever seen it, and still fewer would profit from any system built upon its qualities. Nay, it is a kind of land which hardly requires a system, and would be as prosperous under a bad one, as the general agricultural state of the country would be under the best. It is necessary, however, to suggest this anomalous case, lest we should be led to reason from it, for the purpose of deciding a different case. The most zealous amour patriae will confess that the United States have infinitely less need for a system to improve rich than one to improve poor land; and instead of being blinded by its wishes, should be enlightened by truth, as the only mode of gratifying one of the most amiable of human passions.

The expanse of our territory, generally, is now in a state so far from being able to improve under the double taxation of tillage and grazing, as to require a revolution of our habits to improve under either; and the time has come, when it is equally necessary to discover some mode of raising meats as well as bread, without impoverishing our lands.

It is easy by a good system so wonderfully to alter the case, as to make stocks profitable simply from their manure, exclusive of the labour, meat, tallow, leather, milk and butter, they yield; and to draw from them not only the entire means for their own support, but a surplus for enriching the soil. The mode of doing this has been heretofore explained, but in order to combine with it the subject now under consideration, with more perspicuity, I will take up and consider separately, the mode of managing each species of our domestic animals, usually comprised by the term "stock," upon a tillage farm which requires the nurture of inclosing.

The working animals constitute a species of stock

comprising horses, mules and oxen. The two former ought to inhabit a lot having a stable and stream, and to be excluded wholly from grazing. For two months of the year, clover cut daily, and exposed to six hours sun, to prevent the animal from being hoven, should be their hay. It will add to their health at the season it comes in. After it fails, the best fodder or hay, preserved for the hottest season, succeeds it. Corn stalks serve them from the first of November, whilst they last, and are succeeded by the inferior tops, blades or hay. By littering the stables and yards well in winter, they will make manure sufficing to enrich more land than will produce their corn; as this enrichment is not exhausted by one crop; and as clover, proper cultivation, and inclosing will preserve, and farther improve the land, the working stock exclusive of its labour, subscribes largely to the renovation of the soil instead of its impoverishment by pasturing. The considerations of saving the labour of collecting the working animals from pastures, and avoiding the loss of the morning, so material in a warm climate, are inferior, but additional recommendations of the same system.

The oxen in summer should be penned and fed separately from the other cattle, and in winter the same separation should take place, with a more comfortable cover. They will furnish the same supply of manure as the horses and mules in winter, and more in summer from the removal of their pen, calculated to stand not beyond ten days. Whilst not at work, they may be pastured with the other cattle.

NUMBER 43

Live Stock, Continued

The horned cattle are happily able to encounter the hardships inflicted on them by the impoverishment of our country. These will be gradually decreased by enriching it. Their food for half the year consists of the coarse offal of bread grain in much of the greater portion of the United States, and a system which will increase such crops, will increase their food during that season of the year, when they suffer most, and perish in great numbers, besides affording them a chance from its greater plenty, of participating more copiously of the grain itself. Such an increase of staple crops, begets capital and releases labour, for draining improvements; and speedily points at swamps and marshes of a soil, capable in general of being made one hundred fold more productive in grass, than our exhausted fields. Meadows thus grow out of the enclosing system, if that system increases the staple crops, and are a retribution with accumulating interest to the stock, for the loss of naked fields. This retribution extends to both fall and winter. Meadows should be cut for hay, and grazed with horned cattle, after the second crop has arrived to its most luxuriant state. So far from being deteriorated by it, they are improved, produce cleaner and larger crops of hay, are longer defended against the intrusion of weeds, bushes and coarse grasses, and finally, when tillage becomes necessary for cleansing them, their state for receiving it will be better, and the crop enhanced.

By the increased offal of increased crops, and by the hay of these meadows, stocks will be better provided for during the winter, than under the unlimited grazing system; to which add the grazing of the after math of the meadows, and this superior provision is extended to about eight months of the year. Between three and four months of spring and summer, pasturage only remains to be supplied. An abundant resource for this is one effect of unlimited grazing, and our greatest agrarian calamity. Vast tracts of exhausted country are every where turned out, or left uninclosed, to recover what heart they can in their own way; and their progress in that effort is accelerated by inclosing them as pasturage for cattle alone, or at least excluding hogs. Such fields presently produce shrubs and coarse grass, and lands never cleared, may be inclosed with them, as auxiliaries. Together, they will constitute a pasture for cattle, far better in the spring and summer, than that generally afforded by arable lands, which in the maize country of the United States, are particularly scanty of grass until towards the fall, and then the superior resource of the meadow grazing is provided by the system of inclosing.

It would be too alarming, to subjoin to these reasonings (and probably by its strangeness might destroy them all) the idea of manuring a spacious highland meadow, as a farther auxiliary to the inclosing system; and therefore it will be deferred until crops are trebled by it. But it is indispensably necessary to point out in what way this system is prepared, to satisfy those cravings which cannot be deferred.

As crops increase in a warm and poor country, no department will more suddenly experience an improvement than that of the table. As to beef, it is received from the after math of the meadow, by the pumpkin, and Indian corn, the corn stalks succeed the pumpkins, and it is finished in March on corn and hay. In the interim the knife is at work and the manure is accumulating. During the moderate weather, after leaving the meadow, for the pumpkins, the beeves are penned on successive spots and not littered, the plough succeeding the removal of the pen. When the stalks come in they are placed in their stationary winter's habitation, and copiously littered. And with proper management, the manure thus raised overpays the expense of fattening them. The additional advantage of milk and butter is derived from fattening for beef the old cows yielding milk, through the winter. They may be often made fine meat, and will at least be a valuable acquisition to the stock of salt provisions for the labourers, instead of being devoted to their common fate in a premature age, by want of food.

The best and cheapest mode of raising calves, and of fattening lambs, I have ever tried, is also suggested by the inclosing system. It is that of folding them on red clover from about the twentieth of April, or from the clover's becoming three or four inches high; the calves until frost. Small common fence rails, and the common crooked fences, make folds with less labour and stand better than any I have tried. This pen ought never to stand longer than three days, in which time it ought to be grazed clean. If it stands longer, the grass is injured by treading. When it is to be removed, the calves and sheep are confined in a corner next to the new pen, by using some of the top rails. An acre of fine clover, unless it is disabled by drought, will graze ten calves, ten ewes and ten lambs, through the grass season, allowing for the gradual removal of the sheep, all of which ought to be killed. To make them good meat, they must be allowed other food. Wash of corn meal, or well boiled corn itself, is the best and cheapest I have tried. The acre will be frequently fed over without destroying the clover, and the land will be improved. Calves will make a reimbursement with a profit for this mode of raising them, by their superior value beyond those raised in the common way, and by surrendering at an early age their mother's milk. And its economy is increased by selecting annually the old ewes and their lambs for fattening, comprising, so many, as that a portion of the latter and all the former may be bestowed on the slaves. By harvest, lambs have grown too large and coarse for the table, and the ewes have become good mutton. The mother should die within three days of the lamb, or she falls off. Both furnish a supply of excellent food at that laborious season; and as to have good lambs we must make their mothers fat, the luxury of the master bestows a luxury on the slaves, without an additional expense, and undoubtedly with more economy, than to devote such sheep to their usual destiny. These old ewes thus managed, yield fine lambs, much wool, good mutton, and hides able to bear tanning for the purpose of making pads for the back bands of the plough horses to pass through.

NUMBER 44

Sheep

It is with reluctance that I am about to express my opinion as to this stock, lest they may discredit those upon subjects concerning which I have had more experience. For sixteen years I have laboured to estimate their value and character, upon a small scale, having a flock only of from one to four hundred, daily attended by a shepherd; and my conclusions are, that they require and consume far more food, in proportion to their size, than any other stock, that they are more liable to disease and death, and that they cannot be made a profitable object, throughout the whole extent of the warm dry climate, and sandy soil of the United States, but by banishing tillage from vast tracts of country. These opinions are by no means intended, however, to exclude them as a luxury for the table, capable of being made to repay a considerable portion of the expense it causes.

It is probable that the hot constitution of sheep, produces a rapid digestion, and that insatiable appetite, by

which the fact is accounted for, of their flourishing only
to any extent in fine meadows or extensive wildernesses.
If this voraciousness is not gratified, the animal perishes
or dwindles; if it is, he depopulates the country he inhabits.
The sheep of Spain have probably kept out of existence,
or sent out of it, more people than the wild beasts of the
earth have destroyed from the creation; and those of England may have caused a greater depopulation, than all
her extravagant wars. It may be owing to this animal that
the independence of one country is almost overthrown,
and of the other tottering. In both countries the sufficiency of bread for sheep, may have produced this insufficiency of bread for man, and prejudice may have nurtured
errors, of which our folly may relieve them, just as superstition has been known to seize or steal an idol, which
had long been a curse to the place of its invention. It
is admitted that the wool of sheep is to a certain extent
a necessary, and often a luxury; but if I fancied a pearl,
why should I dive for it myself, when those who love the
employment, wish to supply me; or why should a nation
depopulate itself to gain them, if it can become strong and
populous without pearls? The earth's capacity to produce food and materials for clothes is limited, and by
endowing the brute creation with so much of the former,
as to produce a deficit for man's use, in order to obtain a
surplus of the latter for exportation, the sheep policy is
said to be perfected. It is probable that an acre of the
proper soil in the proper climate, is capable of raising ten
times as much cotton wool, as sheep's, and if we shall only
glance at the vast quantity of the former material for
clothing, exported from a small district of country, thinly

peopled, we shall at once see the capacity of the earth to produce it to any needful extent, without paying depopulation for raiment. Altho' sheep's wool was the best resource for a state of ignorance, it is superceded to a great extent by a state of cotton manufacturing skill; and whilst the English nation have proved the high value of our cotton, and opened an inexhaustible demand for the abundance we can spare, it is certainly a responsible hostage for the small portion of her woollens we may want; and an exchange is probably better than turning our corn fields into sheep pastures. It is exactly the case in which commerce renders a mutual benefit, as we under our warm and dry climate, and in our sandy soil, can raise cotton cheaper than England; and she by the help of her moisture and verdure, can raise wool cheaper than the United States. It is curious that wool should be supplanting cotton here, whilst cotton is supplanting wool in Europe; but as fashions wear out in one country they flee to another.

Their manure is the chief recompense for the expense of sheep, and worth more than their wool, if they are regularly penned. It is true, that this will in some degree injure them, but it is indispensable, unless by surrendering to them a power of grazing at will, the calamitous alternative of speedily reducing the farm to a barren is resorted to.

Moveable pens, as in the case of cattle, are best in the warm seasons of the year; in the cold, a farm pen shelter also, open to the south, and closed to the ground towards the other three cardinal points, will suffice to the 39th degree of North latitude. This pen should be regularly littered with stalks, straw or litter of any kind.

Under the system of inclosing, the sheep may be managed like horned cattle, except that they must be better fed. For this purpose they ought to be attended by a shepherd, that besides the grazing allowed to the cattle, they may be treated with such parts of the enclosed area, as they may benefit or not injure. Of the first description, are grounds infested with the garlic, over which the sheep should be rapidly carried after it has headed, to eat its seed; of the second, the banks of rivers, rivulets or woodland. In winter, the sheep will eat every thing, and the better the food the more they will thrive. A great quantity of corn, caught soft by frost, most of which became quite black, and all of it such as to be refused by hogs, was greedily eaten by sheep; and the supply being copious, made the best flock I ever saw. In winter, their farm pen is made in the field to be cultivated in corn, the following summer, in which field the sheep are then allowed daily to feed under the superintendence of the shepherd. Being covered with the dry litter of clover, the little grass they get under it is of some service to them, and the litter itself is more conveniently disposed for the plough by being trodden down.

NUMBER 45

Hogs

Few animals do us more real mischief, and suffer more unmerited reproach than these. They are the cause of dead wood fences, which render more labour unproductive, than any item of the long agricultural catalogue of practices, portrayed in the miserable countenance of our country. A consumption of labour in making ephemeral fences, which might be employed in making food, clothing or lasting improvements, is a check upon population even greater than the English and Spanish sheep system; but if we add to it, the impoverishment of land, and waste of herbage, by the eradicating license legally conferred on hogs, it will require but a small portion of prophetic skill to anticipate the impeachment of our agricultural system, to be gradually pronounced by the census. We shall, however, long struggle against the admonitions of this unerring logician, by assigning to the allurements of a wilderness, emigrations resulting from a policy and a system, incapable of withstanding these allurements, compared with all the benefits of our cultivation. Our system of agriculture is felt as a greater evil than no system. A country wanting people with actual tillage on its side, is robbed of a great portion of the few it has, by one exposed to every evil except our agricultural system. But we ascribe the expulsions caused by its impoverishments to the attractions of putrefying forests, of an exposure to all weather, of innumerable hardships, and of Indian scalping knives, and lose the faculty of seeing their cause where we tread, by ascribing it to imaginary notions.

The destruction of wood and timber, produced by the mode of raising hogs according to law, exclusive of the depopulation it advances, is itself a calamity grievous in all quarters, but ruinous to those unpossessed of coal for fuel, and stone for fencing. This destruction increases in a ratio correspondent to the diminution of our means to bear it; because the young wood and timber used for fences, fuel and building, is more subject to decay than the old; and a perseverance in prejudice cannot be more amply displayed, than by an expectation of resisting with tender saplings, a practice which has demolished the tough forests of oak.

All the calamities arising from fences of dead wood, are ascribed to these ill-fated animals, as if they had themselves forced upon us the system which has produced these calamities; just as the impoverishment of our lands is ascribed to Indian corn, as if that had dictated the system of agriculture by which it is effected. But it is neither new, nor unnatural, to mistake our best benefactors for our worst enemies.

Yet a single question refutes the calumny. Did the
hogs enact the laws, by which they are turned loose,
without rings in the nose, or yokes on the neck to root
out the herbage, and assail the inclosures? Had they
been legislators, self interest (allowing them wisdom)
would have suggested to them a mode of coming at subsistence, infinitely better than one, by which they are exposed to disasters, hunger, poverty and assassination.

Excluding from the argument all the mischiefs flowing
from the system of raising hogs introduced by law, and
confining the question simply to the mutual interest of
the hog and his owner in the points of comfort, profit and
plenty, we gain conviction of its imperfection, by placing it on its strongest ground.

Meat is the end in view. No animal furnishes better
than the hog. If there is any other which will furnish
more at less expense, in a dry country, or which possesses
more congruity than Indian corn, where that is the chief
fund for subsistence, it ought to be preferred; if not,
the hog deserves more attention than he has hitherto
received. In the maize country, the existence of no such
animal is admitted, by the general recourse to the hog as
the chief resource for meat; and the first question is,
whether he is made to answer the purpose for which he
has thus been selected.

The fact is too notorious to require proof. The maize
Atlantic districts raise an insufficiency of meat for their
own consumption, by means of an animal selected on
account of his peculiar fitness for the object. A failure
in the object with the best means of attaining it, is the
strongest evidence of the misapplication of those means.

Though this supply of meat from hogs is insufficient, it is yet considerable, and far exceeding the quantity furnished by all other animals. But it is still considered by a pecuniary computation as an unprofitable business to raise them. If there is any foundation for this opinion, drawn from a computation which excludes all the mischiefs arising from dead fences, it determines the mode of raising them to be excessively erroneous.

This pecuniary loss must arise from the mode of raising them, in those districts where hogs are the best resource for meat, unless we suppose that nature has treated these districts with such severity, as to provide no animal to supply a moderate comfort, except at an expense which must exclude a great number of people from its use. And as this supposition cannot be admitted, the evil can only be sought for in this mode, where it will be found in the disasters of the hogs, the inattention of their owners, the badness and insufficiency of their food, and the mean quality of their meat. I shall therefore attempt in the next number, to point out a different one, more profitable to the owner, more comfortable to the animal, and entirely exempt from the ruinous vice of operating as an exclusion of live fences.

NUMBER 46

Hogs, Continued

No domestic animal multiplies equally, grows as rapidly, is as thrifty, makes as good salt meat, is as hardy, as healthy, as docile, or eats as little in proportion to size as the hog. A mode of raising him which takes advantage of all these qualities, designating him as the best resource for meat, is a subject worthy of particular attention, and would be a great improvement. My experience is inconsiderable, and my knowledge limited in relation to it. But I shall give the result of the former, without deviating into conjecture, or recurring to books. Indeed, as neither distilleries nor dairies, constitute any resource for the country within my view, little aid could be extracted from the latter.

Indian corn, clover and pumpkins, are my only resources for raising hogs. They are raised within the inclosure of a farm having no cross fences, regularly confined in a pen of nights, and suffered to run at large in the day, in that portion of the farm designed for Indian corn the succeeding year. The farm is divided into four shifts, the greater part of each being left in red clover after wheat, so that shift during the last year of its rest, is well covered. The injury to clover by hogs from grazing, is infinitely less than that from any other animal. No number necessary for domestic consumption will materially affect the field exposed to in this mode. Twenty sheep would injure it more than an hundred hogs. And to prevent rooting, iron rings of the size and shape of a large one for the finger, are constantly kept in the cartilage of the nose.

Until the pumpkins come in, the hogs subsist by grazing, with an allowance of shattered Indian corn, sufficing to keep the sows having pigs, in tolerable heart; other hogs will become very fat upon the same allowance. As soon as the pumpkins are ripe, the whole family are confined to the pen, and fed with as many as they will eat, cut up in troughs, besides a full meal of sound corn daily, raw or boiled as their appetite fluctuates. And those for slaughter are fed with corn about ten days after the pumpkins are expended, to harden and flavor the meat.

By removing the pen with regularity, and ploughing it up, as in the case of cattle, hogs will in my judgment manure land to the value of the whole expense of raising them; and instead of contributing to the ruin of the country by eradicating herbage, and compelling farmers to reject live fences; contribute to its renovation by their manure.

The whole stock exceeding nine months old, except a male and two or three females, is killed annually. If a species is selected which breeds young, and gains its

growth quickly, the litters between the first of June and
the first of March, will furnish an abundance of progeny
for the second killing time. Their mothers will make fat
and small, and the males fat and large meat for the first.
These pigs are accelerated in growth, by being suffered to
share in all the luxuries of the large hogs, unless it may
happen to be necessary to wean a little occasionally, to
gain time for recovering the flesh of its mother. And the
annual clearance of nearly all the old hogs, is a matter
of considerable economy, because the expense is thereby
diminished to a great extent, for above half the year, by
having young ones only to sustain.

The mischiefs from hogs allowed such license, is the
chief objection to be expected to this mode of raising
them. I know not of any agricultural, mechanical or
scientifical object of much value, attainable without effort
or skill. Some degree of both, and but a small one, is
necessary to avoid this objection. The hogs ought whilst
young, to be made quite gentle. Pigs are as docile as
puppies. They will not be inclined to wander far from
their feeding pen in a field of red clover, if care is taken
to secure for them an access to water; and a small boy
with a whip will find it an easy task to discipline them out
of any such inclination. No temptation solicits them at
most seasons of the year, and should they occasionally
light upon one so irresistible as to render them troublesome, they must be confined in their pen, until it is past,
or they are weaned from it.

Hogs are sufficiently hardy to bear the weather, without injury, for eight months of the year; a warm cover
is necessary for them during the other four. This is easily

made and removed by four forks let two feet into the earth, the two in front eight feet, and the two in rear two feet above it, having a secure roof of stalks and straw laid on poles, and the rear and two sides made perfectly close by two courses of rails, one pressing against the forks, and the other against stakes two feet from them all around, with the interval filled tight with straw. The front is open to the South, and a diameter of ten feet each way, will form a comfortable cover for a large stock of hogs.

Small warm huts of a similar construction for the separate use of each sow about to pig in cold weather, is a precaution most useful, and much neglected. Without it, the greater part of the litters will be lost. And such losses diminish considerably the profit arising from a system, an article of which is to compensate by number for the size of hogs brought old to the knife.

NUMBER 47

Hogs, Continued

The reader will discern, that I consider agriculture as a felo de se.* As leading herself to the altar, and inflicting her own death, not with the despatch dictated by humanity even in killing a hog, but by repeated strokes upon every part of her body. By laws of her own making, she has quartered upon herself tribes of factitious capitalists. By laws of her own making, she has adopted the policy of mingling free blacks and slaves, mutually exciting each other to rebellion, teaching one class the trade of living upon herself by theft without labour, and instilling into the other a hatred of her duties. She spontaneously hires overseers, not to improve, but to exhaust her land, with the wisdom of a saint who should expect to advance true religion, by hiring a priesthood to preach and practice idolatry. And she closes her system by a mode of raising hogs, which burdens her defective labour

---

* Self-destroyer.

with the incumbrance of dead and decaying fences; which aids the overseers in substituting a wrong for a right culture; and which has already caused a deficiency of meat, requiring supplies from the western country; supplies destined to fail by an imitation of the system of agriculture, which rendered them necessary.

As these evils united, are obviously killing our lands, any one will cripple them, and therefore a successful effort to remove any one, is not unimportant. If legislatures should persevere in wounding agriculture by endowing hogs with a right of unlimited emigration, to and fro, and exposing them to the usual consequences of licentiousness, namely, poverty, disease and death; yet agriculture may be so far favoured, as to procure some small alleviation of the pains and penalties thus inflicted on her. If hogs were prohibited from going at large, except with a ring in the cartilage of the nose, and a yoke with three projecting wings of six inches long, one at top and one at each side, these pains and penalties would be vastly diminished. The ring, besides putting an end to the eradication of herbage, would counteract the use of the nose as a wedge able to pierce the best live fences, and the wings would powerfully contribute to the same end.

But this remedy would reach a portion only of the evil we are considering, and will leave in full operation the present expensive and insufficient mode of raising meat. By prohibiting hogs from running at large, we should be compelled to recur to a new mode, which might possibly be more adequate to our wants. To form a correct opinion, it behoves us to reflect upon the present mode of raising hogs, and to contrast it with that proposed, or with more promising suggestions. Our subject is closed with a specimen of this mode of reasoning.

By the present mode of raising hogs, vast quantities of wood and timber are annually destroyed; by the proposed, none will be destroyed.

By the present mode, much labour is lost in making mouldering fences; by the proposed, the inhibition on live fences being removed, much will be saved.

By the present mode one half of the pigs and hogs perish, and a considerable portion of the residue are stolen; so that less than half come to the knife; by the proposed, few will perish, fewer will be stolen, and a double supply of meat, may be expected.

By the present mode a great proportion of the meat is lean and dry; by the proposed, most of it will be fat and juicy.

By the present mode, corn, generally hard, being chiefly relied on to raise and fatten hogs, much is used and much is wasted; by the proposed, the use of the pumpkins and clover, vastly lessens the use of corn, and diminishes the expense, whilst it increases the meat.

By the present mode, no return for the food is made by the hog, but that of his carcase; by the proposed, he will pay for it, and in my opinion, more than pay for it, by his manure. If this is wholly true, his meat paid for by the present mode at a price so exorbitant, as to induce some farmers to buy, rather than to raise it, will be gotten for nothing; if partially, this single consideration may at least reduce the cost, far below the usual price.

The value of the clover to hogs is demonstrated by the

fact, that (sows giving suck excepted) they will thrive and grow on it alone if allowed to run at large; and yet make but a small impression on the crop. The addition of corn recommended, is necessary for these sows, and highly improves the other hogs. It is indispensable to gentle and lure all to the pen at night. Clover cut and given green to hogs in a pen, will be eaten greedily, and yet the hogs will fall off; and would I think finally perish; nor is it by any means so efficacious, united with other food, as if gathered by the animal himself. (Note E.)

NUMBER 48

Succession of Crops

This idea, according to the theory of manures advanced in several former numbers of these essays, must contain much error, and all its truth must be limited to the simple facts, that the cultivation of one crop will clean and pulverize the ground for the reception of another, and that some crops will produce these effects better than others, either as requiring more cultivation, like tobacco; as killing grass and weeds by shade, like the pea and pumpkin; or as rendering the earth more friable, like the potatoe. But an opinion that the earth can be enriched by an annual succession of crops, will blast every hope of its improvement, if this can only be effected by manure; because all will prefer the ease and profit of annual tillage, as a mode of fertilizing the earth, to the labour and delay of resting land, reducing tough swards, and raising and applying manure.

In England, a thorough manuring of ground already rich, every five or six years, is allowed by all authors to be indispensably necessary to fulfil the promises of a succession of crops; what then have we to hope from a succession of crops applied to ground already poor without this sexennial manuring? In our gardens a succession of crops is seldom considered as a necessary aid to annual manuring. Draw from the earth as you will, it never fails, if replenished annually with atmospherical matter; let your rotation of crops be what it will, it never lasts, if this replenishment is withheld. Industrious effort, and not lazy theory, can only save our ruining country.

Trust not to the delusive promises of a rotation of crops for restoring our soil. It will aggravate the evil it pretends to remove. It is a remedy which will be greedily seized upon by the annual prime ministers of a Southern farm, whose tenure is precarious, and whose object is sudden income; and they will with joy abandon the labour of manuring and improving for prospective, to gain the bribe of immediate profit.

This disposition is so ruinous already, that I have known an owner with very imperfect management, to manure annually ten times more with equal means at the place of his residence, than on a farm some miles distant entrusted to an overseer. Money wages is one mode of curing an evil sufficient without an ally to ruin our country. But to give this remedy effect, the apocryphal opinion of recovering our lands by a succession of crops ought to be driven out by the more solid reliance upon manuring and inclosing.

Our funds for manuring are sufficient to employ all our energies, and if our energies were employed sufficiently to exclude all worn out land from cultivation, and to produce the sexennial supply of manure, without which a rotation of crops will be delusive, and pernicious effects would follow, as far surpassing in usefulness those of mere rotation theory, as the Atlantic ocean surpasses in extent the lake of Geneva. Many of these funds of manure, ready to pay the drafts of industry, have been heretofore noticed; more perhaps are overlooked. They are scattered every where around us; and Providence has blest our shallow soil with a capacity of suddenly throwing up thickets, constituting a bountiful provision for manuring and curing galls and gullies. I have tried this vegetable manure by strewing the whole surface, by packing it green in large furrows and covering it with the plough, by packing it in such furrows in the same state, and leaving it to be covered with the plough three years afterwards, and by covering it as soon as the leaves were perfectly dry, sowing it previously with plaster. Each experiment of which the result is determined, is highly gratifying. The last on nearly a caput mortuum of a galled and gravelly hill side, exhibits good corn planted over the bushes, as soon as they were covered. It is in vain to begin at the wrong end to improve our system of agriculture. Fertility of soil alone can give success to ingenious theories. These applied to barrenness at best resemble only the beautiful calculations of a speculator, who demonstrates a mode of making fifty thousand dollars from a capital of an hundred thousand, to a man worth only an hundred cents. The capital must precede the profit.

Manuring only can recover this capital, so much of which is already wasted by bad husbandry. It is the great object to be impressed, and all its modes should be tried. When that has provided a fund for experiment, and an excitement to ingenuity, by presenting to industry and genius a fertile area, the time will have arrived for exploring the more recondite principles of agriculture, and descending to the diminutives of improvement.

The effect of manuring and inclosing united, in stopping gullies and curing galls, is an hundred fold greater, than the most ingenious mechanical contrivance. Land filled with roots, covered with litter, aided by buried bushes forming covered drains, protected against the wounds of swine and hoofs, and replenished sexennially with the coarse manure of the farm and stable yards, will not wash. Under such management, the bottoms of the gullies will throw up a growth capable of arresting whatever matters the waters shall convey from the higher lands, soon become the richest parts of the field, and thenceforth gradually fill up. I have long cultivated considerable gullies created by the three shifts, grazing and unmanuring system, and cured in this mode, which produce the best crops, are secured against washing by their great fertility, and are gradually disappearing by deepening their soil.

A succession of crops is utterly incompetent to the ends so necessary to our lands, as it will not produce their renovation; and the portion of truth the theory possesses, if it has any, is so inconsiderable, that it will produce the most ruinous errors, if it leads us to believe, that our efforts to manure them may be safely diminished or superseded, by any rotation of crops, however skilful.

NUMBER 49

Live Fences

This subject, so extremely material to a country requiring to be raised from the dead, by vast and repeated
doses of the only genuine terrene elixir, certifies in every
quarter of the United States, to the scantiness of our
agricultural knowledge; and is one of the presages, that
it is doomed to live and die an infant. If it is an idiot,
its case is hopeless; but if it is only a dunce, it must in
time discern the vast saving of labour to be applied to
draining and manuring, the vast saving of wood and
timber for fuel and building, and the vast accession to
arable, by rendering less woodland necessary, as acquisitions arising from live fences.

In the "Memoirs of the Agricultural Society of Philadelphia," several modes of raising live hedges, suitable
for different soils and climates, are stated and explained.
Two volumes of these memoirs have been published, containing more valuable information upon the subject of
agriculture, than any native book I have seen, and if we

have no relish for the wit, learning and experience, with which they abound, but little good can be expected from these ephemeral essays. To say much upon a subject, copiously handled in a book which every farmer ought to have, would insinuate the existence of a general apathy towards the eminent talents which have presided over, and greatly contributed to its composition; to say nothing, would be a neglect of a subject of the utmost importance.

Several plants are mentioned in these memoirs as proper for making live fences, but I shall confine my observations to one, because my knowledge experimentally, does not extend to the others. The cedar is peculiarly fitted for the purpose, throughout a great district of the United States. It throws out bows near the ground, pliant and capable of being easily woven in to any form. They gradually, however, become stiff. Clipping will make cedar hedges extremely thick. No animal will injure them by browsing. Manured and cultivated, they come rapidly to perfection. The plants are frequently to be found in great abundance without the trouble of raising them. As an evergreen they are preferable to deciduous plants; and they live better than any young trees I have ever tried, planted as follows.

From December to the middle of March, the smallest plants are to be taken up in a sod of a square conformable to the size of the spade used, as deep as possible, which sod is to be deposited unbroken in a hole as deep made by a similar spade; the earth coming out of it being used to fill up the crevices between the sod and the hole for its reception. I plant these cedars on the out and inside of a straight fence, on the ridge of a ditch, the plants in each row being two feet apart both in the direction of and across this ridge; but so that the plants on one side of the fence will be opposite to the centre of the vacancies between those on the other. Each row will be one foot from the fence, so that the top of the ridge will be about eight inches higher than the position of the plants. They should be topt at a foot high, and not suffered to gain above three or four inches yearly in height, such boughs excepted as can be worked into the fence at the ground. Of these great use may be made towards thickening the hedge, by bending them to the ground, and covering them well with earth in the middle, leaving them growing to the stem, and their extremities exposed. Thus they invariably take root and fill up gaps. If these hedges are cultivated properly, and the land is strong, they will form an elegant live evergreen fence, in a shorter time, than is necessary to raise a thorn fence in England, according to the books.

But will they keep out hogs? I am told by travellers that few or none of the hedges in England will do so. Yet hedges are both the chief agricultural ornament, and most valuable improvement of that well cultivated country. But hogs are not there turned loose by law to assail them. I do, however, think that a cedar hedge is far more capable of forming a fence against hogs than the thorn, because one, as a tree, will acquire more strength or stubbornness than the other, a shrub, can ever reach; and because the cedar is capable of being worked into a closer texture than the thorn.

Yet the wedge-like snout of the hog, the hardiness of

his nature, and the toughness of his hide, certainly exhibit him as a dangerous foe to live fences; and the resources of ringing and yoking to control his powers and his disposition, ought to be adverted to, for the sake of an improvement so momentous. These will not shock our prejudices nor violate our habits, and are supported by a consideration of weight, far inferior to the importance of hedging; and yet light as it is, of weight sufficient to justify the recommendation. If hedges are not protected against hogs, at least four rows of plants, and a double width of ridge or bank will be necessary; there must be a double sized ditch to furnish this earth; a double portion of land will be occupied by the hedge and ditch; and more than double labour, owing to the inconvenience arising from great breadth, will be always required to keep the hedge in order. Something less than moieties in all these cases will suffice for hedges capable of fencing out every other animal, if the legal rights of hogs are only modified, and besides the narrow hedges will be far more beautiful. (Note F.)

NUMBER 50

Orchards

In our warm and dry climate, I consider live fences as the matrix for apple orchards. These are the only species of orchards at a distance from cities, capable of producing sufficient profit and comfort, to become a considerable object to a farmer. Distilling from fruit is precarious, troublesome, trifling and out of his province. But the apple will furnish some food for his hogs, a luxury for his family in winter, and a healthy liquor for himself and his labourers all the year. Independent of any surplus of cyder he may spare, it is an object of solid profit, and easy acquisition. In the Southern states, the premature decay and death of apple trees, is the chief obstacle to its attainment. And this my experience tells me is generally occasioned by a stroke of the sun on the body of the tree. Hedges in a great variety of positions will afford shelter to trees against this stroke.

This conclusion has been drawn from many facts, but a single case only shall be stated. Some years past the following experiment was tried. An area of above an acre was inclosed by a cedar hedge, in the form of a square, with each side presented to a cardinal point of the compass. Soon after, a young apple orchard was planted on the outside around the hedge three feet from it, and at twenty feet distance between the trees. The hedge shaded the bodies of the trees when it could do so, and has been for some years thick and high. Not a single tree has decayed or died on the North or East side of it, many have on the West, and several on the South; and the general thriftiness of the trees on the North and East aspects, greatly exceeds that on the two others.

If the result of this experiment can be depended on, for uniting live fences and orchards, the same culture will answer for both, and a vast saving of land, a great saving of trees, a great accession of comforts and profit, and a useful and ornamental border of roads will ensue. The same experiment tends to recommend low or short bodies, as some preservative for fruit trees against strokes of the sun.

Next to this cause of the death of apple trees, the residence under, and subsistence upon the bark of the bodies and roots below the surface of the ground, during winter, of the field rat, has been the most common. The remedy against this animal, perhaps the mole also, and probably against the whole family of insects, is to dig away so much of the earth from the roots near the body, to remain open during the winter, as will make the place too uncomfortable a residence for them, during that season, in which they are most apt to feed on the bark.

A saving of much time and trouble, and an acquisition

of sounder trees would result from an easy practice, to which I have of late years conformed. By earthing up the young grafts gradually as they grow, to about six inches above the junction of the slip and the stalk, roots will invariably shoot out above this junction, and by cutting off the stalk just above it, when the young tree is transplanted, you get rid of the defects in its constitution, sometimes occasioned by the operation of engrafting, and what is infinitely more important, all the scions sprouting up from its roots, during the whole life of the tree, will be of the true fruit, and furnish spontaneously and permanently healthier orchards, than can be obtained by the labour and art of engrafting.

Good cyder would be a national saving of wealth, by expelling foreign liquors; and of life, by expelling the use of ardent spirits. The cyder counties of England are said to exhibit the healthiest population of the kingdom. Even hard cyder would be a useful beverage to our slaves. Reduced to vinegar it is considered as a luxury, and allowed to be wholesome. But the extreme ignorance of mankind in making cyder is demonstrated, by an uncertainty whether the manufacture shall turn out to be sweet, hard or sour. It often happens that things of most value are not perfected, because perfection is easily attainable. A thousand times more ingenuity has been expended on steam engines, than would have sufficed for discovering the best modes of agriculture; and the art of making cyder is in its infancy, whilst that of making wine has been brought to maturity. Yet the former liquor would furnish infinitely more comfort, at infinitely less expense to mankind, than the latter, if the art of making it had been equally perfected.

It is probable that a similarity exists in the best process for making both liquors, and that useful hints may be collected from the details as to wine, towards forming a process for making cyder. From this source I have extracted a practice, though undoubtedly imperfect, yet tolerably sufficing for family purposes. It is this:

When the fermentation of the must is half over, so that it is considerably sweeter than it ought to remain, it is drawn off (throwing away the sediment at the bottom of the cask) and boiled moderately about one hour in a copper, during which the impurities rising to the top are taken off by a skimmer with holes in it, to let the cyder through. Twelve eggs for each thirty three gallons, yolks and whites, are beat up, pouring gently to them some of the boiling cyder, until the mixture amounts to about a gallon. This mixture is gradually poured into the boiling cyder and well mixed with it by stirring. It then boils gently five minutes longer, when it is returned hot into the cask. In eight or ten days it is drawn off, leaving the sediment to be thrown away, and put into a clean cask, with six quarts of rum or brandy to thirty-three gallons. The cask is made completely full and stopt close. For this purpose a sufficient provision of cyder must be made. The cyder is bottled in the spring.

The chief object in making cyder, must be the management of the fermentation, so as to avail ourselves of the spirituous, and avoid the acetous. In the fall it is accomplished by the above process. But cyder is subject to a second fermentation in the spring like wine, which often demolishes bottles or ends in acidity. To manage this so as to make it keep good in casks, is an object highly desirable, but which I have not attempted to accomplish. Perhaps it is attainable by racking it off in the spring and making a second addition of spirit. The simple process above stated, will carry it well through the winter, and furnish good bottled cyder; but it promises nothing more. By cutting off the corks even with the bottle, and dipping its mouth in boiling pitch, it is as completely closed, as the best waxed bottled claret or burgundy.

NUMBER 51

Draining

Prejudices have assailed, and will continue to assail, every species of improvement, and theory instead of experience will often sow opinion. It is frequently believed, that draining, clearing and reducing to cultivation marshes, bogs and swamps, will add to the insalubrity of the air, because vegetables feed upon certain qualities of it, unfit for animal respiration; and thus render it purer for that purpose. But why should we load the atmosphere with poison, because vegetables will absorb a portion of it? Countries kept damp by endless forests, though abounding in the utmost degree with these absorbents of atmospherical miasma, are peculiarly unwholesome; and first settlers unexceptionably become victims to the fact. It proves that the air may be contaminated beyond the purifying power of an entire vegetable wilderness, and that a reliance for its salubrity upon the eaters of poison, would be equivalent to a reliance upon the eaters of carrion for its purification, if shambles were as extensive as bogs. After having made the air as pure as possible by every means in our power, the vegetable chymistry by absorption, is a means provided by providence, for its last filter; but to infer from this natural operation, that our efforts to render it purer by draining are pernicious, would be an equivalent inference to the idea, that the cultivation of the earth is pernicious because it is capable of spontaneous productions.

Campania* and some other flat and marshy districts of Italy, are recorded in history as having been made so healthy and delightful in the flourishing period of the Roman Empire by draining, as to have been selected by the opulent for country retirement, and splendid palaces. The drains neglected by the barbarous conquerors of Italy, have never been re-established by its modern inhabitants; and the swamps and marshes have restored to these districts an uninhabitable atmosphere, by having their waters, their trees, and their verdure restored to them.

As new countries are cleared and ploughed, they become more healthy. The draining effects of these two operations exceed those of any other, and by drying the earth very extensively, furnish the strongest evidence for ascertaining the effects of draining wetter lands. If the

---

* Campania is a territorial division of Italy, south of Rome, bound on the north by the mountains of Aurunci, on the east by the Apennines, on the south by a spur of these mountains which ends near Sorrento, and on the south and west by the sea. The region was, in antiquity, fabled for its fertility.

healthiness of a country is increased by these modes of draining, it will not be diminished by auxiliary modes.

The connexion between draining or drying the earth, and human subsistence, furnishes a kind of argument, neither logical nor demonstrative, and yet of conclusive force to my mind. Can it be believed that the author of creation, has committed the egregious blunder, of exposing man to the alternative of eating bad food, or of breathing bad air? If not, draining whether by the sun, the plough or the spade, being indispensable to avoid the first, cannot wreck him on the second evil.

From the great improvement made in the health of the Eastern parts of the Union, if we may trust in recent history, by opening the lands to the sun, and with the plough; I long since concluded, that this improvement would be vastly extended by resorting to every other species of draining. And having removed some years past to a farm, reported to be extremely liable to billious fevers, I threw several small streams into deep ditches, dried a wet road leading to the house, by open or covered drains, and cleared and drained some acres of springy swamp, closely covered with swamp wood, lying four or five hundred yards south of the house. The multitude of springs in this swamp, made deep, central, and double lateral ditches, entering into it every six yards necessary throughout the ground. The labour was great, but the wet thicket is now a clean dry meadow. Perhaps an attachment to a theory may have caused me to imagine, that the improvement in the healthiness of my family and the draining improvements, have kept pace with each other; but I am under no delusion in asserting, that the healthiness of no part of the world, according to the tables of mortality which I have seen, has equalled it.

A very large proportion of the country on the Eastern waters consists of level land, swamps, bogs and marshes. The first is chiefly cleaned and exhausted; the two last are chiefly in a natural state; and all generate poison for want of proper draining by the plough, by ditches, and by dams, instead of producing the richest crops of every kind for man and beast, of any other part of the country, without infecting the air.

The swamps, bogs and marshes, constitute one of our best resources for recovering the exhausted high lands, as furnishing employment for labour, and funds for manure; to the farmer, they offer a certainty of profit, in exchange for the frequency of loss; and to the worn out land, an intermission of its tortures, and a cure for its wounds.

If the bounties of draining include an improvement in salubrity, in subsistence, in profit, and of exhausted lands, they ought to excite an ardour which will presently leave behind the few and plain remarks which I shall make upon the subject; or at least to awaken great districts of country to the facts, that their best lands, those capable of yielding the most profit, if not those, only capable, of yielding any or much profit; lands able to support more people than those at present under culture, lie wholly useless; except it may be useful to kill people who are employed in killing land, and thus shelter the survivors in some measure against the evils of penury.

NUMBER 52

Draining, Continued

The simplest mode of draining is by the plough, and yet even this is rare. Considerable districts of flat, stiff and close land, are soured by stagnant water and baked by the sun, for want of this plain operation; so as to increase labour, diminish crops and taint the air. Sometimes this rigid land, though intended for Indian corn, is left unbroken thro' the winter, and retains its excessive moisture, for want of a declivity to discharge it; at others, being fallowed level, the water becomes a menstruum for melting down the soil into a brick like cover, which is generally rendered excessively hard by the sun, before the water is evaporated sufficiently to admit the plough. If the glutinous quality of water had not been demonstrated in the familiar operation of brick making, it ought to have been instantly perceived in the case under consideration. This soil holds it upon the surface with such surprising retentiveness, as often to shew it in a rut or some other small aperture, at a time when the crop is suffering by drought. Being naturally adapted to extract and retain the gluten in water, a surface is formed which obstructs absorption, and suspends the water excessively exposed to evaporation; so that the crops suffer more than those of any other kinds of land, both from its excess and deficiency, under the flat culture habit.

For both these misfortunes, draining is the only remedy, and in most cases it can be effected by the plough. This will make ridges and furrows, differing in their level in proportion to the breadth of the former. The wider the ridge, the deeper the furrow may be made; and in ridges calculated for Indian corn, of five feet and an half wide, the bottom of the furrow may easily be made fifteen inches lower than the top of the ridge. Land of the nature described, from the worst, is capable by skilful plough-drainings, of being converted into the best of our soils. If a habit had existed of draining wet meadow lands, first by cutting lines of ditches from North to South over the whole surface of the meadow, and then by filling them all up, in cutting the same number from East to West, and so cutting and filling ditches alternately; all the arguments in favour of this mode of draining meadows, would apply against the only practicable mode of draining cornfields by the plough; for the latter object can only be effected by abolishing the habit of cross ploughing.

The difference of the level between the ridge and the furrow, in almost every case, enables us to seize upon some descent in the field (as the smallest will suffice) by which to dispose of the superfluous moisture. However distant, a descent comes at last, and adjoining land holders would find a mutual benefit by uniting in the operation, because stagnant water on the higher field, does an injury to the lower, only capable of being removed by allowing it a passage.

Supposing, however, the unusual case of a perfect level, essential benefit will yet accrue from the proposed mode of draining by the plough. The climate of the country under consideration is by no means a wet one, and therefore, even in this case an instance would rarely happen of a fall of rain so excessive, as to drench the earth, fill the proposed furrows, and overflow the ridges; because the earth of these ridges having been retrieved from a saturity of moisture, keeping it in winter constantly unsusceptible of an addition, and having been rendered friable by lying in ridges exposed to frost, will absorb infinitely more than the same earth in its flat compact state; because the deep furrows having passed below the crust caused by the union between the earth of the surface, and the gluiness of the water, will thereby have opened new channels for absorption; and because the capacity of the furrows if properly constructed, will generally or invariably be adequate to the quantity of superfluous water.

An infallible mode, however, of perfecting the operation of draining by the plough, exists in subjoining it to a dry ditch, which in no case need be above eighteen inches deep, and twenty-four wide, to be placed on the side of the field most proper for conveying off the water. If there is any descent, this ditch must run at its foot; if none, it must receive the water nearest to some descent, to which the ditch must be continued. In both cases every furrow of the field must deliver its water into the ditch.

Those readers who have seen large flats of close, wet land on the Eastern water courses, employed in killing teams, poisoning the air, and disappointing the hopes of the husbandman, will not consider the suggestions of this number, as useless. Our agriculture is hardly prepared for the plainest improvements, and an attempt to introduce those of a complicated nature, would of course be unsuccessful. The double paradox however contended for, having been the result of experience, may safely be referred to the same tribunal, with a word or two to solicit a fair trial. It is asserted that the flat surface in the kind of soil I have been speaking of, will produce the evils, both of too much and too little moisture; and that the high ridges and deep furrows earnestly recommended, will prevent both. In addition to the previous observations in this number, applying to the reconciliation of these apparent contradictions, the reader will be pleased to recollect those in a former one, designed to prove that evaporation will be greater from a flat than from a ridged surface, and therefore in winter when it is too slow, the furrows may carry off the superfluous water, and in summer when it is too rapid, the ridges may obstruct it.

If twenty inches of rain falls in the year, which would retain moisture in droughts longest; a level iron pan of an hundred acres area, or an hundred acres of earth of a soil absorbing all that fell? The soil I have been speaking of, flat and undrained, is somewhat of the nature of the pan; drained by ridges and deep furrows, it is converted into one more absorbent.

NUMBER 53

Draining, Continued

The next species of draining to be considered is nearly as simple, as useful, and as much neglected, as that we have just past. A great part of the country below the mountains is of a sandy soil, and abounds with a multitude of creeks, bogs and rivulets, generally furnishing fine land up to their very springs, if they were drained. But instead of doing this, the labour of the country has been applied with great perseverance and success, to draining the hills of their barren sands, for the purpose of pouring them upon these rich vallies. To arrest and repair so ruinous an evil, would be the means of bringing under culture an immense body of land, infinitely more fertile than that in cultivation; and if health and plenty are bad motives for the undertaking, this fertility ought to suggest the folly of neglecting the smallest slipe of these wet lands, from pecuniary considerations only.

If, however, the wonderful manner in which the Eastern states are watered, is adverted to, the very great quantity of these wet lands will strike the mind, and disclose to it at once a capacity as great for causing unhealthiness, as for producing profit; and as in reaping the good we remove the evil, an admiration of human nature is awakened, when we see it brave the worst climates, and court death abroad for the sake of wealth, rather than acquire it at home by highly improving a tolerable one, and courting long life.

There is hardly a habitation in most of the Eastern states, however distant from the larger rivers, without the atmospherical influence of this vast mass of creeks, bogs and rivulets; and accordingly their effect is almost every where in some degree, experienced. Few of their channels retain any appearance of their natural state, being every where obstructed by sands, bogs, bushes and rubbish, so as to form innumerable putrid puddles, pools and bogs, upon the occurrence of every drought; to several of which, all our summers and autumns are liable. By stopping and spreading the waters of our creeks and rivulets, they soon cease to flow in droughts, and the water which might be carried off in a healthy current at all times, in wet seasons, poisons the earth, and in dry, the air, because then evaporation becomes its only channel.

Every rational being will acknowledge, that nothing can be more ridiculous than to kill ourselves for the sake of remaining poor, and nothing wiser than to lengthen our lives for the sake of becoming daily more comfortable. The latter objects will both be certainly accomplished by draining our creeks, rivulets and bogs, so as to bestow on them unobstructed currents, and to cultivate their borders. In sandy countries, where they are most extensive, valuable and pernicious, their last quality is most easily removed, as I shall endeavour to shew.

Side and straight ditches, where ditching is necessary, ought generally to be abandoned, and the stream trained nearly to its natural course, avoiding acute angles, and aiming at gentle sinuosities. The loose texture of a sandy soil suggests these precautions. In consequence of it, side ditches are speedily filled up. Straight ditches give an impetus to the current, exposing a crumbling soil to a constant abrasion, and devoting the point upon which it expends its greatest fury, to great injury. Acute angles create strong currents and are unable to withstand weak ones. The lowest ground is naturally the best for drains. And gentle bends check the impetuosity of currents. From adhering to the lowest ground or natural course of the stream, we may avail ourselves to great extent of the stream itself towards perfecting the drain, by periodically removing such obstructions as it is unable to remove, or discloses in cutting a ditch for itself. These in the sandy countries, consist generally of old wood, occasionally of veins of some more rigid species of earth; the first to be removed, the latter to be cut through. In cutting ditches, widening channels, pairing off points, cleaning and deepening drains of any kind, one of the most obvious, and most common errors, is to leave the earth on their borders, so as to dam out a considerable portion of the water the drain was intended to receive, and to destroy all the crop within its influence. This earth ought unexceptionably to be employed in curing hollows, leaving the edges of the drain every where lower than the adjacent ground. By this means floods will seldomer occur, and more rapidly return to the channel; because as the water is every where trickling into the drain as the rain falls, it has more time to dispose of it, and for the same reason, an excess will sooner be reduced. Both the rapid and complete reduction of floods is of great importance to crops, few of which will sustain much injury from a very short immersion. They are ruined for want of a remedy against stagnant water. Drains in the lowest ground, with edges lower than the ground designed to be dried, aided by ridges and furrows, emptying into the drains, will afford this remedy, in the most perfect manner.

NUMBER 54

Draining, Continued

As all our streams have others falling into them, and are attended with a multitude of springs breaking out at the termination of the high land, some substitute for the side ditches so unsuccessfully tried for the purpose of intercepting these rills and springs, is indispensable. I have tried three with entire success, at an expense of labour infinitely less than that so frequently lost by adhering to side ditches, in such cases as we are considering. If the tributary stream rises beyond the ground we are draining, it is managed by the same principles as the chief stream, so far upwards, as is necessary. If it rises in a bold spring at the junction of the hills with the flat we are reclaiming, a channel is made for it in the lowest ground, and by the shortest distance, to the central drain, as narrow as the spade will allow, never more than eighteen inches deep, with perpendicular sides, which in these narrow cuts last much longer than slopes, because they are not equally exposed to frosts. If springs ooze in a continued line at the junction of the hill and flat, a side cut as narrow as possible and deep enough to intersect them all, with a direct cut as above to the main drain, is one remedy. The labour of these cuts is trifling. The last, however, like all ditches above the lowest ground in sandy soils, is liable to be filled up. To obviate this inconvenience (which in these small cuts is not very great) I have frequently tried covered drains, constructed as follows, with invariable success.

A ditch at least four feet deep is cut so as completely to intersect the whole line of these oozing springs, to the depth of about three feet, and it is continued to the open drain into which it must discharge its water, by the route affording the most convenient fall for that purpose. The ditch is cut gradually narrower from the top to the bottom, where it is not above eight inches wide. A row of poles of such a size as nearly, but not entirely to touch, is laid on each side of the ditch at bottom. Green or seasoned brush, without leaves, trimmed to lie close, is then packed into the ditch, with the small ends downwards, and touching the poles, beginning at the upper end of the ditch. The inclination of the brush must be up stream, at an angle of about forty-five degrees with the bottom of the ditch; it must be packed as close with the hand as possible, and cut into lengths proper for the end of filling the ditch within ten inches of the top. The brush is then to be covered with four inches of dry sound leaves of any kind, and the whole of the earth to be returned upon the ditch and well rammed. It will press down the brush and leaves low enough to admit of any species of culture without disturbing them. The oozing water will be received by the former, and must trickle through the apertures caused by having its small ends at bottom, and by the poles, down to the open drain, and the soured ground will lose every boggy appearance.

This mode of draining seems in description to be more troublesome, than I have found it to be in practice. Unless its duration could be ascertained, we cannot certainly pronounce as to its cheapness. The oldest I have had an opportunity of attending to, was constructed about ten years past. Its objects were to render a road dry, and about two acres of soured barren land better, by sinking a line of oozing springs lying collaterally with the road, which made it a quagmire in wet weather, and rendered the two acres barren. The road has been ever since dry and firm, and the land, of the best in the field. I cannot help thinking that a well constructed drain of this kind, will last a century. Where stones can be had, they may be made to last forever, but I doubt whether brick work would be equal to the brush.

But this is like shooting speculation a century beyond hope. It is superfluous to invent modes of preserving spots, whilst we are destroying districts. I will therefore return to the subject, as it relates to draining the vast body of land lying on creeks and small rivers. There is no species of draining so cheap or beneficial, as where there is water sufficient to perform a chief part of the work. Most streams can perform some of it. In either case, the removal of obstructions of wood or loose stone, requires infinitely less labour, than to dig an equivalent canal; and the water thus aided, will continue to deepen its channel, until its efforts are controlled by withholding the assistance. The earth it scoops out of the channel, becomes an alluvion for curing an abundance of chasms and inequalities, the fruit of torrents and obstructions. And by correcting some angles, and deepening the channels of the creeks, and small rivers, a very large quantity of the best land now yielding foul air, may be brought at a trifling expense to yield fine crops.

For the introduction of this mode of draining, the cheapest, the most practicable, and the most profitable, a law is necessary. I do not know that Coke's summa ratio provides for the case, and the absurdities to be found in the code, upon which this exalted encomium is pronounced, are records of human folly sufficient to shake a confidence in the good sense and justice of an entire nation, however plain the case may be.* A proprietor below may perhaps be found, blind to the clear moral obligations which require him to remove the obstructions against the draining of a proprietor above; whilst one above may be so lynx-eyed, as to see injuries to himself from draining land below. And yet the prosperity and the health of the whole nation is at least as deeply affected by the object, as by the establishment of roads; nor would a lower county which should stop all the roads leading

---

* Sir Edward Coke (1552–1634) is the father of the common law tradition. His work appears in his periodic *Reports* and the *Institutes* (1628). He was Lord Chief Justice (1613–1616). Lord Coke called the prescriptive common law of England "the perfection of reason." See Herbert Butterfield, *The Englishman and His History* (Hamden, Ct.: Archon Books, 1970). Such Whig traditionalists were far more important in the political thought of early America than the "natural rights" speculations of John Locke, for every lawyer cut his teeth on Coke, and most of the authors of our national independence studied some law.

from above, act as unjustly or absurdly as those who stop the drains from above. It would not injure the climate, and by arresting commodities, it would establish some monopoly beneficial to itself; but the obstructor of draining gains no exclusive advantage, and shares in the general calamity of a bad climate.

Such laws are not novel. Pennsylvania is indebted to them for some of her finest farms. I much question whether the state legislatures have a power to pass any laws, equally beneficial. They might try the experiment, short of that requiring social embankments, by only imposing the simple and easy obligation of keeping up a social current, sufficient to drain all lands above, in every stream lying above tide water. Such laws might at first be limited to the removal of obstructions of wood or earth, until experience should decide, whether they might not be beneficially extended even to obstructions of stone.

NUMBER 55

Draining, Continued

The residue of this subject contains in every view its most important division, and unfortunately meets with less capacity to do it justice. The benefits arising from draining the kind of ground we have passed over, though great in themselves, are inconsiderable, compared with those which would result from draining the marshes and sunken grounds upon tide water. A new country and climate would be gained by it. We know that the Dutch in both hemispheres, have reclaimed rich countries from the ocean, whilst we abandon them to the rivers; but I do not recollect to have heard of a book upon draining and banking. My whole experience is confined to a single experiment, yet unfinished, the occurrences of which I shall relate, so far as they may be useful. It is made on ground similar to the body of marsh and wet land, abounding on the tide rivers and creeks of the Eastern States, to an extent, sufficient if reclaimed, to dispense wealth and comfort, and unreclaimed, unwholesomeness and death.

About two hundred acres of such land, three fourths of which were subject to the tides, which fluctuate to the extent of about three feet, and within half a mile of a large river, is the subject of the experiment. The remaining fourth, though a few inches above tide water, was sunken land, covered with the usual growth of such ground. A large portion was soft marsh, subject to common tides, and nearly as much a sheet of water, shallow at low tides. On one side of this area, has been constructed a canal about eighteen feet wide, to conduct a creek sufficiently large for two mills above; and on the other, one half as wide, to receive and convey several small streams, and a great number of springs. At the termination of the work, these canals are connected by a dam nearly two hundred yards long, one half crossing the soft marsh, and the other the space constituting the former bed of the creek. These canals are between four and five miles long, and have been constructed cautiously and leisurely, to diminish the loss of the adventure, should it prove unsuccessful.

The experiment was commenced by cutting a ditch on the left side of the small canal, about four feet wide, and two deep, near the dry land, but wholly in the soil of the wet. It was found to yield too little earth to make a bank high and strong enough to resist either inundations or high tides; that the earth became so porous, on drying, as to produce leaks and breaches; and that it was yet so adhesive as to admit of the burrowing of muskrats, with which the place abounded. Thus the first attempt failed, and a considerable ditch became wholly useless.

As this spongy and fibrous soil extended to the base of the hills on both sides, the next attempt was made by driving a double row of stakes and puncheons round and split, being six feet long, two feet into the wet ground, about eighteen from the dry, fitted together as close as possible, and covering them with the same kind of soil, dug out of the canal for conducting the creek, which afforded earth when cut about one foot deep, to cover the stakes. The result was, that the wooden wall under this spongy and fibrous earth, was no security against the muskrats, and that the bank was pierced by them at pleasure. The labour in wood was therefore lost, but not the insufficient channel nor the bank.

The channel being about twelve inches deeper than the adjacent sunken ground, would contain and conduct the creek except in inundations, and as the bank hitherto described, was in every view insufficient, chasms of fifteen or twenty feet wide were made in it at about three hundred yards apart, to let the water pass out when high. The creek was turned into this canal, with a view of floating the sand from above, and depositing it along the bottom, conveniently for removal to the bank in order to oppose its friable nature to the architectural skill of the muskrats.

At some convenient season once a year (for the experiment proceeded for years) the water of the creek being turned successively through these chasms above, left its bottom below of firm sand, which was very easily raised upon the bank. By the pressure of this annual alluvion of sand, upon the spongy soil, the channel of the creek became deeper, and the alluvion was increased, so that finally the first embankment, being greatly raised and completely covered with the sand filtered by the water into a state for the object, became a fortification proof against the skill of these troublesome animals.

The chasms left for inundations being of the kind of soil described, were not liable to be cut by the water into new channels, and their edges or banks, being higher than the bottom of the creek, very little sand could escape through them.

As the body of water on the left side, was too inconsiderable for the alluvion process, it became necessary to abandon the old ditch, and to commence a new one, so far touching upon the base of the rising dry land, as to secure a sufficiency of sand for the bank, and yet to be able to penetrate to the springs, which created a perpetual pond and bog in a portion of the area to be drained. It is now cut throughout its whole course of about three miles, so deep as to have reached many of the springs, with a bank able to command inundations and tides. The bank was composed of sand only (the wooden staccade having turned out to be useless), and being of considerable size, proved a complete barrier against the muskrats, in the following cases excepted: In three several places the bog or marsh, protruded into the dry land at right angles with the course of the ditch, in narrow necks not worth the expense of including. Two of these were about thirty yards wide, and the third near ten. All were crossed, and to save the trouble of getting sand for the bank, a more careful trial was made of the staccade and spongy soil. They proved in all three places insufficient to confine the water, or resist the muskrats. A sandy soil lay on both sides of these guts, but still it would be considerable labour to remove a quantity of it sufficient for the whole bank; to save this labour, a ditch was cut on the inner or lower side of the bank close to its base, three feet wide,

and as many deep, quite across the mouths of the two
largest guts, and filled with the adjacent sandy soil; and
this thread of sand was continued on the back of the
spongy part of the bank above high water mark in the
canal. At the narrow gut the bank was well coated above
ground with sand. At all three, success was complete.

Before the inefficacy of the staccade was discovered,
it was resorted to in making the dam across the creek
and marsh. Stakes and puncheons of about nine feet
long, were driven about three into the earth across both,
in the centre of the intended dam, and in a triple row.
Nine feet from this staccade on each side, a close and
strong wattled fence of green cedar was made, for the
purpose of holding the moist soil of the marsh, so far as
the dam was to be compounded of it, and of arresting
the sand, where it was to be made by an alluvion. By
laying plank for the labourers on each side at fifteen feet
distance from these wattlings, and working backwards
towards them, cutting out the earth as deeply as the
labourers could reach, marsh earth was easily obtained
at low tides to raise the dam to a sufficient height, so far
as the marsh extended; but though it was eighteen feet
wide, it proved unable to resist either the water or the
muskrats. It therefore became necessary to cut a ditch
along the whole length of this moiety of the dam, binding on the centre or staccade, four feet wide, and two
feet deeper than the summit of the marsh, and to fill it
with a thread of well filtered alluvion sand. This remedy
has hitherto been sufficient, but nine months only having
elapsed, since it was tried, it is not entirely confided in.

NUMBER 56

Draining, Continued

The remaining moiety of the dam was entirely composed of alluvion sand. For this object, the canal for the creek was made to terminate at a steep sandy hill, being cut close to its base. Care was taken to keep the bottom of the creek two feet above low water mark, for the sake of a current, which being directed into the two nine feet lanes, made by the staccade and the wattlings, gradually conveyed the sand into them, and forced the creek to retire into a narrow channel. To accelerate the operation, the sand of the hill was occasionally thrown into the creek, and to lessen the labour of doing it, the channel, as the canal widened by drafts of sand from the hill, was kept near its base. This was done by occasionally removing the stones and pebbles, generally found in sandy soils, and left behind by the filtration, to the base of the bank, where they produced the indispensable end of preventing the attrition of the current.

As much sand being thus conveyed and deposited as

the descent would allow, two close parallel green cedar wattlings were made eighteen feet below the lowest hitherto mentioned, from the highland to the marsh; the cut through the marsh on the lower side, made in raising that part of the dam, was converted into a channel for the creek to the opposite high land, and a short canal was cut through a neck of marsh, to conduct it from thence to tide water below. And thenceforth the sand was deposited by the current along the whole extent of the dam, from whence it was occasionally with great ease removed upon it, by taking off the creek in low tides and dry seasons, in which there is no difficulty.

In carrying the staccade across the creek, great care was taken to make its top one foot higher than the highest tides, and on covering it with the sand, the aperture left for the tides was closed. The dam was, however, twice broken by high tides, before it was conjectured, that the sand by its weight, had compressed the porous marsh soil of which the bottom of the creek was composed, and lowered the whole staccade with it. Upon a strict attention to this idea, however, it was concluded, that such a compressure, in proportion to weight and compressibility took place throughout the dam and banks; and that though it required occasional additions to both, to preserve their level at least two feet above the highest tides and inundations, its effect of obstructing the percolation of the surrounding water into the space to be drained, admitted by the nature of the soil to a great extent, was a full retribution for the labour thus expended.

The dam and banks being closed quite around, to get rid of the internal water, constituted the remaining difficulty. It was necessary to construct a gate to discharge it at low times. A tide gate in the centre of the dam was unsuccessfully tried. And finally a trunk made of two inch oak plank, sixteen feet long, with a cavity three feet wide and one deep, answered the end much better than any other experiment. The water on the inside passes along the dam, parallel to the water on the out, in the channel cut for raising the dam across the marsh, to the small canal near the junction of its bank, with the dam. At this spot the foundation is an unctuous fullers earth. The place being made by bay-dams, was dug out to the precise level of low water, and the trunk accurately laid down upon it. Plank one foot wide was sunk quite around it edgeways, so as to lap two inches on the bottom of the trunk, and the whole was covered with earth, and well rammed to within two feet of the ends, so as to discharge the water into the small canal. At each aperture of the trunk, is a door made of a single plank, fitted to the outside, having four folds of coarse woollen cloth, dipped in hot tar, nailed on so as to fit the mouths of the box, fixed by strong hinges made for the purpose, and latched under water by the help of a long handle attached to the latch. The defect hitherto discovered, is, that the trunk is not long enough by about six feet.

This species of trunk was first tried to save the water of a small branch for grinding gypsum, in a simple tub mill, built for that purpose. Only one door, and no latch was necessary. The pressure of the water in the pond was such, that when high, a strong chain attached well to the door, worked with a small lever, was necessary to open it. A hole of two inches diameter, kept closed with a large peg, to be pulled out by a pole fastened to it, was resorted to for diminishing the resistance of the water, and caused the door to open more easily. And the end of saving the water was very well effected.

It was discovered that the interval water to be voided by the trunk, was vastly increased by springs passing under the canals, for which there was no remedy but to deepen them. This remedy was applied to the small one with such effect, that its continuance, until the bottom in its whole course shall be brought to a level with the water at low tide, is confidently considered as a certain cure for the evil. The number and size of the springs discovered, were beyond expectation, and the interception of the residue is considered as certain. The large canal could not be deepened hitherto, because it has not quite finished the work of alluvion. But there will be no difficulty in cutting off the springs beneath it, by a narrow ditch in the centre. For when this work is done, the obstructions to prevent the creek from deepening itself, will be removed, and that operation will both lessen the work of penetrating to the springs, and also bestow upon the bank a more perfect degree of strength.

The efforts used to prevent the abrasion of the water in acute angles, eddies or strong currents, consisted of single or double wattles of green cedar, in proper declivities to resist water, and to retain earth; and of throwing all stones and gravel washed from the base of the hills cut by the canal, to the base of the bank. The bank also, generally, had covered itself before its apertures, for allowing a passage to inundations, were closed, with a strong tegument of shrubs, weeds or grass; and these several remedies against the attrition of the current have hitherto been effectual. A portion of the land heretofore flooded by common tides, is quite dry, and will be this year cultivated. After widening the dam by alluvion, to about thirty feet, the creek will no longer be kept parallel with it, but will be sent straight on from the right bank. And the bank is destined to the use of apple trees.

The sandy soil approximating upon most or all of the marshes and sunken grounds of the Eastern States, seems to be the providential provision of the means for reclaiming them; and the multitude of currents passing through this soil, are like vehicles for conveying these means to the necessary positions. They are vehicles which disregard distance, travel constantly and never decay. They will calk the most porous soil, overwhelm the strongest vermin, and follow the slightest direction. Their efforts may be aided by the plough, by removing obstructions, and by tumbling into them sandy declivities with little labour, near to which they should be guided for that purpose.

NUMBER 57

Tobacco

The extent of country yet devoted to the cultivation of this plant, entitles it to a place in an agricultural ephemeris, the object of which is, to kill bad habits, and to be killed itself by a complete system. The preservableness of tobacco, endows it with the rare capacity of waiting for a market, and constituted a recommendation which induced me to cultivate it attentively during two years. Both crops succeeded beyond the medium calculation, and the experiments still exhibited results conclusively proving the propriety of its abandonment. These results were all with ease reduced to figures. It was easy to fix the value of labour bestowed on an acre of tobacco, and on its crop after severance; and on an acre of corn or wheat, with the preparation of its crop also for market. It was as easy to ascertain the produce of equal soils, and prices were settled by sales. Such estimates demonstrated the loss of growing tobacco, merely on the score of annual profit, without taking into the account, the formidable obstacle it constitutes to the improvement of land.

This objection is not founded upon the erroneous opinion, that it is peculiarly an impoverisher. On the contrary, my impression was, that it was less so, than any other crop I knew of, except cotton and the sweet potatoe. But upon its enormous consumption of labour, and its diminutive returns of manure. It would startle even an old planter, to see an exact account of the labour devoured by an acre of tobacco, and the preparation of the crop for market. Even supposing that crop to amount to the extraordinary quantity of one thousand pounds, he would find it seldom, if ever, producing a profit upon a fair calculation. He would be astonished to discover how often he had passed over the land, and the tobacco, through his hands, in fallowing, hilling, cutting off hills, planting, replantings, toppings, succourings, weedings, cuttings, picking up, removing out of the ground by hand, hanging, striking, stripping, stemming, and prizing, and that the same labour, devoted to almost any other employment, would have produced a better return by ordinary success, than tobacco does by the extravagant crop I have supposed.

Though its profit is small or nothing, its quality of starving every thing, exceeds that of every other crop. It starves the earth by producing but little litter, and it starves its cultivators, by producing nothing to eat. Whatever plenty or splendour it may bestow on its owner, the soil it feeds on must necessarily become cadaverous, and its cultivators squalid. Nor can it possibly diffuse over the face of the earth, or the faces of its inhabitants, the exuberance which flows from fertilization, nor the happiness which flows from plenty.

A substitute is the object of inquiry, after we are convinced of the detrimental nature of any crop. When flour sells for as much as tobacco, by the pound, wheat would be a complete one, at any distance from water carriage; but as that is seldom the case, others must be sought after. The extent and population of the country, within reach of navigable water, opens to the tobacco districts a wide market, for the disposal of many better substitutions. Horses, mules, beef and pork, would more than suffice to replace all the advantages lost by relinquishing the culture of tobacco; and materials for manufacturing, with manufacturing itself, would amply provide for any possible deficiency. The market for live stock and meat, is so great and valuable in the bread stuff districts of the Eastern waters, as to attract supplies from quarters far beyond the narrow tobacco belt, with which they are immediately surrounded; and if it is a question in the best cultivated countries, whether grazing and breeding live stock, even upon the margin of navigation, is not the most profitable agricultural employment; every doubt vanishes in comparing it with the culture of tobacco, in situations where the capacity of walking to market, will create a considerable item of that comparison.

The system of agriculture, for a bread stuff farm, according to the experience I have had, requires live stock sufficient to consume and reduce to manure, every species of provender and litter; in effecting which, a sufficiency of meat may be provided for the labourers, either without expense, or even producing a profit. But if I am right in concluding, that the live stock of such a farm ought to stop at that point, whenever its situation renders the expense of transporting its grain to market trivial, it follows, that a vast market would remain for the meat and live stock of the tobacco district, consisting of towns, artizans, all who live by professions and the interest of money; and of the bread stuff farmers themselves, as to horses and mules, the breeding of which is excluded by this system; and as to pork also, wherever a better mode of raising it than the present, shall not be adopted.

Having had no experience of a farm devoted to raising live stock, my observations are conjectural. It seems to me that manuring might be carried much farther, where the whole produce was consumed on the land, than when a part of it was exported; that the product might be therefore more rapidly increased, and the space cultivated, diminished; and that the herbaceous and succulent crops would so far banish the use of those more exhausting, as greatly to accelerate the improvement of the exhausted tobacco district, and to insure an immediate or very near return of profit, exclusively of a return of comfort, far exceeding that to which it has been accustomed.

NUMBER 58

The Economy of Agriculture

There is no subject less understood, nor more generally mistaken than this; nor any more essential to the prosperity of agriculture. Sufficient to afford matter for an entire treatise, it cannot be embraced by a short chapter. But a short chapter may put minds upon the tract, able to unfold its involutions with every branch of agriculture, and more specially to disclose its value.

Diminutions of comfort, necessaries and expense, are too often mistaken for the means of producing the ends they obstruct; and the rapacity which starves, frequently receives the just retribution of a disappointment, begotten by a vicious mode of avoiding it. From the master down to the meanest utensil, the best capacity for fulfilling the contemplated ends, is invariably the best economy; and the same reasoning which demonstrates the bad economy of a shattered loom, will demonstrate the bad economy of a shattered constitution, or an imperfect state of body. The cottagers who inflict upon themselves and their families the discomfort of cold houses, bad bedding and insufficient clothing, to acquire wealth, destroy the vigour both of the mind and body, necessary for obtaining the contemplated end, at which, of course, they can never arrive. The farmer who starves his slaves, is a still greater sufferer. He loses the profits produced by health, strength and alacrity; and suffers the losses caused by disease, short life, weakness and dejection. A portion, or the whole of the profit, arising from their increase is also lost. Moreover, he is exposed to various injuries from the vices inspired by severe privations, and rejects the best sponsor for his happiness, as well as prosperity, by banishing the solace of labour. In like manner, the more perfect, the more profitable are working animals and implements, and every saving by which the capacity of either to fulfil their destiny in the best manner is diminished, terminates with certainty in some portion of loss, and not unfrequently in extravagant waste. Even the object of manuring is vastly affected by the plight of those animals by which it is aided.

A pinching miserly system of agriculture, may indeed keep a farmer out of a prison, but it will never lodge him in a palace. Great profit depends on great improvements of the soil, and great improvements can never be made by penurious efforts. The discrimination between useful and productive, and useless and barren expenses, contains the agricultural secret, for acquiring happiness and wealth. A good farmer will sow the first with an open hand, and eradicate every seed of the other.

Liberality constitutes the economy of agriculture, and perhaps it is the solitary human occupation, to which the adage, "the more we give, the more we shall receive," can be justly applied. Liberality to the earth in manuring and culture, is the fountain of its bounty to us. Liberality to slaves and working animals, is the fountain of their profit. Liberality to domestic brutes, is the fountain of manure. By raising in proper modes a sufficiency of meat for our labourers, we bestow a strength upon their bodies, and a fertility upon the ground, either of which will recompense us for the expense of the meat, and the other will be a profit. The good work of a strong team, causes a profit beyond the bad work of a weak one, after deducting the additional expense of feeding it; and it saves moreover half the labour of a driver, sunk in following a bad one. Liberality in warm houses produces health, strength and comfort; preserves the lives of a multitude of domestic animals; causes all animals to thrive on less food; and secures from damage all kinds of crops. And liberality in the utensils of husbandry, saves labour to a vast extent, by providing the proper tools for doing the work both well and expeditiously.

Foresight is another item in the economy of agriculture. It consists in preparing work for all weather, and doing all work in proper weather, and at proper times. The climate of the United States makes the first easy, and the second less difficult than in most countries. Ruinous violations of this important rule are yet frequent from temper and impatience. Nothing is more common than a persistence in ploughing, making hay, cutting wheat, and other works, when a small delay might have escaped a great loss; and the labour employed to destroy, would have been employed to save. Crops of all kinds are often planted or sown at improper periods or unseasonably, in relation to the state of the weather, to their detriment or destruction, from the want of an arrangement of the work on a farm, calculated for doing every species of it precisely at the periods, and in the seasons, most likely to enhance its profit.

A third item in the economy of agriculture is not to kill time by doing the same thing twice over. However laboriously at work, we are doing nothing during one of the operations, and frequently worse than nothing, on account of the double detriment of tools, teams and clothing. The losses to farmers occasionally by this error, are prodigious under every defective system of agriculture, and under ours are enormously enhanced by the habit of sharing in the crop with an annual overseer. Shifts and contrivances innumerable are resorted to, for saving present time, by bad and perishable work, at an enormous loss of future time, until at length the several fragments of time thus destroyed, visibly appear spread over a farm, in the form of ruined houses, fences, orchards and soil; demonstrating that every advantage of such shifts is the parent of many disadvantages, and that a habit of finishing every species of work in the best mode, is the best economy.

The high importance of this article of agricultural economy, demands an illustration. Let us suppose that dead wood fencing will consume ten per centum of a farmer's time, which supposition devotes about thirty-six days in the year to that object. It would cost him five whole years in fifty. If his farm afforded stone, and his force could in one whole year make his enclosures of that lasting material, he would save four whole years by this more perfect operation; exclusive of the benefits gained by a longer life, or transmitted to his posterity. If his farm did not furnish stone, as live fences can be made with infinitely less labour than stone, his saving of time would be greater by raising them, but the donation to posterity less, from their more perishable nature. It seems to me that the time necessary to rear and repair live fences, is less than one tenth of that consumed by those of dead wood. By doing this article of work in a mode thus surpassing the present miserable fencing shifts in use, our farmers would gain the enormous profit of four years and a half in fifty, and an entire country, that of nine years in each hundred. Time constitutes profit or loss in agriculture, and many other employments. Such an enormous loss is itself sufficient to bankrupt the soil of a fine country. Transformed into an equivalent gain, the difference of eighteen percentum to the same country might retrieve it. The case simply consists of the difference between paying and receiving enormous usury, for the sake of growing rich.

I have selected a few items merely to attract the reader's attention to the economy of agriculture, that his own sagacity may pursue the subject beyond the limits assigned to these essays. It is one highly necessary to all practical men, and worthy of the minute consideration of the most profound mind; nor do I know one exhibiting to experience and talents a stronger invitation to make themselves useful.

NUMBER 59

The Pleasures of Agriculture

In free countries, are more, and in enslaved, fewer, than the pleasures of most other employments. The reason of it is, that agriculture both from its nature, and also as being generally the employment of a great portion of a nation, cannot be united with power, considered as an exclusive interest. It must of course be enslaved, wherever despotism exists, and its masters will enjoy more pleasures in that case, than it can ever reach. On the contrary, where power is not an exclusive, but a general interest, agriculture can employ its own energies for the attainment of its own happiness.

Under a free government it has before it the inexhaustible sources of human pleasure, of fitting ideas to substances, and substances to ideas; and of a constant rotation of hope and fruition.

The novelty, frequency and exactness of accommodations between our ideas and operations, constitutes the most exquisite source of mental pleasure. Agriculture feeds it with endless supplies in the natures of soils, plants, climates, manures, instruments of culture and domestic animals. Their combinations are inexhaustible, the novelty of results is endless, discrimination and adaption are never idle, and an unsatiated interest receives gratification in quick succession.

Benevolence is so closely associated with this interest, that its exertion in numberless instances, is necessary to foster it. Liberality in supplying its labourers with the comforts of life, is the best sponsor for the prosperity of agriculture, and the practice of almost every moral virtue is amply remunerated in this world, whilst it is also the best surety for attaining the blessings of the next. Poetry, in allowing more virtue to agriculture, than to any other profession, has abandoned her privilege of fiction, and yielded to the natural moral effect of the absence of temptation. The same fact is commemorated by religion, upon an occasion the most solemn, within the scope of the human imagination. At the awful day of judgment, the discrimination of the good from the wicked, is not made by the criterion of sects or of dogmas, but by one which constitutes the daily employment and the great end of agriculture. The judge upon this occasion has by anticipation pronounced, that to feed the hungry, clothe the naked, and give drink to the thirsty, are the passports to future happiness; and the divine intelligence which selected an agricultural state as a paradise for its first favourites, has here again prescribed the agricultural virtues as the means for the admission of their posterity into heaven.

With the pleasures of religion, agriculture unites those

of patriotism, and among the worthy competitors for pre-eminence in the practice of this cardinal virtue, a profound author assigns a high station to him who has made two blades of grass grow instead of one; an idea capable of a signal amplification, by a comparison between a system of agriculture which doubles the fertility of a country, and a successful war which doubles its territory. By the first the territory itself is also substantially doubled, without wasting the lives, the wealth, or the liberty of the nation which has thus subdued sterility, and drawn prosperity from a willing source. By the second, the blood pretended to be enriched, is spilt; the wealth pretended to be increased, is wasted; the liberty said to be secured, is immolated to the patriotism of a victorious army; and desolation in every form is made to stalk in the glittering garb of false glory, throughout some neighbouring country. Moral law decides the preference with undeviating consistency, in assigning to the nation, which elects true patriotism, the recompense of truth, and to the electors of the false, the expiation of error. To the respective agents, the same law assigns the remorses of a conquerour, and the quiet conscience of the agriculturist.

The capacity of agriculture for affording luxuries to the body, is not less conspicuous than its capacity for affording luxuries to the mind; it being a science singularly possessing the double qualities of feeding with unbounded liberality, both the moral appetites of the one, and the physical wants of the other. It can even feed a morbid love of money, whilst it is habituating us to the practice of virtue; and whilst it provides for the wants of the philosopher, it affords him ample room for the most curious and yet useful researches. In short, by the exercise it gives both to the body and to the mind, it secures health and vigour to both; and by combining a thorough knowledge of the real affairs of life, with a necessity for investigating the arcana of nature, and the strongest invitations to the practice of morality, it becomes the best architect of a complete man.

If this eulogy should succeed in awakening the attention of men of science to a skilful practice of agriculture, they will become models for individuals, and guardians for national happiness. The discoveries of the learned will be practiced by the ignorant; and a system which sheds happiness, plenty and virtue all around, will be gradually substituted for one, which fosters vice, breeds want, and begets misery.

Politicians (who ought to know the most, and generally know the least, of a science in which the United States are more deeply interested than in any other) will appear, of more practical knowledge, or at least of better theoretical instruction; and the hopeless habit of confiding our greatest interest to people most ignorant of it, will be abandoned.

The errors of politicians ignorant of agriculture, or their projects designed to oppress it, can only rob it of its pleasures, and consign it to contempt and misery. This revolution of its natural state, is invariably effected by war, armies, heavy taxes, or exclusive privileges. In two cases alone, have nations ever gained any thing by war. Those of repelling invasion and emigrating into a more fruitful territory. In every other case, the industrious of all professions suffer by war, the effects of which in its modern form, are precisely the same to the victorious and the vanquished nation. The least evil to be apprehended from victorious armies, is a permanent system of heavy taxation, than which, nothing can more vitally wound or kill the pleasures of agriculture. Of the same stamp, are exclusive privileges in every form; and to pillage or steal under the sanction of the statute books, is no less fatal to the happiness of agriculture, than the hierarchical tyranny over the soul, under the pretended sanction of God, or the feudal tyranny over the body, under the equally fraudulent pretence of defending the nation. In a climate and soil, where good culture never fails to beget plenty, where bad cannot produce famine, begirt by nature against the risque of invasion, and favoured by accident with the power of self government, agriculture can only lose its happiness by the folly or fraud of statesmen, or by its own ignorance.

NUMBER 60

The Rights of Agriculture

It is lamentable to confess, that this, to be a true, must be almost a negative number. This most useful and virtuous interest, enjoys no rights, except in the United States; and there it enjoys no exclusive rights, whilst the few in which it shares are daily contracted by the various arts of ambition and avarice. Every where else, agriculture is a slave; here she is only a dupe. Abroad she is condemned by avowed force to feed voluptuousness, avarice and ambition; here, she is deluded by flattery and craft, during fits of joy or of fury, to squander her property, to mortgage her labourers, and to shackle her freedom. Abroad, she suffers contempt, and is sensible of her degradation; here, she is a blind Quixote, mounted on a wooden horse, and persuaded by the acclamations of her foes, that she is soaring to the stars, whilst she is ready to tumble into the dust.

Privileges are rearing by laws all around at her expense, and whilst she is taught to believe that they will only take from her a few inconsiderable slips, they will at length draw a spacious circumvallation, within which will gradually grow up a power, beyond her control. Tricks, as well as inventions, are daily fortified with legal bulwarks, called charters, to transfer her wealth, and to secure frauds against her efforts. Capital in every form, save that of agriculture, is fed by taxes and by bounties, which she must pay; whilst not a single bounty is paid to her by capital in any form; and instead of being favored with some prizes in the lottery of society, she pays most, and is rewarded herself by the blanks of underwriting the projects of statesmen, and bearing the burthens of government.

The use of society, is to secure the fruits of his own industry and talents to each associator. Its abuse consists in artifice or force, for transferring those fruits from some partners to others. Of this abuse, that interest covering the majority of partners is the victim. And the difficulty of discriminating laws, transferring such fruits for the benefit of society, from those having in view the gratification of avarice and ambition, produces a sympathy and combination between these distinct kinds of law. As the members of the government, and members of legal frauds, both extract power and income from the majority, they are apt to coalesce; and each party to favour the designs of its ally, in their operations upon the common enemy. Hence governments love to create exclusive rights, and exclusive rights cling to governments. The ligament of parent and child, binds them together, and the power creating these abuses, must make them props for its support, or instruments for its subversion. Its election between these alternatives is certain, and society is thus unavoidably thrown into two divisions. One containing all those who pay, and the other those who receive contributions, required either for public use, or to foster private avarice or ambition. Good government is graduated by this latter kind of contribution thus unfortunately allied to the former. The highest amount constitutes the worst, and the lowest, the best possible species of government. But as both are drawn from the majority of every society, whenever the agricultural interest covers that majority, this interest is the victim of the coalition; and as it almost universally does cover this majority, the agricultural interest is almost universally its slaves.

The consequences to agriculture will be demonstrated by converting this coalition between government and its creatures, or of all who receive tolls given by law, into a political pope, and placing in his mouth an address to agriculture, in a parody of Ernulphus's form of excommunication.*

"May you be taxed in your lands, your slaves, your houses, your carriages, your horses, your clothing, your liquors, your coffee, your tea, and your salt. May you be taxed by banks, by protecting duties, by embargoes, and by charters of a thousand different forms. May the exemption of your exports from taxation be removed, and may you then be taxed through your wheat, your corn,

---

* Modeled on the oft-quoted curse of Ernulphus, Bishop of Rochester (1040–1124). A probable source for Taylor's knowledge of this proverbial figure is Book III, chapters 10-11 of Laurence Sterne's *Life and Opinions of Tristram Shandy* (1759–1767), where the curse appears in full.

your tobacco, your cotton, your rice, your indigo, your sugar, your hemp, your live stock, your beef, your pork, your tar, pitch and turpentine, your onions, your cheese, and your potatoes. May you be taxed for the support of government, or to enrich exclusive or chartered interests, through every article you import, and through every article you export, by duties called protecting, but intended to take away your constitutional protection against taxation for the benefit of capitalists. May you be taxed through every article produced by your labour or necessary to your subsistence, comfort and pleasure, by exercises. And whilst every species of your products, and of your consumption are thus taxed, may your capital, being visible, be moreover taxed in various modes. May all these taxes whether plain or intricate (after deducting the small sum necessary to produce the genuine end of society) be employed in enriching capitalists, and buying soldiers, placemen and contractors, to make you submissive to usurpations, and as quiet under your burthens, as a martyr tied to the stake, under the flames. After you have been taxed as far as you can pay, may you by the bounty of God Almighty be moreover mortgaged up to your value or credit, for the benefit of the said coalition of capitalists. And finally, may none of this good and useful coalition, to whom is given the wealth of this world, as the kingdom of heaven is to the pope and his clergy, be taxed in their stock or principal held under any law or charter whatsoever; nor in their capital employed in any manufacture or speculation, nor in any profit drawn from such principal stock or capital; nor through any of their sinecures, salaries, contracts or incomes; but on the contrary, may such stock, principal, capital, profits, salaries, contracts, and sinecures, be constantly fostered by bounties in various injurious forms, to be paid by you, you damned dirty working, productive bitch, agriculture." Throughout the world, agriculture, like one of Ernulphus's contrite excommunicants, responds, amen, to this pious invocation.

Throughout the world, agriculture has enjoyed, and in England, continues to enjoy, one of the rights in which she has a share in the United States; that of a voice in elections. And throughout the world, this right has been unable to shield her against an anathema, which prescribes for her as perfect a hell, as the formula of Ernulphus prescribes for his heretick. Let the agricultural interest of the United States, pause here and look around. Is a blind confidence in a right so universally ineffectual, a sufficient safeguard for its freedom and happiness? To me it seems, that an interest can never be long free, which blindly confides in a coalition, whose object it is to draw from that interest, power and wealth. That the major interest must be as cunning, as wise and as watchful, as the minor, or that the minor interest will enslave it. And that agriculture must as attentively keep her eyes upon the coalition, to avoid its operations upon her, as the coalition does upon agriculture, for the purpose of transferring to its members portions of her power and wealth, whenever she slumbers.

Hence have arisen the political suggestions to be found in these essays. I cannot discern much good in an improvement of agriculture, to get luxury, voluptuousness and tyranny for a few, and wretchedness for a multitude.

The best cultivated country in the world, abounds most in paupers and thieves. Agriculture must be a politician to avoid this fate; and those who ridicule her pretensions to knowledge in this science, intend by persuading her to repose in a blind confidence, built upon the frail right of election, to expose her to it. How can she even judiciously elect, if she cannot or will not judge of publick measures, by the light of her own interest?

The moral consequence of this supineness or ignorance, is, that social happiness gradually becomes the dependent of a minority, and of course it is provided for, by continually subtracting from the happiness of a majority. The visible immorality of this, demonstrates the virtue, as well as wisdom of suggestions designed to obstruct it.

The remaining right in which agriculture participates, in common with all other interests, having any thing to export, is bestowed by the constitutional prohibition of duties upon exports. This right originated in state jealousies, and not from a disposition to favour agriculture, but yet it is her best security, for the preservation of that portion of our government, which will longest be sensible of her elective influence; and its relinquishment will be the most fatal wound which can be inflicted on her. The coalition I have described will try every art in her most unguarded moments, to snatch it from her, and it will be the last relinquishment it will need. To determine whether her elective influence can bear further wounds, let agriculture re-survey the legislation of our whole term of independence, and compare the catalogues she may select, of laws for creating or fostering privileges and exclusive interests, with those for fostering herself; and let this comparison form the criterion for ascertaining her legislative influence. Thus only can she judiciously increase this influence, if it has settled too low, or diminish it, if it has raised too high. There is no fair mode of judging, except by these legislative acts. To infer, that the agricultural interest influences legislatures, because it chiefly elects them, would be like inferring, that the French nation influences the tribunate, because they wholly elect it. Let agriculture therefore hold fast the solitary security she enjoys in common with her industrious associates, against the ambition of usurpers, and the avarice of capitalists, nor be deluded into the absurd notion, that it is wise to relinquish the only peculium of industry, for the sake of some temporary operation upon foreign nations, inevitably resulting upon herself in the form of retaliation, whilst the protection of exports against taxation, will be gone forever.

NUMBER 61

Agriculture and the Militia

The rocks of our salvation; as they are called by legislatures, presidents, governours, and toast-makers,
throughout the United States; and hard rocks indeed they
need be, to withstand the saws, wedges, and chisels, made
by law, to cut, split and chip them to pieces. It is probable that more talents were wasted upon the bank of the
United States, at each of its epochs, than have been expended for the improvement of these national fortresses,
for securing wealth and independence, since the revolution. Edifice, after edifice, has been raised upon their
ruins; but the new structures resemble the venerable fab-
ricks from whence they are torn, as the modern huts
raised of its ruins resemble the ancient city of Palmyra.

A pernicious little army (pernicious as constituting a
reason for neglecting the militia), a species of marine
preparation, whose most striking features are decay, imbecility and expense; and an awful unconstitutional precedent, for resorting to a volunteer militia, officered by the

President instead of the States, have dismantled one fortress, and all the arts to enrich capital and speculation legerdemain, by paper, at the expense of property and industry, as practised in England, are playing upon the other.

When the future historian of our republick, shall search for acts of patriotism, and matter for biography, the contrast between the heroes who have created, and the politicians who have ruined a nation, will afford him ample room for exhausting the strongest phrases of eulogy and censure. The first was not effected by enfeebling the heart, nor will the second be avoided by impoverishing the soil and its cultivators; by beguiling the militia of its power and importance, with substitutions founded in the pretext of diminishing its duty, but preparing the means of usurpation for some ambitious president; and by taxing agriculture in various crafty modes, under pretence of enriching it, but in fact to enrich capitalists at its expense.

The patriots of the revolution have chiefly retired to the enjoyment of a treasure, deposited beyond the schemes of craft, leaving to their successors two specious fields as productive of glory, as the field of war was to them. Far from exhausting the resources for gaining the transporting consciousness of having benefited our country, they left for these successors the creation of a proud militia and a fertile country, as equally meriting national admiration and gratitude, with the feats which secured our independence, and placed prosperity within our reach. But of what avail is it, that one set of patriots should have cut away the causes which enfeebled our militia, and impoverished our agriculture, if another does not enable us to reap from their valour the rewards which excited it? After wading through the calamities of war near to these rewards, to reject them, one by neglect, and the other by the preference of a harpy which always eats and never feeds, seems only consistent with the policy of the British parliament, which excited the resistance of the revolutionary heroes. Had they been told that they were fighting to destroy the militia, and to make agriculture food for charter and paper capital, they would have discerned no reason for making themselves food for powder.

It would be easy to shew that agriculture never can experience fair treatment without a sound militia, but it is a subject too extensive and important to be considered in this light way, and therefore they are only exhibited in union, in the concluding essay, to remind the reader, that they are political twins, one of whom never lives long free, after the other dies.

Executive, legislative and festive encomiums of these twins, which ought to be called "Liberty and prosperity," though the unhappy delusions of fervour, produce the knavish effects of flattery; they prevent us from acquiring a militia and an agriculture, which deserve praise (false praise always excludes real merit), and keep us without laws for raising either to mediocrity, much less to perfection. I do not believe that these encomiums are generally the artifices of deliberate vice and secret purpose, to impose upon the enthusiastic and unwary, in pursuance of the precedents so often exhibited by rapacious priests clothed in the garb of sanctity; but yet rapacity may sometimes assume the language of patriotism, to keep the people blind to the dangers which threaten, and to the measures which can save them.

The good humour of the festive board will bear illustrations of these assertions, with less discomfort than cold design, or deluded negligence; and therefore, however inconsistent it may be with the gravity and importance of our subject, an aversion for giving pain to any one, induces me to supply it with the following toasts.

THE MILITIA . . . The Rock of our Liberty.

Unarmed, undisciplined, and without uniformity, substituted by an ineffectual navy, an ineffectual army, and paper volunteers, officered by the president.

Unpatronized even at the expense of a gun boat.

Flattered and despised.

Taught self contempt, instead of a proud and erect spirit. *Nine cheers.*

AGRICULTURE . . . The fountain of our wealth.

A land killer.

A payer of bounties and receiver of none.

A beautifier of towns and a sacrificer of the country.

A cultivator for stock, without stock for cultivation.

Giving its money to those who will give it flattery.

A weight in the legislative scales of the United States, as much heavier than a feather, as a feather is heavier than nothing.

Its labour steeped in an infusion of thievery, dissatisfaction and sedition, by a mixture of bond and free negroes.

Producing 40,000,000 dollars annually for exportation, bearing most taxes for publick benefit, and taxed in various modes for the private benefit of 300,000,000 dollars worth of capitalists who pay no taxes.

Out of a remnant of the 40,000,000 dollars exported, compelled by protecting duties to pay heavy bounties for the encouragement of manufactures, already amounting to above 150,000,000 dollars annually. *Nine cheers more.*

A few words, at parting, to the reader, will close these essays. If he is of the courteous nature which loves to give and to receive flattery; or if his interest tugs him violently against them, he may disbelieve the plainest truths they contain, or at least reject them as being told in too blunt a style. If he is ignorant of agriculture or a devotee of a party or an idol, he will rather presume, that our agriculture is perfect and undefrauded, than take the trouble of enabling himself to judge; or silently swallow the grossest errours, than give up his superstition. These papers never contemplated the desperate hope of obtaining the attention of any one of these characters. Half the profit of agriculture, must undoubtedly convince the several tribes of capitalists, that it flourishes exceedingly. The idolator will rather embrace the stake than truth, and the agriculturist who prefers ignorance to knowledge, though these hasty essays constituted a complete system of husbandry, would be as little benefited by them, as a lawyer or a physician who practised by deputy, would be by the reports of Coke, or the dispensatory of Cullen.* Yet to those who would think and inquire, opinions slowly and cautiously admitted, upon various views of national interest, without a motive likely to mislead or deceive, might afford suggestions capable of becoming subservient to better talents, awakened to the discussion of subjects so momentous to national happiness. To awaken such, was the summit of the author's design. (Note G.)

---

* William Cullen (1710–1790), the famous Scots physician, noted for his skill in diagnosis and as a teacher in his discipline.

NUMBER 62

Cotton

The cultivation of this crop, so important to the United States, was not overlooked, but omitted, because it was probably better understood by others. But not having seen any thing published in relation to it, and having paid some attention to it for many years, it is not any longer neglected. The root of cotton sinks deep into the earth. Hence it requires deep culture. This is not as attainable by the hoe as by the plough. The best mode of effecting it which I have tried, is to lay off the ground in four feet ridges, raising those ridges as high as possible, and opening the middle furrows as deep as possible. This operation should take place in the fall or early in the winter, leaving the land in that state until it is time to plant the seed. Then these ridges should be reversed, making them very high upon the furrows. The exposure of the furrows to the atmosphere through the winter, will render the earth more friable at their bottoms, and more pervious to the roots of the cotton. Its benefit will be more or less, as the soil may be light or stiff; but the fertilizing qualities of the atmosphere will make it of some value, even to sandy soils. Further, the first deep ploughing in raising the ridges, will bury whatever vegetable matter may lie on the surface, reduce it by the spring to some degree of putrescence, and cause it to be converted into food for the cotton, through the summer. And the second will bury the seeds of grass or weeds so deep, that many of them will fail to vegetate, and thereby the labour of cultivation will be diminished, whilst the crop, being less infested with those rivals for subsistence, will be increased. As the cotton plant grows until frost, it is generally made more productive by early planting. The quickest mode of planting I have tried, is to open the tops of the ridges with a small trowel hoe plough, drawn by two horses, that one may walk in each furrow, and a straight line may be made to receive the seed. This plough has a mould board on each side, to raise and deposit on both sides of its furrow, earth sufficient to cover the seed. A line is carried fastened to a staff at each end, across the ridges, having marks of coloured stuff at the distances designed for the plant. The planters follow the line, each taking one row, drop the seed at the marks, and cover it with the earth provided on each side by the plough, using the hand which deposits the seed for that purpose. This mode of planting is, however, only calculated for those districts wherein cotton is cultivated on a small scale, merely for family use. Whenever it is cultivated for exportation, a drill plough ought undoubtedly to be resorted to. I have seen one made so as to deposit Indian corn at such a distance and in such quantity as was required, opening the furrow, placing and covering the corn all at one operation. Such ploughs ought to be used upon the ridges I have de-

scribed, previously bringing the cotton seed by the use of
ashes and water, or by substituting gypsum for the ashes,
and a little rubbing, into a state of easy separation. I have
tried gypsum in the proportion of a bushel to the same
quantity of seed, and was satisfied of its benefits; but the
experiment was only made two or three times, on account
of the unfavourable nature of the climate where I live,
for the culture of cotton. If gypsum, as I believe, may be
so applied, as gradually to enrich land, then it must ultimately benefit this plant. If its effect in reducing vegetable
matter into vegetable food constitutes the mode of its
operation, then it is peculiarly adapted to this reduction of
the cotton stalks, whenever the same field is successively
cultivated. The soil best adapted to cotton, is peculiarly
proper for the use of the drill plough, as clods or stones
constitute the only serious obstacle to it. In good land I
plant the cotton at the distance of two feet, and thin it to
two stalks, so that it stands at four feet by two apart, with
two stalks at a place. But the thickness of the plant must
be graduated by the quality of the land. Topping and suc-
couring also, in the climate I am used to, increases the
crop and improves the staple. The first is speedily performed by a keen small scythe with a proper handle, and
should take place when the cotton has disclosed as much
bloom, as it may have time to bring to perfection. Useless
bloom, which it will continue to throw out if permitted,
will impoverish the crop, and impair the quality of the
wool. The little success which has attended the raising
of sheep's wool, in those states adapted to cotton, renders
the latter an object of great importance. There is no article
of our agriculture, the raising of food excepted, more
worthy of attention.

NUMBER 63

Hay and Fodder

G reat losses are annually sustained in some parts of the United States in making hay, and in others, in curing corn blades, commonly called fodder. Mine, in a course of many years, have I think amounted to a moiety, of the crops; and most of the expedients I have resorted to for avoiding these losses, have been but partially beneficial. Grass loses much both in quantity and substance by an exposure to the sun in curing it, and fodder more, being thus exposed in small bundles. Both, and particularly the last, suffer greatly by dews and rains. This year I have made the most promising experiment for remedying these evils. A large meadow in bottom land, of a grass called red top or herd's grass, was cut in dry weather, and shocked in large shocks quite green, but dry, that is, not wet with either dew or rain; in the following mode. Four sticks of five feet long, of the thickness of a man's wrist or more, were set up in a square of two feet wide at bottom, and meeting at top in a pyramidal form, where the shock was to stand. One at least of these sticks should be forked at top, to keep them steady whilst the hay is putting round them. A round log, about six feet long and six inches in diameter, was laid upon the ground, with one end reaching to the centre of the two feet square, between the sticks, and the other raised upon a fork about eighteen inches, for the purpose of enlarging the flue presently mentioned, lest it should be closed by the pressure of the hay, and that the log may be more easily drawn out, when the shock is finished. Around and over the sticks, the shock was made, its top reaching two or three feet above the top of the sticks. The purpose of the log, was to make a flue for the admission of fresh air into the centre of the shock, and the expulsion of the air heated by the fermentation of the grass in curing. The flues were made to face the point from which the wind usually blows at the time of hay making. If any flues happened to be closed by the pressure of the grass, they were easily opened by a smaller and pointed log; or when the largeness of a shock threatened this inconvenience, it was effectually prevented by inserting into the flue a short forked stick as soon as the log was removed, to hold up the hay. As the logs are removed as soon as the shock is finished, two or three are sufficient for following a dozen mowers. The hay thus made is the best I ever saw, and the efficacy of the mode of curing it, was strongly supported, by the growing grass under the shocks having been uninjured, whereas I never left shocks so long in one spot before, without its having been killed by the undissipated fermentation of the hay in curing. Corn blades, or fodder, sustain an immense loss, even in dry weather, by two or three days' exposure to the sun and dews; and in wet they are nearly ruined. For an experiment, I shocked them in the mode just explained, quite green and dry; but I chiefly allowed them from four to eight hours sun, before they were shocked. Thus was made the best fodder I have seen. But the weather was favourable. The ends of the blades were laid outwards, and the shocks bound at top by a rope made of the blades.

NUMBER 64

The Present and Political State of Agriculture

After all, in these topicks, which occupy the twelve first numbers of this book, must the remedy be found for the decreasing fertility of a great portion of the United States, which if not arrested, must terminate in want, famine, and depopulation. All classes of people have a deep interest in preventing these dreadful evils. The towns are already suffering from mean, dear, and insufficient supplies. The decay of agriculture, and a bad police, are certainly the causes of these conspicuous effects. A bad police produces a fraudulent traffick by slaves, free people of colour, and a few bad citizens, discourages honest labour, and compels it to require compensation in its prices, for the risque of theft, or to shrink from the losses and vexations it occasions. So far as the evil is caused by this bad police, the remedy obviously lies in a better. A better can only be effected by laws, which by rendering the products of labour more secure, would tend to its encouragement, and greatly advance the comfort, virtue, and happiness of the community. Of this nature would be laws for protecting live fences. They would prevent wasteful trespasses, produce judicious grazing, increase the quality and quantity of meats, as well as of vegetables, and vastly improve the cadaverous aspect of a great portion of the United States.

But the root of the evil lies still deeper. Why is it, whilst our free form of government has bestowed life and energy on every other occupation, that agriculture alone languishes? Patriotism and benevolence, conscious of this calamity, have unfortunately turned their eyes towards the local projects of roads and canals, which however desirable, are remedies incapable of reaching the true cause of the calamity; and even capable of aggravating it in some degree, by causing an unthrifty expense, generally oppressive, for the sake of local advantages of uncompensating value. Such undertakings are naturally begotten by a previous flourishing state of agriculture, without which they would be destitute of the food necessary for their subsistence. Success even then must depend upon the interest, economy and industry of individuals. When a republick becomes an undertaker of agricultural improvements, the expenditure of the public money terminates in the same way, as if it should purchase and cultivate a great number of farms for the public benefit. It only awakens efforts for salary, and results in loss and disappointment. The honour or contempt arising from such projects in free governments, is so widely divided, as to leave little or no excitement for labour, and industry in their execution, save what arises from a competition for contracts, and a struggle for appropriations. Hence the example of a tyrant or a monarch, who reaps all he sows, and is therefore stimulated by his personal interest, popularity and glory, is no precedent for us. He, indeed, by his power, can force nature for a time out of her course, raise cities in deserts at the expense of his subjects, or erect stupendous works of art, without a benefit to mankind, correspondent to their cost. But nature should be our guide. This has decreed that a good state of agriculture must precede that which it begets. It inevitably produces, by an easy birth, the best modes of transportation, by awakening the efforts of individuals.

The bad state of agriculture on the navigable waters, demonstrates, that its cause does not lie in any inconveniences of transportation, and therefore I can discern no other cause of sufficient force to produce this visible effect, except the combined weight of taxation, banking and protecting duties, lying heavily upon agricultural effort. The peculiar state of our agriculture, in constituting almost the only source of national income, and in being obliged to find foreign markets, leaves it almost exclusively exposed to these burdens, because the consumers of that portion of its labours, from which its profit arises, live beyond their reach, and contribute nothing towards their alleviation. They contribute towards the alleviation of agricultural burdens at home. Such is the case with the consumers of the corn, wheat, cotton, rice and tobacco, of the United States. The bounties paid by agriculture to manufacturers, probably exceed the amount of their contributions. And banking being wholly supported by productive labor, whilst it also withdraws from taxation a great portion of the wealth of the nation, is itself a heavy item of these burdens, instead of sharing in them. In this accumulated pressure upon agriculture, is, in my opinion, to be found the true cause of its bad and declining state. I question whether there is an object of taxation so heavily burdened in proportion to its ability, in any other country. Its exports are the only resource for meeting the demands upon it, direct and indirect, and such of its wants which must be supplied by money. The computation in reference to these in the preceding part of this book, is already left far behind, by the rapid accumulation of its burdens, to demonstrate which, the progress of taxation only, is exhibited by the following extracts from official reports, from its two extremes and its medium.

By an estimate of the secretary of the treasury (Mr. Hamilton) of January 1, 1791, the expenses of the federal government for that year, excluding interest on the national debt, and including the extraordinary expense of an existing Indian war, amounted to $ 740,232

By his estimate, dated Jan. 23, 1792, including the interest of the national debt, these expenses amounted to 3,688,043

By an estimate of the secretary of the treasury (Mr. Gallatin) dated October 24, 1803, these expenses, excluding the interest of the public debt, amounted to 2,500,000

By the same estimate including that interest, to 6,300,000

By an estimate of the secretary of the treasury (Mr. Dallas), these expenses for the year 1816, amounted to } $42,884,269

But deducting all articles supposed by him to be temporary, the permanent expenses of the government amounted to } 19,288,669

In 1794 the exports of the United States of articles both foreign and domestic, by the official report, amounted to } 26,011,788

From these documents it appears, that the expenses of the federal government were above fifty-seven times higher in 1816 than in 1791, and near seven times higher than in 1803. That the ordinary or permanent expenses of the government had trebled between 1791 and 1803; that in 1816, they were above twenty-two times higher than in 1791, and near three times higher than in 1803.

In 1794, excluding foreign articles, re-exported, the native were about $20,000,000 in value; now they may amount to forty millions. And it may be assumed as a fact, that the population of the United States has about doubled since 1791 or 1794. If either the increase of people or of exports had graduated taxation, it ought in 1816, to have exhibited only double the amount of the taxes of 1792. But taxes are in all countries graduated by cunning, rapacity and ambition, and in none, by these scales.

The idea, however, of justifying an increase of taxation by an increase of either, is fallacious. It makes people the property of governments and not the wealth and strength of nations. When an increase of people, by producing a greater division of public burdens, diminishes the contribution of every individual, it is thus, and thus only, an increase of national wealth. But if the contributions of every individual, remain as high as before this increase of people, it inflicts an additional degree of poverty upon the former inhabitants, upon whom the difficulty of subsistence is increased by an accession of population, to any given space; and this accession to the expense of subsistence, brought by an accession to the population, is a real loss to the former inhabitants, unless their burdens are rendered lighter, by being divided among more people. But if the burdens of the former inhabitants are increased under the pretext of an additional population, this increase, added to the increased difficulty of living, converts an increased population, which ought to be a blessing, into a curse, and from being a cause of wealth, into an instrument of oppression, and the author of poverty. In like manner an accession to population, used as a pretext for increasing standing armies, produces national weakness, instead of national strength, by the expense of their maintenance, by their gradual transformation into a counterpoise to the nation, and by fostering an unmilitary reliance upon them. Thus, by using an increase of population as a pretext for increasing taxation and standing armies, the maxim, "that it adds to the wealth and strength of nations," is completely reversed, by making it the cause of poverty, and weakness. Let the facts to sustain this reversal, be glanced at. In 1791, our neighbouring enemies, the Indians, were much more numerous than at present, and our own population only half as much. What then can justify a great addition to our standing army, except that the nation is much weaker now than it was then? With respect to taxation, it is still more evident, that an increase of population is made to produce national poverty, when it is considered to what an extent it has been used as a pretext for increasing it, whilst our exports of native commodities and population, have preserved a close alliance with each other. The state of agriculture, in consequence of a reversal of the old maxim, "that people are the wealth and strength of nations," into the new one, "that they are the property of governments," is the effect of our increase of taxation for the permanent expenses of government, from $3,688,043 to $17,288,669, in twenty four years. Add to this item, the state taxes, the bounties to banks and manufacturers, the increased difficulty of subsistence, and unavoidable private expenses, and it will be evident, that as the far greater part of the total must fall upon agriculture, the demands upon her have, at length, exceeded the whole amount of her share of the national exports. From this cause, therefore, I deduce the bad state of agriculture in the United States.

Another idea has been urged as an auxiliary to that we have just examined, still more fallacious, and equally ruinous to agriculture; namely, "that a depreciation of money, makes it just to increase salaries and taxation." Our agriculture cannot reimburse itself for our local depreciation, because its prices are fixed chiefly by prices abroad. All other interests can, because their prices are not regulated by foreign prices. As agriculture is the chief victim of this local depreciation, instead of redress, to present her with a new calamity, because she is suffering a great one already, is manifestly unjust. Such a doctrine exposes our governments to great temptation. By producing a local and temporary depreciation of an artificial currency, and making it a pretext for raising salaries, and then removing the device, they might make what stock-jobbers call "a good speculation." An occasional temporary advance abroad of agricultural prices, would also furnish them with frequent pretexts of the same kind; and as the salaries are never diminished because agricultural prices fall, the effect to agriculture, from nominal high prices, produced by a local depreciation, is a real increase of taxation, and from temporary high prices, a permanent increase of taxation; so that high prices of all kinds, instead of relieving her, are only in the end, an aggravation of her oppressions. The case of a famine displays their pretext for increasing salaries in its true countenance. A famine of bread, tobacco, cotton, or rice abroad, or of specie at home, will cause an increase of prices. Are such famines, particularly the last, good reasons for increasing salaries? In like manner, prices will rise as the fertility of land diminishes. Does the remedy lie in taxing these lands higher, the poorer they become? But if the fluctuation of prices is a proper rule for graduating salaries, then a fair reciprocity between the government and the people, re-requires their reduction when prices fall, as well as their increase when prices rise, in order to comply with the rule itself; yet governments never remember this pretended principle, when its application is in favour of the people.

It is further said, that salaries ought to be graduated by a reference to the computed value of the acceptor's time, and that high salaries obtain the most merit and talents.

Under the first idea, every member of a legislature ought to have a different salary, each man's time being of distinct value; or if the salaries are to be alike, however different each member's time may be in value to himself, then to do justice to a few whose time may be of great value, a manifest injustice must be done to the public, by giving equal salaries to a multitude, far beyond this value. And therefore if this idea should regulate salaries, it is not improbable that those who pay themselves may highly respect the motive of compensating a few great men for their time, whilst it will also amply appreciate their own. But this rule for compensations can never be observed. The public service most detrimental to the personal and private affairs of individuals, is that of the militia. Compare the risque of life and health, and the loss of time often necessary for the subsistence of a helpless family, with the sacrifice made even by the most eminent member of congress; or compare the mass of suffering in both these lines of public service. Is it not obvious that this rule for compensations, neither has nor can be fairly carried into execution.

Whether high salaries invite talents and open the door to merit, is a fact, depending upon history. From this, truth seems to me to lie in the reverse of the proposition. They appear rather to have excited rapacity, and opened the door to arts for gratifying ambition and selfishness. The case of the British parliament is, I think, unfortunately cited to prove the affirmative of the proposition. And to make it answer this purpose, an assertion that its members receive no compensation, is coupled with the citation. But the truth is, that these members do receive, by pensions and offices, compensations so enormous, as to have produced a disregard for the direct moderate compensation, and yet to have awakened all the energies and frauds of avarice and ambition to carry elections, and to acquire the fruits of success. Has the great profit arising from a seat in the house of commons, carried into that body merit and talents, or artifice and corruption? If the English parliament should now endow themselves with a high direct compensation, retaining the indirect compensation of executive patronage, would it be purged of corruption, and regenerated into patriotism? This would place it nearly in the state of our congress. At home it is such, whether more merit or talents have appeared in legislatures, as they have been more amply replenished with wages and patronage, the chance of drawing a prize from which, is often valued even here more highly than the direct wages. As to the argument that high wages open to the poor, the door of dignity, it is only the plausible pretext of those pleading for an increase of their own income, at the expense of the poor whom they pretend to favour.

Another argument remains of itself sufficient to destroy the policy of high wages, and its effect, heavy taxation, if all those hitherto urged, were feeble. They beget inveterate parties and factions, which successively resort to every pausible pretext of increasing their income and power; transmit to their successors precedents which operate as salves for conscience, and poisons for patriotism, and universally terminate in the subversion of a free and moderate government.

Some principle, by which to settle the important question of wages, is still wanting, capable of guarding the people against temporary pretext, and individual selfishness; and it seems to me to reside in the following ideas. Public servants are either public property or mere hirelings. In the first character they owe something to society beyond the services purchased by wages. This debt is due for the multitude of benefits derived from society, and ought therefore to constitute a greater portion of their compensation, as the government is freer. To the militia it constitutes the chief compensation for their services. What can be more manifestly unjust, than to make social duty the chief compensation for the hard sufferings of militia services, and yet to bestow on civil services a compensation capable of exciting faction, avarice and ambition, and of gradually destroying those blessings purchased by the great body of the people by the greatest sacrifices, almost gratuitous? If public servants are to be considered as mere hirelings, then the principle ought to be extended to military services, and in both cases, the public and its servants ought to be considered as free contracting parties, and in both the price of the commodity ought to be settled by the rate of the market, by a mutual agreement. But as the militia are coerced, and as civil public servants possess the valuable and exclusive privilege of refusing to serve, is it not highly unjust to the nation, to give a price for the commodity, not only higher than the same thing, of a quality as good and even better can be bought at, for the end of killing its free and easy government by a poisonous plethora of expense and taxation. In my opinion, high salaries, by awakening avarice, faction and intrigue, have a tendency to destroy a sense of duty, virtue, honour and patriotism; and that low salaries have universally produced the best public servants. I conclude that salaries ought to be graduated by the public good, and not for the benefit of individuals.

Taxation ought to be governed by some principle, and when understood, this principle ought to be enforced by the people, to shield themselves against those frauds of faction, avarice, and ambition, used in modern times to steal the liberties of nations, in lieu of the braver modes resorted to by the tyrants of antiquity.

What, it may be asked, have these remarks to do with agriculture? The answer must depend upon the opinion of the reader. Should he think with me, that the burdens heaped upon it constitute a chief cause of its decay, nothing can restore it to health and prosperity but its own knowledge of this fact, by which it may be induced to remove some of the pressures under which it is languishing; and therefore none of the subjects of this book, can be more instrumentally connected with the prosperity of agriculture. In England, the pressure upon agriculture and manufactures is defended by armies and the difficulties of emigration, yet it is sorely felt; here, where the inferiority of soil, renders it much less capable of bearing this pressure, the same arts of taxation and paper frauds, will, I fear, produce still more calamitous consequences.

NOTES

NOTE A

(Page 114)

U pon a review of the foregoing essays, originally offered to the pubic in a newspaper, without foreseeing
that they would appear in a book, a few expressions have
been expunged, lest their political doctrines should be
ascribed to party motives. These proceeded from an
opinion, that the inculcation of sound political principles,
was the only mode of avoiding the evils incident to a
blind zeal in favour of the projects of any set of men
exercising power; or of preserving a consistency between professions and actions. To an union between
public interest and public knowledge, the world is indebted for the benefit it has derived from the Grecian
and Roman republics, and to the want of such an union,
the regions which once sustained them, for their present
state of slavery. No association to inflict or to avoid
oppression, can succeed, if it is ignorant of the means
for procuring success in both objects. Political knowledge is necessary to the people for one end, as to princes,

orders, factions, and usurpers, for the other. Without it, the lords of the soil in the United States, must gradually become the slaves of some legal aristocracy; and exposed by political ignorance to the rapine of an endless catalogue of exclusive factitious interests, would soon resemble monkies stript by the superior intelligence of man, of diamonds they had dug out of the earth. As agriculture, with its dependencies, almost covers the whole public interest of the United States, so degrading a consequence of its political ignorance, demonstrates how intimate its connexion ought to be with politics. The first produces; the latter secures. Exclusive political knowledge, creates exclusive legal interests. A complete agricultural treatise, would comprise the soundest agricultural principles, chymical, experimental and political; and the inutility of the two first items might be more plausibly asserted, because they only teach men how to labour, than that of the last, which teaches them how to live happily.

Funding, legal enrichment of all kinds, and the perpetual effort of those who exercise power to increase it, may here, as every where else, enslave the majority and the public interest. By funding only, agriculture may be soon made tributary to the dealers in credit, chiefly located by the nature of their employment in a few large cities. The dispersed situation of the agricultural and of every general interest, renders its share of the vast acquisitions to be made by the credit trade, trifling; and the circumstance of its constituting the chief item of the general interest, renders its share of the contributions to support it enormous. It is a trade for getting premiums and interest without money, upon the credit of those who pay both; and for inflicting an annual tribute on those who have the credit, until they prove its goodness by paying coin for paper. If agriculture or the public interest borrows ten millions in paper notes, furnished by the partnership between banking and funding, at a premium of ten per centum and an annual interest of six, in fifteen years it pays a sum in specie, equal to the debt, but both the debt and annual tribute still remain. The public interest cannot transform itself into an exclusive interest for carrying on this credit trade, because it must be the payer not the receiver; nor can it have any thing of consequence to lend, because the projects requiring loans, incapacitate it for a lender, especially so far as it is agricultural. A liability to pay, and an inability to lend, generate exactly the same relative situation, between these two interests, which subsists between two nations, when one is tributary to the other. Upon the credit of this liability, that of the paper loaned to governments, depends. The government in fact gives the public credit to associations for vending paper stock, which these associations sell back to the government for a good premium and a perpetual interest, for which premium and interest the only consideration they pay, is an adherence to the will of the donor, against the will of the public interest, by which the donation is paid. The impoverishment produced by this species of tribute, is demonstrated by the difference in the price of products in the paying and receiving districts, by their different agricultural appearances, and by emigrations. The effects of a tribute, collected in distant provinces, and expended at particular places, are uniformly the same, inflicted either by a tyrant or a patriot. Ought not agriculture to understand this political machine?

An amendment to the constitution for empowering the general government to tax exports and to make local regulations, would comprise a boundless power of sacrificing agricultural and exporting districts to the interest of credit dealers, to transitory political projects of men in power, and to the passions of non-exporting districts; and although the apparent favours to the latter would be delusive and entrapping, they would suffice to divide agriculture itself, into two parties neutralizing each other's defensive ability, and to subject both like all large inert bodies, to less powerful, but more intelligent and active exclusive interests. Ought it not to understand political principles to meet occurrences of this kind?

As no interest covering the majority of a nation can avoid oppression except under a free form of government, because the end of every other form, is to foster partial interests, should not agriculture be able to see the importance of maintaining the division of power between the general and state governments? The latter are her intimate associates and allies. The general government is already in a far greater degree, the associate and ally of patronage, funding, armies, and of many other interests subsisting upon her. If it should by new powers be enabled to enlist still more of such dangerous auxiliaries, to break over the boundary between general and local concerns, in a single place, the breach will produce consequences similar to those produced by that of the Tartars in the great wall of the Chinese.

A fanatical love or hatred of individuals or parties, is

equally inconsistent with a free form of government. Political enthusiasm enslaves parties to leaders, as religion enslaves sectaries to priests. Politicians never love or hate from passion. All their enmities and connexions flow from interest, according to which they reconcile or break them, without any of those sensibilities excited in ignorance by its own imaginary idols. As this idolatry is an universal cause of oppression, should the truth be concealed from agriculture, that she may become the victim of that enthusiastic confidence, which falsehood and mystery only are able to inspire? A political bigot is as certainly the slave of some party leader, as a religious bigot is of some priest.

These few cases are cited to shew, that agriculture without political knowledge, cannot expect justice, or retain liberty. The correctness of the political opinions expressed in these essays is another question. The author has suggested such as his mind suggested to him, to awaken agriculture to the importance of this species of knowledge to its prosperity and happiness, that it may by its own understanding detect his errors or its apathy.

NOTE B

(Page 125)

The slave-holding states have been deterred from making agricultural improvements, and establishing any
tolerable system of police for the management of slaves,
by the lazy and hopeless conclusion, that the destruction of their lands, and the irregularities of their negroes,
were incurable consequences of slavery. A refutation of
these errors must precede the possibility of any considerable agricultural improvement. The first is occasionally
detected by the rare efforts of individuals. But these can
never make a wide and lasting impression, whilst they
are defeated by the second. This obstacle can only be removed by legislative power. Until a better police for the
regulation of slaves is invented, than has hitherto existed, no considerable improvement can possibly take
place in a system of agriculture to be executed by them.
A bad police will forever draw back agriculture with
more force, than individual exertions can drive it forward;
nor can the most violent efforts over-rule its baleful in-

fluence, any more than the destruction of a tyrant can over-rule bad principles of government, and extract liberty from the causes of oppression. The creation of a free-negro class has been noticed as a great defect in this police; but its defectiveness in relation to the slaves themselves, was overlooked. Nothing effectual has been done by law, for controlling the irregularities of the slaves or the errors of their owners, by which a multitude of mischiefs to themselves and others are produced, together with the ruinous national misfortune of an impoverishing and depopulating system of agriculture. As the remedy for these evils lies only within the reach of law, it is the duty of the government to find it. Should it require a farther limitation of the prerogatives of ownership, public and private good will unite in their recommendation of such a measure. As the laws now stand, an owner, by withholding from his slave even a necessary subsistence, may compel him to steal it from others, and thereby increase the profit of his labour; or he might drive him into the resource of absconding, and prowling like a wolf for food. Ought the prerogatives of ownership be to inflict such unjust calamities upon a free people? Are they not infinitely more grievous than the ancient royal prerogative of purveyance? One grievance robbed openly, the other robs secretly; one was subject to some legal regulation, the other is subject to none; one paid something, the other pays nothing. Can agriculture or industry flourish here under the burden of having an infinite number of roguish and runaway slaves living at free quarter upon them, when they could not in England bear the purveyance of a single king? The slave himself may have imbibed from a vicious disposition, a habit of indiscriminate theft, so ruinous and disheartening to industry; nor can any excuse justify his robberies from the innocent. The insufficiency of the laws to correct these evils, will be discerned by comparing the number of such robberies, with the instances of their receiving any species of punishment. The object of punishment is to deter by example, and not to gratify the passion of revenge. But this trivial risque amounts almost to the encouragement of impunity; and leaves only to the public that security against the thefts of slaves, arising from their love of moral rectitude, without any apprehension of punishment. Agriculture in the slave states, is every where languishing under this mortifying and consuming malady. She possesses no moveable which she can call her own. Bleeding continually under these numberless scarifications, legislatures continue to act towards her, like surgeons who should desert a patient covered with wounds, because he was not quite dead. It would be better to cure her by protecting her property. A law, compelling the sale of every negro who should run away or be convicted of theft, out of the state, or at a considerable distance from his place of residence, would operate considerably towards correcting these great evils. If its execution was insured, as might easily be effected, it would strongly influence both the master and the slave; it would only retrench in a very small degree the prerogatives of ownership, for their common good, and it would render the remaining mass of those prerogatives infinitely less detrimental to national prosperity.

NOTE C

(Page 175)

The foregoing essays having been written several years past, subsequent experience has made some change in a few of the author's opinions. Those in relation to the essential article of manuring are stated in this note.

The extent of surface now manured upon the same farm, by a more careful employment of the same resources, has so far exceeded his expectations, as to have transferred his preference as means of improving the soil from inclosing to manuring, without, however, lessening the value of the former in his opinion. A field of two hundred acres aided by both, produced last year a crop of Indian corn averaging fifty bushels an acre, and another of eighty, aided only by inclosing and gypsum, a crop of twenty-five. The first being nearly double, and the second, one third beyond their respective products when last in culture. Under a diminution of the stocks quoted, the surface manured last year exceeded an hundred acres, and will this extend to one hundred and

thirty. It is contemplated to extend it, until it reaches
annually a space sufficient for the whole Indian corn crop
of the farm. The regular increase of crops furnishes additional vegetable matter; the chief basis of this rapid improvement. Tull's position "that ten cultivated acres, will
not produce the means of manuring one" is quite erroneous. Four acres already produce offal capable of manuring one, from the corn and wheat crops, exclusive of the
bread stuff they produce for sale. By removing the cattle
and sheep early in the spring from the farm pens, and
forbearing to return them thither until late in the fall,
the space manured by penning is greatly extended, and
the manure raised in the farm pens but little diminished,
because its quantity is regulated by litter. This is in a
small degree diminished by extending the period of penning, and as both cattle and sheep will require some food,
early in the spring and late in the fall in these pens, the
litter arising from that food will enable the farmer more
frequently to remove the pens at these seasons, whilst a
mixture of various manures causes a greater benefit to
soil. These pens on removal are fallowed in high ridges
five and an half feet wide, and those thus treated before
the middle of August, if the land is strong, cover themselves with a heavy coat of grass, furnishing a fine pabulum for a bushel of gypsum, to the acre, to be sown
thereon. This cover, by reversing the ridges, is completely
buried, and bestows on the ground a second valuable manuring. The hog pens are managed in the same way,
excluding the litter, not because it would be useless, but
because it is used otherwise. For these, stiff cold soils are
selected. Thus the same stocks have been brought to ma-

nure by penning, nearly double the surface quoted. In the winter, all the farm pens are littered daily and copiously with corn stalks. Each ten ordinary sheep will by this means, exclusive of the summer's penning, raise manure sufficient for one acre; and that raised in the stable and its yard, and in the farm pens of the cattle, calves and fatlings, has sufficed to produce the result stated in this note. Instead of applying the corn cobs in the former mode, they are weekly scattered in the pens or stable yard to preserve them from the fire, where they absorb a rich moisture to be bestowed upon the earth as they gradually decay; thus constituting a valuable addition to the manure, and saving the labour of their separate removal, and more tedious application in the former mode. The augmentation of manure thus produced, requires a commencement of its removal early in March, and by appropriating a small portion of the labour of the farm to this object for one month before the commencement of corn planting, that left to be subsequently carried out will be finished in good time. The holes for depositing the manure, are more judiciously arranged under the direction of a person on horseback (whose elevation and sole attention to that object, will enable him accurately to distinguish the variations in the quality of the land, and to bestow the manure accordingly), than by the labourer who walks, measures, and digs. By equalizing the fertility of a field, the crops are increased, because it bestows on the whole surface, a capacity to sustain the same quantity of seed, and renders unnecessary a multitude of discriminations too intricate to be correctly made. The rider pronounces aloud the number at which the walker is to make each hole, extended or contracting the distance according to the variations of the soil; and the walker counts aloud his own steps to this number, at which he digs a hole as a mark for depositing each load of manure. To a farmer, this occupation furnishes an agreeable mental amusement.

Two great errors in relation to the use of corn stalks as manure, are prevalent. One, that they ought to be trodden to pieces; the other, that when it is too late to effect this, it is good management to gather and lay them in the furrows, to remain uncovered for a year or two. When the stalk is saturated with the moisture of the farm pen, it has acquired all the fertilizing principles it can hold, in that state. It acquires none from being trodden. Its porous texture enables it speedily to absorb what it can contain. After this is effected, it is only necessary to bring it into a putrescent state. When the stalks are all in, this is soon done, by covering them with straw, chaff or tops. It will not require above ten days in the common March weather after a rain. Thus they will be made sufficiently soft and brittle to raise, spread and plough well in. Their richness as a manure will be discerned by their capacity to extract salts from the atmosphere whilst moist, after they are raised, in a quantity sufficient suddenly to change their colour. The excessive waste or loss they sustain, left in furrows on the surface, arises from the same quality by which the rich moisture of the farm pen throughout the winter, is absorbed and saved, namely, their extreme porousness. Their surface is dry, nothing evaporates, and nothing runs from them, if the depth of litter is as considerable as I make it. As absorbents, no litter equals them; but exposed on the surface, they suffer more than any other from evaporation.

A common question discloses another general error in relation to manuring. When the surface manured is stated, an inquiry after the number of stocks follows. We shall never succeed to a great extent, if we consider animal manure in any other light, than as a kind of sugar to sweeten the copious repasts of vegetables, with which we ought to feed the earth. It may also, mingled with vegetable matter, dispose the mass at particular periods of its putrescency, to extract salts from the atmosphere. But however useful it may be, the epithet "animal" is only to be admitted connected with a recollection of its origin. This is vegetable matter, of which animal manure is only a remnant, having undergone one or two secretions, and the diminution arising from animal perspiration. Vegetable matter therefore is the visible origin of manure. If atmosphere is its source, that can only be reduced to a visible substance by vegetable instrumentality. Manuring must consequently be regulated, not by the number of stocks, but by skill and industry in raising and applying vegetable matter. Let us then banish from the agricultural dialect this misleading question; which blinds us by insinuating a falsehood; and substitute for it one, which discloses truth, the thorough belief of which must precede agricultural improvement. The correct question is "how many acres do you manure for each labourer employed on the farm?" It took me more years to reach one, than to exceed four, and my stocks were rather diminished, as the space manured increased. During the first period, the delusion of the first question misguided my efforts; during the second, they were directed to the raising, preserving and applying vegetable matter in the most beneficial mode I could. How far manuring may be carried, is not to be foreseen, but I think I can discern through the remnant of the mist which long hid from me the idea of its being pushed to four acres for each labourer, a possibility of its being extended to double that quantity.

In this calculation I exclude gypsum, lime, marle and inclosing. The more valuable auxiliaries they may be to our vegetable resources, the more our success will be accelerated. Vegetable matter only, can bestow on gypsum a boundless fertilizing power, and perhaps it may be also a necessary associate of lime and marle, with neither of which I have been able to make any satisfactory experiments; at least, the universal capacity of creating it every where in great quantities, establishes its vast superiority over every other species of manure; and designates it as the basis of agriculture. Applied in green bushes it is much more beneficial in curing galled declivities, than animal manure. I use it with great advantage for that purpose, and also for manuring level land in the following mode. The brush is laid in furrows, made in cultivating corn, as deep and wide as explained in these essays, moderately thick and then cut to make it lie close, that it may not be removed by the winds. There it remains uncovered for three years. By applying the brush, the winter succeeding the culture of the land in corn, in a course of four shifts, it is ready for the plough at the proper time. Even the ridges, as well as the furrows, will be highly improved by the brush, from the scattering power of air and moisture. These ridges on the fourth year are reversed to cover the brush, by this time in a putrescent state, and thus prepared to rot under ground. The objections to the other modes of using brush wood, which I have tried, are these. Spread over the whole surface, it does not rot sufficiently in three years to admit of being ploughed in, without greatly encumbering the plough. Left sufficiently long to avoid this inconvenience, much time is lost without any retribution; and much of the manure during the latter period of its decay, by evaporation. Drilled green and speedily covered with earth, the wood will not rot under ground so as not to incommode the plough when the ridges are reversed in the fourth year afterwards. This preservation of the wood, diminishes or delays its efficacy as a manure. Drilled green, lying uncovered three years, then covered by the plough without disturbing it, and lying four years more until the ridges come in course to be reversed, the wood is made useful as a manure, without producing these inconveniencies. I have used all kinds of brush wood, but chiefly pine and cedar. The latter are preferable in a small degree to other green wood, when both are applied in the winter, because of their leaves. A confidence in the benefit of this mode of manuring, has induced me this year to cut down a thicket on the broken ground of a creek around a level field, and to apply the brush to the furrows of the weakest parts. All wood of above two inches diameter, was used as fuel. The residue bestowed a handsome dressing on double the surface it grew on. The land it came from was not capable of cultivation, and the growth was lean. Being enclosed, it will rapidly grow up thicker, and afford periodical cuttings for the same purpose. The wood pays for the labour, and the manure necessarily disengaged from the fuel wood, is an additional donation from such lands (in which we unfortunately abound), capable of extending our means for manuring very considerably, and of conveniently improving fields inconveniently situated for folding or farm pens.

NOTE D

(Page 214)

Instead of laying the plough aside, until the first hand-hoeing of Indian corn takes place, it is probably better to run a deep furrow with a large plough drawn by two horses, and having a long mould board, on each side of the corn, immediately preceding this hand-hoeing. As the corn is very low, this furrow must be run so far from it that the earth raised by the mould board will not quite reach it, but be left on each side, so as to form a narrow trough on the ridge in which the corn stands, to be filled up by the hand-hoeing immediately following this furrow. The hoe will have little else to do, and two thirds of the labour usually attending this operation, will be saved. It is better performed. The deep furrow destroys all the grass in its range. In rows five and an half feet wide, the earth moved by the helve on the left of the share, meets and covers the grass in the water furrows between the ridges. And the earth thrown up by the share and the mould board towards the corn, is used to stifle

the grass in the trough on the top of the ridge and about
the young corn. A hand-hoeing in the usual way, is
infinitely more laborious, and in humid seasons, from its
shallowness, infinitely less effectual in destroying the
grass, whence it is often enabled suddenly to take root
and grow with renovated vigour; somewhat similar to
the effect of scarifications applied to green swards even
of wheat. The deep ploughing of this suggestion, its ac-
celeration of the first hand-hoeing, and its suppression
of the grass whilst it is young and weak by a cover of
earth, will both obstruct this misfortune and enable the
corn to reap great benefit from the genial weather which
occurs in the early part of the summer, instead of often
being destroyed by it.

If Indian corn is a crop of such value, as it is supposed to be in these essays, the selection of the best species is an object of importance. The little said of this,
arose from the necessity of the different climates of the
United States for different kinds. But the vast number
of varieties abounding in the same latitudes, disclose a
want of spirit for fixing so important a preference as
that of the best over the whole rabble, by careful experiments. Those which I have made have inculcated the
opinion, that the species which combines the three circumstances of producing the most stalk, the largest cob,
and the longest grain, is the best for the latitude of 38
degrees north. The small flinty forward kind producing
from 2 to 6 ears on a stalk, inspired the most hope, and
produced the most disappointment of any I have tried.
Its superiority of weight was counterbalanced by many
disadvantages. Early kinds are unexceptionably dwarf-

ish, and the latest I have procured has the largest stalk. The length of the grain, supposing the cob to be equally long and large, decisively settles the superiority of farinaceous product. The longest and the thickest cob, if the length of the grain is equal, produces the most corn. The size of the stalk is important, if vegetable matter possesses the high value contended for in these essays, and if it is chiefly extracted from the atmosphere. The size of the plant produces some economy of labour, besides augmenting our drafts from the fertilizing atmospherical treasury because we can gather far more grain, stalk, blade, top, shuck, and cob in the same time, when the plant is large, than when it is small. I have discovered no good reason for a recent preference of yellow to white corn, except that a foreign fashion causes the former at this juncture to sell best, nor any benefit from several trials of planting seed saved from twin ears. In the before mentioned latitude, corn constantly pushes out barren shoots, or more than it can fill with grain, which probably serve to impoverish such as succeed. If so, there would be no advantage gained, could we increase their number by planting from twins.

NOTE E

(Page 263)

The mode of raising hogs has continued to attract my attention, on account of the vast importance it derives from its connexion with live fences. If it can supply us with meat, without obstructing an improvement, by which the agricultural state of the Union would be more benefited than by any other, its usefulness would be great; but if it will also supply us with more meat than the present mode, no legislature will much longer suffer a state to languish under the evil of dead fencing, for the sake of diminishing both meat and bread. Sensible of the enthusiasm with which human nature embraces all opinions it ardently wishes to realize, I have endeavoured in these essays to confine myself to the decisions of experience, and to avoid the delusions of hope. My experience of the recommended mode of raising hogs, has for several years resulted in a far more plentiful supply of pork without purchasing, than I could previously afford to obtain by purchasing. It has also as strongly convinced me, as I can be convinced without an exact experiment, that the expenses of raising it is reimbursed, or nearly so, by the manure of the hogs; and that the alternative for public preference, really lies between an expensive and insufficient supply of pork, accompanied with dead fences; and an expenseless and sufficient supply of the same article, accompanied with live. The recommended mode of raising hogs is improved, by reserving a sufficient number of breeding sows to insure the dependence upon those under one year old for keeping up the stock; by separating the large and small hogs in cold weather, to prevent the latter from being smothered; by increasing the size of a pen for one hundred of different ages, to an acre; by removing it once a fortnight, when the hogs are constantly confined, or every four weeks, when penned of nights only, and instantly ploughing up the ground in high five feet and an half ridges, to be reversed when cultivated; by soaking corn until it is sour, in a number of barrels sufficient to provide in succession, according to the warmth of the season, their chief food in this state; by giving them the sour water to drink as each barrel is emptied; by a small allowance of any vegetable food after the pumpkins are expended (they will eat corn stalks in the early part of the winter); by penning them without rings if such food is scarce, on ground well covered with any kind of grass, the roots of which will contribute to their health, whilst they prepare the land for the plough; and by using them in the same way to eradicate the garlic, than which no food is healthier.

NOTE F

(Page 271)

Since these essays were written, my experiments in cedar hedging have become two or three years older, and have removed every doubt of its cheapness, practicability and importance. They were commenced by planting a single row of cedars on the inside of a fence, two feet apart, about eight inches below the summit of the bank of a ditch. The errors of neglecting to cultivate the young plants, to crop or to manure them, and to plant a second row on the outside of the fence, were for several years committed. Struggling with hungry rivals for a scanty food, they grew slowly, were meager and spindling. The lower branches began to perish from omitting to check the perpendicular growth by cropping, and the hope of training the cedar into a hedge seemed almost desperate. Though the land is generally poor, manuring (a small dressing with bushes excepted) has hitherto been neglected. But topping, clipping the lateral branches, culture, and filling gaps by bending into them and covering boughs to take root, leaving out their ends have been imperfectly practiced for two years. Another row of cedars has also been planted on the outside of the fence. The old hedge has been so highly improved by these inconsiderable aids, as to have assumed a handsome appearance, and to promise a speedy exhibition of a large farm enclosed by a live fence.

The cedar planted in a good soil, well manured and properly cultivated, cropped at one year's old and annually, so that it rises only as it spreads; and clipped at the ends of its branches, those excepted, buried about their middle to fill gaps; will thicken near to the ground like box; and after it is brought to the intended height, by raising the bank of the ditch, will be in close contact with it. My experiment has been more imperfectly made from the circumstance of its embracing at once a large farm; made upon a smaller scale and more skilfully, an example would speedily appear, which would be ardently copied.

Green pine or cedar brush has been used as a dressing to the hedge as follows. The earth is shaved downwards on each face of the bank of the ditch, so as just to take off the grass, and not to injure the roots of the young hedge, and left in a ridge. The brush is laid in a line with the hedge eighteen inches wide, so as to cover the ground. After it is in danger of being perforated by weeds or grass, the ridge of earth shaved down is thrown upon it. To the other benefits of this process, that of protecting the young cedars against the sun, which strikes the face of banks with great force, is to be added. In some situations this protection is indispensable. By drawing down and returning this mixture of earth and brush alternately, as the hedge requires weeding, it receives both manure and cultivation, at a very trivial expense of labour.

No doubt can exist, that the thin population of a great portion of the United States, proceeds from the poverty of the soil, whether it be natural or artificial. In the latter case, patriotism ought to sicken with the anticipation of the censure which posterity will see written in the face of the country. These words will be engraved on it. "Your ancestors, like Indians, proved their regard for their children by scalping the mother." In the former, is it wise, patriotic or pious, to neglect the means for its improvement? Live fences attended with apple trees would, I have no doubt, more than double the population of the eastern sandy portions of the United States. Let the reader compute before he decides upon this opinion, and test it by figures. The savings of wood, of labour, and of the expense in foreign liquors, are items going to an increase of population, because these savings must be carried into some productive object for its sustenance. The conversion of the brushwood now lost in making dead fences, into manure, is a smaller item of the same nature. But the single advantage of securing to agriculture the benefit of making a permanent and constant use of atmospherical manure, arising from the security of live inclosures, alone suffices to sustain the opinion. By gradually spreading fertility over barrenness, inclosing will increase population to an extent commensurate with its own progress. For a system of closing the pores of the earth against the inhalation of those qualities of the atmosphere, by which its surface is fertilized, it will enable us to open them.

Wealth instead of poverty; national strength instead of weakness; and perhaps liberty instead of slavery, march in the train of permanent inclosures. But we are blinded against computations founded in figures, by comparisons arising from superficial prejudices. Beggary admires the luxury of competence, and its mediocrity chuckles over her wealth, when she beholds poverty. So we draw opinions concerning the fertility and improvement of a whole country, from comparisons made among ourselves, always shedding darkness upon truth, because always influenced by several of the worst or weakest passions of human nature. To provide prosperity for nations by the cool calculations of reason, and not to devote posterity to wretchedness from the odious prejudices implanted by such shallow comparisons, constitutes the duty of legislatures, and the real virtue of patriots. The appalling difference between the average product of wheat in this country and in England, ought to dissipate our delusion as to the present quality of our soil, to awaken our inquiries after the causes of an inferiority so deplorable, and to rouse all our capacities in search of a remedy. Our wretched, expensive and ineffectual mode of inclosing, is in my view the chief of those causes. No history has preserved, and no country exhibits, a good system of agriculture in union with dead wood fences. Homer, in his description of a Phoeatian garden, informs us, that *green* fences were understood and used in his time.

Four acres was the allotted space of ground,
Fenced with a *green* enclosure all around.*

---

* *Odyssey*, VII, lines 112–116 (Pope's version).

He mentions stone and thorn inclosures, selects the green
to adorn his most splendid horticultural scene, and is
utterly silent as to dead wood fences. Were they exploded
above three thousand years ago, to be now revived as an
evidence of man's rotary disposition? But we need not
dive into antiquity, nor travel over the globe to settle the
question. At home we see the waste of soil graduated
from north to south, by some inexplicable circumstance,
distinct from original fertility. The different modes of
fencing are probably that circumstance. In Connecticut, I
have seen many fields apparently so naturally poor and
stoney, that I could never account for their fertility, until
I discovered the advantages of permanent inclosures, and
recollected that they were surrounded by stone fences.
Prejudice, sustained by conscience, is too strong to be subdued by reason, and too respectable on account of its honesty, to deserve contempt. Yet it ought to be persuaded
by its senses, and to be induced to follow its own interest
by the plainest evidence. Though at length convinced
through its eyes, of the benefits arising from inclosing,
it will not be convinced through its mouth, that the old
mode of raising meat by ranges (as they are called) is insufficient for the supply of a thin population, and that the
effect of its conviction of one error is defeated, by its persistence in another. Dead wooden fences are too transitory, too subject to imperfections arising from idleness
or accident, and too easily impaired by thoughtless or
malicious trespassers, to guarantee to a nation the benefits of an inclosing system. They are here to-day and
gone tomorrow. Live, possess the rights and the respect
of a freehold. Attached to the soil, they soon efface the

unjust and ruinous prejudice, nurtured by their evanescent rival "that arable lands, when out of actual culture, ought to be turned into a common." This opinion, suggested by a national wish to obtain good and sufficient supplies of grass, and gratified throughout a great portion of the union, as a wish for such supplies of horses, would be gratified by throwing open every stable to all who wanted them, is undoubtedly entitled to denunciation as a prejudice if prejudice exists among mankind.

My wish for a better understanding was never stronger than in considering this subject, from a conviction that its gratification could never have been more useful to the public. Throughout the world, countries inclosed by stone or live fences, and those inclosed by dead wood, exhibit the contrast between cadaverous decrepitude and blooming youth. The richest county of Virginia below the mountains, painted on the same canvass, would be a foil to the poorest of Connecticut. The incapacity of the first, for rendering inclosing subservient to the improvement of land, by excluding ruinous or injudicious grazing; and the capacity of the latter to avail itself of this agricultural panacea, is a chief cause of the contrast. In Britain, live fences are substituted for stone, where the latter is not to be had, and often preferred to it; and are by wide experience demonstrated to be a sound sponsor for an excellent state of agriculture: here, the demonstration that dead wooden fences ensure a bad state of agriculture is as wide. Does truth require more than two demonstrations?

If permanent fences are indispensable for the purpose of changing the state of our agriculture from bad to good, they are also necessary for the preservation of our happiness. The portion of liberty and happiness enjoyed under the expensive system of government existing in Britain, is owing to the productiveness of labour; and not to the operations of the paper, patronage, party, and official conspiracy for pilfering that labour as the ingenious conspirators pretend. Though her average product of wheat is thirty-five bushels, worth at least one hundred and five dollars, she finds it better to convert so much of her land and labour to the still more profitable objects of raising wool, cheese, meat, with other agricultural products, and to manufacturing, as to have occasion for the importation of bread stuff. To this great productiveness of labour it is owing, that she is the happiest and freest country of Europe, under the greatest load of pecuniary expenditure. In the United States, agriculture must for ages graduate the productiveness of labour, in spite of the projects of statesmen, and the fallacy of stock-jobbing. If we rush into English extravagance without gaining the productiveness in that occupation which must feed it, the majority of the people must be speedily ground down to a degree of poverty, below an ability to preserve a free government, or to acquire personal happiness. Let us therefore provide the foundation, before we rear this splendid superstructure, by abolishing a mode of inclosing lands which produces nothing, consumes a great portion of our labour, and by impoverishing the soil, daily diminishes the productiveness of the residue.

NOTE G

(Page 329)

A date being necessary for estimating the opinions contained in the foregoing essays, the reader is informed, that they appeared in the ephemeral columns of a newspaper, before the year 1810, and that the notes were written in the beginning of the year 1814. Though the last number was better calculated for the place of its original appearance (as well as some other parts of the work) than for that it now unexpectedly occupies, it is suffered to remain, because however light, it is true; but lest its tone may infect its matter, it seems proper to advert to the same subject more seriously.

Society is unavoidably made up of two interests only, in one of which all special and particular modifications of interest are included; namely, one subsisting by industry; the other, by law. Government is instituted for the happiness of the first interest, but belonging itself to the second, it is perpetually drawn towards that by the strongest cords. Therefore, unless the first is able very accurately to distinguish between laws calculated to do it a benefit or an injury, it must be gradually sacrificed to the appetites of the second, because government, a member of the second, legislates. All men enjoying honour, power or wealth by law, or striving to acquire either through that channel, are like coin struck with the same dies. The engravers, avarice and ambition, constantly mark the same etching, and the aqua fortis, self-interest, indelibly imprints it on the human mind. From this fact, the preference of a republican government is deduced, as being calculated for checking the natural disposition of legislatures or the government, to favour the minor class, composed of legal or factitious interests, at the expense of the major class, composed of natural interests; including all who subsist, not by means of legal donations, but by useful talents in every form, such as those employed in agriculture, manufacturing, tuition, physic, and all trades and scientific professions. The propensity of law to sacrifice the great or natural interest of nations, to the class of little or factitious interests, arises from two causes; one, the government being the matrix of the latter, views her progeny with the eyes of an owl and considers them as beautiful; the other, that although law can enable the small class to live upon the great one, it cannot enable the great class to live on the small one; uniting to produce this propensity in a degree so violent, that mankind have pronounced it irresistible, except by a countervailing union between strong republican fetters upon government, and a degree of political knowledge in the major class, sufficient to prevent these fetters from being broken by laws. The remedy is so rare, that many honest men doubt of its existence; and have concluded in despair, that the major class or general interest of a nation, must inevitably become the slave of the minor or factitious interest in some mode. Others believe, that by exciting the general interest to watch, to think, and to judge for itself, its intellect will be brightened, and its rights preserved. But all agree, that neither any individual nor any interest dictated to by another, can prosper; and that political ignorance universally implies political slavery. Election has no power beyond a charter or a commission, to prevent the elected from being transferred by his election from the great class of the general interest, to the little class of factitious or legal interest; on the contrary, the structure of republican government is raised upon the principle, that it necessarily transfers him from one to the other, at least in most instances. This is unanimously admitted by the elected themselves. They separate into two parties, called inns and outs. The inns say that the outs are influenced by a desire to get in, and the outs, that the inns are influenced by a desire to keep in. Agreeing that both belong to the minor class and neither to the major class, which can neither get in nor keep in; these two members of the minor class vote in constant opposition, because they stand in each other's way, which could not possibly happen if they were genuine members of the general interest class. How then can the major class expect happiness from this species of political gambling for a rich stake which it pays, and the gamblers alternately win, if it has no skill in the game?

Agriculture is the most powerful member of the class constituting the general interest, but if her sons are too ignorant to use this power with discretion (like a body of elephants thrown into confusion in a battle), they rush in every direction, trampling down friends and foes for a short time, and inevitably become an easy prey to their enemies. As the most powerful individual constituting the major class of general interest, the political ignorance of agriculture, would of course destroy the rights of the whole class. If she divides herself between any of the members of the inferior class, each of her moieties enlist under an aristocratical or monarchical power; whether it be called executive, legislative, credit or charter, and the member obtaining the victory by her aid, becomes her master. Just as in a division of her forces between a king and a nobility, the king or the nobility, and not agriculture, gains a victory, both over her, and over all her weaker associates in the class of the general interest.

As there are two classes of interest only in society, there are also only two political codes, each appropriated by nature to one class. The code of the minor class is constituted of intrigues and stratagems to beguile the major class, and to advance the separate interests of the individuals, parties and legal combinations, of which the minor class is compounded. The code of the major class consists of good moral principles, by which the national rights and happiness can only be preserved. The guilt of offensive war, and the virtue of defensive, are the essential qualities of the respective codes. One is compounded of the best, and the other of the worst qualities of human nature; and the members of the general or natural interest of society, can never avoid oppression nor sustain a just and free government, unless they are skilled in both.

As the extension of comfort and happiness is the only good motive for writing an agricultural book, whatever would defeat the end belongs to the subject; and as a legal profusion in overstocking a nation with members of the minor class, is the solitary process for enslaving it, unless the major class understands the sublime branch of ethics, namely, political morality, it cannot counteract this process. Thus only can it distinguish between laws and projects calculated for benefiting or injuring the nation. This science only can prevent the liberty, the virtue, the happiness, the bravery and the talents of the nation from being extinguished. The treasury of the United States has been cited as a proper subject for its application. If the agricultural and other members of the major class should discern that the president had become a king of the treasury, surrounded with nominal checks and balances appointed by himself; if they should discern that the representatives of the people were convinced of a great waste of public money, and yet ignorant of the modes by which it was effected; if they should recollect the consequences of such an error in the English form of government; and if they knew that nations were enslaved by a corrupting application of their own treasure, would not the correction of the evil be founded in genuine political morality, and be plainly adverse to the erroneous and flagitious political code of the minor class.

The intimate connexion between agriculture and the militia, arises from their being both interests belonging to the major or general class of national interest, of such magnitude, that they must live or perish, politically together; and the rights of the whole class will be lost by

the subjection of either. By transferring the power of
the purse from agriculture to the stock-jobbers, or the
power of the sword from the militia to a mercenary army,
the destruction of a free form of government naturally
ensues.* This single consequence suffices to refute two
hundred thousand artifices, eternally practiced by the
sundry members of the minor class, to discredit the
militia. They might be refuted by an hundred thousand
facts. The most eminent periods of Greece and Rome,
were inspired by an union between a militia and a considerable degree of political knowledge in the major class.
Thermopylae was defended, and Xerxes defeated by militia. The Roman empire was created and destroyed by
militia. England and the Indians have often felt the
militia of the United States. Europe was repulsed by
the militia of France, and the career of France arrested by
the militia of Spain. The pride, the habits and the interests
of mercenary armies are, however, its historiographer,
and the hatred of government and parties, its patron.
These convert its eulogy into a crime. "It is unfit," say
they, "for the execution of the projects of statesmen, and
hence diminishes the energy of the government." But it
is the best security against foreign conquest, and the only

---

* Horror of a standing, professional army is a convention of the "old
Whig" doctrine from which Taylor derives. Despots are made possible
by such a force and the independent virtue of the subject population is
destroyed. Republicans of Taylor's school had been disturbed by the
Federalist monopoly of influence in the "new" American army developed
by the late 1790s. They feared it might intrude upon the regular process
of our national politics, and their fears were not groundless. See Richard
H. Kohn, *Eagle and Sword: The Beginnings of the Military Establishment
in America* (New York: The Free Press, 1975).

security against domestic oppression from a combination among the members of the minor interest; nor will any project plainly calculated to advance the happiness or secure the liberty of the general interest ever fail of finding a complete security in the power of a militia, organized to sustain and not to betray that interest. How often have the zeal, virtue and courage of a militia, burst through the artifices or neglect of the minor interest for suppressing all three, and demonstrated their natural alliance with political morality and national liberty.

INDEX